Contemporary British Autoethnogra

THE UNIVERSITY OF
WINCHESTER

STUDIES IN PROFESSIONAL LIFE AND WORK
Volume 9

Editor
Ivor Goodson
Education Research Centre, University of Brighton, UK

Editorial Board
J. M. Pancheco, *University of Minho, Portugal*
David Labaree, *Stanford University*
Sverker Lindblad, *University of Gothenburg*
Leslie Siskin, *NYU/Steinhardt Institute for Education & Social Policy*

Scope
The series will commission books in the broad area of professional life and work. This is a burgeoning area of study now in educational research with more and more books coming out on teachers' lives and work, on nurses' life and work, and on the whole interface between professional knowledge and professional lives.

The focus on life and work has been growing rapidly in the last two decades. There are a number of rationales for this. Firstly, there is a methodological impulse: many new studies are adopting a life history approach. The life history tradition aims to understand the interface between people's life and work and to explore the historical context and the socio-political circumstances in which people's professional life and work is located. The growth in life history studies demands a series of books which allow people to explore this methodological focus within the context of professional settings.

The second rationale for growth in this area is a huge range of restructuring initiatives taking place throughout the world. There is in fact a world movement to restructure education and health. In most forms this takes the introduction of more targets, tests and tables and increasing accountability and performativity regimes. These initiatives have been introduced at governmental level – in most cases without detailed consultation with the teaching and nursing workforces. As a result there is growing evidence of a clash between people's professional life and work missions and the restructuring initiatives which aim to transform these missions. One way of exploring this increasingly acute clash of values is through studies of professional life and work. Hence the European Commission, for instance, have begun to commission quite large studies of professional life and work focussing on teachers and nurses. One of these projects – the Professional Knowledge Network project has studied teachers' and nurses' life and work in seven countries. There will be a range of books coming out from this project and it is intended to commission the main books on nurses and on teachers for this series.

The series will begin with a number of works which aim to define and delineate the field of professional life and work. One of the first books 'Investigating the Teacher's Life and Work' by Ivor Goodson will attempt to bring together the methodological and substantive approaches in one book. This is something of a 'how to do' book in that it looks at how such studies can be undertaken as well as what kind of generic findings might be anticipated.

Future books in the series might expect to look at either the methodological approach of studying professional life and work or provide substantive findings from research projects which aim to investigate professional life and work particularly in education and health settings.

Contemporary British Autoethnography

Edited by

Nigel P. Short
Informal Associate, School of Psychology, University of Sussex, UK

Lydia Turner
School of Psychology, University of Sussex, UK and
Sussex Partnership NHS Foundation Trust, UK

and

Alec Grant
SNM, Faculty of Health and Social Science, University of Brighton,
East Sussex, UK

SENSE PUBLISHERS
ROTTERDAM/BOSTON/TAIPEI

A C.I.P. record for this book is available from the Library of Congress.

ISBN: 978-94-6209-408-6 (paperback)
ISBN: 978-94-6209-409-3 (hardback)
ISBN: 978-94-6209-410-9 (e-book)

Published by: Sense Publishers,
P.O. Box 21858,
3001 AW Rotterdam,
The Netherlands
https://www.sensepublishers.com/

Printed on acid-free paper

TABLE OF CONTENTS

ACKNOWLEDGEMENTS

This book was developed over a number of conversations with many people over many years. To all of them we say thank you. As editors, we have all, inevitably, had very different autoethnographic experiences of autoethnography. It was our unique and different positions that encouraged and prompted us to want to collect a number of chapters from different perspectives and disciplines, showing how some of the many forms and guises that constitute autoethnography can be presented.

Appropriately, in a book about narratives and storytelling, our achievement has not been done alone. We would like to thank all the contributing authors for their generosity and enthusiasm and promptness; this has helped to make editing the book a gratifying project.

We are indebted to Peter de Liefde and his colleagues at Sense for guidance, support help and flexibility, Professor Ivor Goodson for including this volume as part of his Studies in Professional Life and Work series, and Mike Hayler for facilitating this project through previously publishing with Sense.

We would also like to acknowledge the 'All together for Autoethnography' (A4A) group at the University of Brighton. This group has provided a convivial and dialogical environment for discussions associated with Autoethnography.

Thanks go to Josh Turner and Robin Harris for providing the book's sleeve (JT) and back (RH) sleeve photographs and to Professor Kim Etherington for providing the book's blurb.

The intent of the book was to help give a voice to the voiceless, the invisible to become visible *and* to make differences noticeable; invisibility is, in the end, intolerable.

ALEC GRANT, NIGEL P. SHORT & LYDIA TURNER

INTRODUCTION: STORYING LIFE AND LIVES

Rotten and rusted; a five-bar gate
Lies felled in the mud, letting the fields escape

The Present
Simon Armitage

Like much of British poetry, this book has a place: a place where numerous histories came together in one unplanned space. The three of us were sat together in the atrium of the Checkland building at the University of Brighton, having accidentally bumped into each other in the autumn of 2011. The idea of this book morphed from an initially spontaneous, then ever-developing, conversation. Similar to the casual sharing of thoughts about a recipe book, our ideas converged like the different ingredients that go to make up a new and novel dish. In the company of our invited contributing authors, this book is the resultant mix of many different autoethnographic ingredients.

Contemporary British Autoethnography considers, presents, analyses and discusses multiple autoethnographic representations, illustrating the fluid nature of identities as these move with shifting contexts. The chapters in the book display competing tensions within autoethnographic inquiry at paradigmatic, methodological and representational levels, around performance, identity and voice, in relation to the sociocultural. We hope it will also raise questions about the iconoclastic and boundary changing nature of autoethnography at all of those levels. We believe that this book contributes a necessary and timely challenge to mainstream qualitative research practices which, in our experience, can be characterised by oppressive and inflexible institutional rules, restrictions and normative assumptions.

DEFINING AUTOETHNOGRAPHY

The meaning, function and onto-epistemological characteristics of autoethnography have been subject to an ongoing, vigorous, and sometimes heated debate in recent years (see eg Anderson, 2006; Ellis & Bochner, 2006; Jackson & Mazzei, 2008, 2009; Muncey, 2010). However, at a general level, there appears to be consensus among the autoethnographic communities around acceptance of the description of the approach provided by Ellis and Bochner (2000). This is that autoethnography is a contemporary qualitative research methodology, demanding unusually rigorous, multi-layered levels of researcher reflexivity, given that the researcher/s and the researched are normally the same people.

N. P. Short et al. (Eds.), Contemporary British Autoethnography, 1–16.

Proceeding from the above broad description, as both a methodology and method of diverse interdisciplinary practices, autoethnography is concerned with producing creatively written, detailed, local and evocative first person accounts of the relationship between personal autobiography and culture. Accounts might be highly charged, thumping the reader firmly in the solar plexus, leaving them metaphorically gasping for breath, or they may be gentle and meandering, allowing the reader space and time for reflection.

The creativity with which autoethnographic pieces are often written, opens up a reflexive world in which the researcher/researched join with the reader to create a story. This iterative process of reflection and reflexivity within the autoethnographic process does not lend itself to linear chronological progression, specificity and concreteness; instead, the text might wander, twist and turn, changing direction unexpectedly. It might jump from one thought/feeling/memory or experience up or down or backwards, forwards or sideways to another. Fractions of an experience link to other fractions of another experience becoming 'felted', with 'no separation of threads, no intertwining, only an entanglement of fibres.....it is in principle infinite, open, and unlimited in every direction' (Deleuze & Guattari, 1987, p. 525), lacking specificity and defined authenticity. Thus the story might change, develop and grow throughout the reader's experience of the writing, and almost certainly changes and grows as the author authors and re-authors their writing:

> The point of any present story is its potential for revision and redistribution in future stories. This principle of perpetual generation means that narrative analysis can never claim any last word about what a story means or represents. Instead, narrative analysis, like the story itself, can only look toward an open future. (Frank, 2005, p. 967)

These accounts represent lives that may range from being very similar to very different from the lives of others and it is in this context that the situated nature of self with others in social and cultural milieus is critically interrogated (Spry, 2001). In relation to autoethnography, a seminal but provisional definition of 'culture', to be unpacked, problematised and discussed further below, is the meaning construction woven in human and material contexts as people go about and through their lives (Bochner & Ellis, 1996).

In the above vein, autoethnography has been usefully defined by Ellis (2004, p. xix) as follows:

> … research, writing, and method that connect the autobiographical and personal to the cultural and social. The form usually features concrete action, emotion, embodiment, self-consciousness, and introspection … (and) claims the conventions of literary writing.

> Thus, autoethnography, an approach as close to the arts and humanities as it is to the social and human sciences, celebrates and prizes subjectivity rather than

viewing it as an irritant, and can be distinguished from biography or memoir by its commitment to rigorous cultural interrogation and analysis.

HISTORICAL ROOTS AND CONTEXTS WITHIN QUALITATIVE RESEARCH

In the context of the tensions within the autoethnographic community about the characteristics of the approach, several possible histories could be written about its emergence. One significant historical strand relates to critical tensions in the philosophy of science governing qualitative research: specifically, in the ongoing postmodern and poststructuralist critiques of the knowledge claims, representational practices and effective dissemination of traditional qualitative approaches. This critique initially emerged in the late twentieth century, and is associated with two inter-related onto-epistemological phenomena: the so-called 'triple crisis' and the 'narrative turn' in human and social science inquiry (Denzin & Lincoln, 1005; Spry, 2001).

The triple crisis – of representation, legitemation and authority (Holman Jones, 2005) – signifies scepticism toward positivist-informed 'master' or 'grand' narratives, which claim objectivity, authority and researcher neutrality in the study of social and cultural life. In this context, the representational practices associated with positivist science have been subject to challenge. This critique has extended to a rejection of the assumed ubiquity of stable meanings, existing independently of culture, social context and researcher activity and interpretation.

In related terms, the narrative turn in the human and social sciences has triggered a shift from a single, monolithic conception of what should constitute scholarly work in favour of a developing pluralism. Paving the way for autoethnography among other contemporary qualitative methodologies, this pluralistic agenda has resulted in the recognition and promotion of multiple forms of experience in diverse research and representational practices. Included and celebrated among these are local, short stories (for example, Bochner, 2001; Grant & Zeeman, 2012; Reissman, 1993, 2008); indeed many autoethnographic writers consider local narratives essential in balancing, and destabilising the exclusivity of grand narrative accounts.

This has impacted on a corresponding emergent shift in autoethnographic researcher value position, where the privileging of the distanced spectator and writer of essays is rejected in favour of the embodied, feeling, culturally engaged and vulnerable observer and teller of creative, evocative stories (Bochner, 2001). In this context, the function and purpose of human and social science texts also changes. With regard to the relationship between the writers and readers of autoethnography, disinterested, 'objective' instruction gives way to evocative, emotionally-resonant connection.

In summary, in the context of the above sustained intellectual context, critique and practices, the interdisciplinary genre of autoethnography, as both methodology and method, has developed as a radical alternative to conventional, realist social science practices and writing. Significantly, researchers within the burgeoning autoethnographic movement have eschewed the assumptions and practices of traditional qualitative approaches, including the privileging of researcher over the subject, an over-concern with method at the expense of story, and pre-occupations with outmoded conceptions of validity, truth, and generalizability (Denzin, 1992; Spry, 2001). Thus, grand theorising, the façade of objectivity, the decontextualising of research participant and the search for single truths are all rejected. This allows for the emergence of new forms of subjectivist writing, which focus on the local and the particular, and which synthesise autobiography with cultural critique, utilising creative written and analytical practices, including literary tropes (Ellis, 2004; Grant, 2010a; Richardson, 2000; Richardson and St. Pierre, 2005). Autoethnographic work thus emerges as an ideal way of creatively celebrating the locally and temporally situated nature of identity, fieldwork and cultural interpretation and analysis (Holman Jones, 2005; Jones, 1996; Spry, 2001).

AUTOETHNOGRAPHY AND THE PERSONAL AS POLITICAL

An important implication emerging from the above is that cultural interrogation constitutes the exploration of multiple ways of experiencing and representing lives. In this regard, autoethnography actively promotes political inquiry (Denzin, 2006; Ellingson, 2006; Ellis, Bochner, Denzin, Lincoln, Morse, Pelias & Richardson, 2008; Spry, 2001), related ethical dilemmas (Berger, 2001; Ellis, 2007; Rambo, 2007), and the experiences of people who feel they have been culturally excluded and marginalised (Short & Grant, 2009; Short, 2010).

Writing about how identities are compromised by dominant cultural meanings, at odds with subjective and relational experiences of the world, gives the lie to the often taken for granted master narratives about how life is or is supposed to be. Autoethnography, therefore, often explicitly challenges the exclusivity of supposedly value-neutral, rationally-based categorical thinking and abstracted theory in explicitly celebrating emotionality, political standpoint position and social activism. Many autoethnographers, explicitly and implicitly, do this in pursuit of a social justice agenda, aiming for the reduction of the oppression of individuals and groups within broader socio-political structures (Fine & Weis, 2005). The aim of this pursuit is to positively impact on and change the world, in line with an aspirational utopian ideal (Holman Jones, 2005).

THE POLITICS OF SUBJECTIVISM

In this context, subjectivism is welcomed and seen as a resource (McLeod, 2011), as the body is assumed to be a central site for socio-political meaning making (Spry, 2011). However, as Sparkes (2003) robustly argues, subjectivism should not be confused with solipsism or self-indulgence. The subjectivist stance in autoethnography is predicated on quite the opposite: that culture flows through self and vice versa (Ellis & Bochner, 1996), and that people are inscribed within dialogic, socially shared, linguistic and representational practices (Bakhtin, 1984; Frank, 2005) through their daily occupations. The self is therefore understood as a social and relational rather than an autonomous phenomenon (Church, 1995). Although this position undoubtedly provokes turf wars about the proper focus of the social and human sciences and polarises positions within these areas, these are perhaps irresolvable issues which amount to 'difference(s) to be lived with' (Rorty, 1982, p. 197).

FUNCTIONS

Given the argument so far, writing autoethnography demands high, rigorous, courageous and challenging levels of personal, relational, cultural, theoretical and political reflexivity. Pillow (2003) describes this in terms of uncomfortable reflexive practices, within which autoethnographic researchers critically explore and interrogate the sociocultural forces and discursive practices that have shaped and influenced their emerging subjectivities. This provides unique opportunities for authors to reflect on what they bring to their different forms of autoethnographic inquiry. Not surprisingly, such reflexive work often results in and characterises autoethnography as social and cultural critique, experienced and perceived as social transgression (Park-Fuller, 2000). In this context, an important function of autoethnography is to expose 'the elephants in the room' of cultural context: social and organisational practices which beg robust scrutiny and critique but which are taken for granted as unquestioned, normative 'business as usual'. Thus, the autoethnographer fulfils the dual role of cultural trickster (McLeod, 2011) and cultural conscience agent (Grant, 2010a; Short, Grant & Clarke, 2007).

At this point, it may be useful to develop and problematize the discussion around the nature of autoethnographic 'culture' from the straightforward Bochner and Ellis (1996) definition described earlier. The description by these seminal autoethnographic authors of culture as straightforward social meaning construction may lend itself to a normative reading of culture as a kind of folksy form of liberal participation. This reading suggests people endlessly, uncomplainingly and uncomplicatedly assimilated in the stitching together of the quilt of life, or at least with complaints that can be documented in such a way that does little to explicitly contest the pre-determined shape, texture, pattern and purpose of the quilt. Reflecting an ideology of hegemonic cultural practice, the smooth operation and management of social, political and organisational structures is thus left minimally challenged or disturbed. This is played out in the politics of autoethnographic representational practices, with normative cultural assumptions arguably frequently forming the framing backdrop in autoethnographies which tend towards the tradition of conventional qualitative inquiry and voice, to be discussed in greater depth below.

In contrast, those in the autoethnographic communities who embrace more of a critical and poststructural edge to their work might regard such representational practices as anathema to trenchant and reflexive cultural interrogation. Textual practices which expose oppressive, deadening and creativity-stifling societal practices and experiences are key in challenging cultural hegemony.

To this end, as will also be argued further below, the use of fictional and other devices can be employed to trouble the assumptions of conventional autoethnographic voice. One such device, arguably useful for critical autoethnographic work, is satire. Used effectively in epochs from ancient to modern, including by such notable figures as Aristophanes, Jonathan Swift and Joseph Heller, satire involves the strategic use of humour to exaggerate and lampoon the paradoxes, contradictions and flaws inscribed within established cultural practices in order to expose their absurdities and oppressive social consequences. An illustrative example of the use of satirical strategies in this volume is provided by Alec Grant, in an autoethnography that critically interrogates the neoliberal cultural 'partnership' between higher education and mental health services.

This example suggests that satire has a logical functional place in those autoethnographies aspiring to a social justice agenda. The attempt to raise awareness of cultural contradictions and their insidious consequences can stimulate connection among developing communities of writers and readers. In terms of utopian, aspirational and social emancipation politics, such a connection may contribute to a weakening of cultural hegemony and the gradual emergence of new storied communities.

The use of satire and other textual practices in the service of cultural critique points to the contingent nature of 'culture' and 'identity'. This signals a further significant function of autoethnography, which is to challenge, deconstruct, and expose as socially constructed rather than foundational or essential, binaries such as: self/other, inner/outer, public/private, individual/society (Sparkes, 2002). The issue of the deconstruction of self/other binaries links to a significant dimension of autoethnographic representational practices. Arguably, qualitative researchers have for too long frequently neglected the first-hand knowledge that they alone possess in the execution of their research ventures (Riemer, 1977). Autoethnographers are, by definition, exemplars of the research and professional ethic of engaging with and reporting on something first hand rather than vicariously. In this regard, they undermine the potentially benevolent stigmatizing and othering, colonialist research that can inform normative ethnographic practices (Jackson & Mazzei, 2009). However, the politics of representation is shot through with philosophical problems around voice, signifying a relatively new and major poststructural challenge to autoethnographic writing.

VOICE

In conventional approaches to qualitative research generally and some variants of autoethnography specifically, it is often implicitly assumed that the voices of participants and researchers authentically and directly correspond to their narrative identities. Associated with this assumption is a tacit acceptance of the 'metaphysics of presence': a self-knowing subject is pre-supposed who can speak for her/himself and others (Denzin, 1989; Lather, 2009). The well-intentioned task in conventional approaches is thus to facilitate the production and dissemination of this authentic voice (Lather, 2009; Mazzei & Jackson, 2009; MacLure, 2009).

The metaphysics of presence assumes real, coherent, stable individuals living lives of equivalent meaning. In line with the seminal work of Husserl, Schutz, Sartre and others, the research task related to this proposition is to access and uncover these meanings from the inner life of the person being studied via the clear window of language. This task applies whether the researcher is studying her or himself, as in autoethnography, or in more mainstream, participant-based, research approaches.

Following Derrida, the poststructural objection to the above is that the ideas of voice as a clear window into the inner life of the self (Denzin, 1989), and of self and voice as identical, are both untenable (MacLure, 2009). The argument that voice is inevitably dialogic (Bakhtin, 1981; Holquist, 2002) coheres with a postmodern understanding of a cacophony of voices inhabiting and constituting a self. These voices are often contradictory, sometimes inhabiting the foreground, sometimes erased, invalidated or distorted by historical and contemporary relations of power (Chaudhry, 2009).

Given the above, voice cannot be considered an innocent and straightforward way to account for a 'self'. Power, subjectivity and desire shape the ways in which individuals speak of their present situation and of their lives. Further, consciousness can never be fully present to itself through language (Jackson, 2009). The light of human meaning is always refracted through the dark glass of language, signs and the process of signification, and language is always unstable. Any expectation of indisputable meaning is confounded by language that is forever constituted by myriad significatory traces of words containing and referring to other words. If it is accepted that there can never be a clear unambiguous statement of anything, then all stories have the status of simply being one story in place of another (Mazzei, 2009). Written and spoken voice is thus forever condemned to insufficiency: 'Neither can deliver the fullness and immediacy that fuels the dream of presence' (MacLure, 2009, p. 100).

On this basis, the act of writing autoethnography influenced by poststructural sensibilities constitutes the performance of provisional 'truths', in textual strategies that evoke fragmented and estranged subjectivities within a temporal landscape of discontinuity and displacement (Gannon, 2006). There is nothing before or behind such language use and autoethnographic performance constitutes speaking oneself into existence within relations of power. In this context, following Deleuze, Davies (2009) argues that an individual, rather than being a self-conscious 'I', is a location where thoughts may emerge. The act of writing opens the writer to becoming what is not yet known and what can never be contained in words.

Writing should therefore aspire to open up other ways of knowing and seeing differently (Davies, 2009; Richardson & St Pierre, 2005). However, in contrast to the kind of risk-embracing writing urged from a poststructural perspective, some examples of autoethnography share the tendency of much mainstream qualitative research in 'playing it safe'. The net result of this at worst is that ambiguity, complexity, power, history and specificity are erased in a *literal* voice which, in a research context, must respond to charges of being insular, parochial, partial and a-theoretical. This is often in spite of well intentioned attempts to produce rigorous qualitative inquiry.

Such attempts betray telling and tacitly accepted theoretical and philosophical governing principles. Despite its traditional associations with interpretivism, an unquestioned assumption of the metaphysics of presence in conventional qualitative and autoethnographic inquiry links to other paradigmatic and methodological positions, although this may not be acknowledged explicitly by researchers (Lather, 2009). These positions include modernism, realism, positivism, phenomenology, and at a broader sociocultural level liberal-humanism. The resultant product is the voice of the coherent humanistic participant or researcher, assumed to be already 'formed' prior to her inscription within culture, who 'knows who she is, says what she means and means what she says' (MacLure, 2009, p. 104). Such a conscious, stable, unified, coherent, rational, knowing and a-historic self is assumed to have a will, freedom and intentionality which is subsequently transferred through language to public action (St. Pierre, 2009). The developing and increasing accrual of experience of this self is equally assumed to provide a stable and reliable source of knowledge and knowing. In the process of knowledge production, so-called 'lived' experience is regarded as necessarily preceding consciousness and reflection. Next comes the writing, transmission and dissemination of such knowledge which has the self of the researcher at its heart as privileged and authentic (Jackson & Mazzei, 2008). In an attempt to both instruct, connect with and reassure readers, this product might be called the narrating voice of the predetermined I.

Narrative postructural voice rejects the assumption of such stable identity in subjectivity in aspiring to speak from its inevitable inscription within overlapping, intersecting, and often contradictory discourses. The poststructural 'voice' is a constant performance of shifting, plural and often discordant combinations of discursive power and positioning (Jackson, 2009). In this context, voice is always provisional and contingent, always becoming. The task of writing research is thus more to show how subjectivity is produced rather than to display a privileged and secure, transcendent narrative identity position, confidently working in synchrony with a backdrop of unfolding history (Jackson & Mazzei, 2008). As product, this might be described as the poststructural narrating voice of the emerging 'I'.

In contrast, textual practices in conventional qualitative and autoethnographic approaches often work with a set of much more straightforward implicit assumptions around writer and reader ethics. This is that the role of the empathic voice is to give voice to the voiceless, reflected in neat, linear and tidy narratives, which make a rhetorical appeal to readers to identify with well-rehearsed forms of suffering (Lather, 2009). Such research activity and knowledge building in and around the empathic voice is equally informed by hegemonic assumptions of universally shared reality positions, and can be seen in some examples of evocative and therapeutic autoethnography (eg Ellis, 2001, 2004; Ellis & Bochner, 2000).

Poststructuralist qualitative researchers such as Lather (2009) argue in opposition that the representation of voice should not be reassuring and should resist easy identification by acknowledging a politics of difference rather than sameness. A main reason for this argument is that associations made between empathic connection and sameness often signal colonising research tendencies. At the levels of writing and reading qualitative research, the empathic voice facilitates a kind of reassuring and voyeuristic cultural tourism while simultaneously obscuring structures of cultural discrimination and power imbalances, thus undermining the social justice agenda of contemporary qualitative research.

From this perspective, the extent to which we appear the same can erase necessary and important differences between us. Thus, empathy can function as a kind of violence – a will to absorb the other in a demand for a totality, or a 'capture and tame' form of conquest disguised as intimacy. On this basis, Lather (2009) argues for poststructural writing practices within which the liberal embrace of empathic understanding is rejected in favour of an 'interpretive reticence' towards a becoming voice – towards a voice that can never be fully known.

Such a poststructural epistemology allows for confusion, difference and saying the unsayable and uncomfortable. This can be conveyed through the use of de-authoring and decentring devices to disrupt authoritative voice and presence (St. Pierre, 2009), including the use of messy texts which undermine a clear sense of linear time (eg Grant 2010 a, b; Short, Grant & Clarke, 2007). As discussed earlier, the use of fictional devices also undermine authenticity and challenge privileged cultural voice and coherent identity positions. These further trouble any sense of a fundamental, essential, foundational position of ultimate truth beyond a narrative which has discursive rather than ontological reality (Chaudhry, 2009).

The poststructural critique of voice in conventional qualitative and autoethnographic approaches extends to an over-reliance on the rationality of words expressed through normative syntax and grammar, written or spoken. Mazzei (2009) critiques researcher investment in such a straightforward, rational, linear and coherent expression of words. Instead, she argues for a re-focus of interest in, in her terms, the impossibly full voice of boundless identity. This is expressed in cracks in meaning, and is detectable in words that shift and cavort, in subtleties of wording and expression, in indirect and oblique responses, and in communication with silences. Mazzei urges a researcher response which resists theoretical and analytical imposition and listens to voices in a way that signals the abandonment of investment in the normative voice. In her view, 'working the limits of voice' enables voices that would otherwise be silenced to be heard, and allows us to listen to ourselves listening and explore the politics of silence.

In related terms, MacLure (2009) calls for a privileging of the distinctive voice. This refers to properties of voice, including laughter and humour, mimicry, mockery, irony, secrecy, silences, inconsistence and masks. These are often regarded as irritants, irrelevancies or blocks to analysis in conventional qualitative approaches. MacLure believes in contrast that they should be accorded analytic respect because of their function as strategies of resistance to the absorption of voice into the colonising normative cultural agenda of sameness, discussed above. This suggests that a kind of reverse airbrushing is called for in the process of acknowledging how voices 'complicate their own transparency and authenticity' (p. 109).

The problematic of voice links to questions around where and what constitutes autoethnographic data (St Pierre, 2009). Is it in the time-space of where it should be 'officially', for procedural ethical purposes? Or is it outside this – in informal conversations, sleep dreams or daydreams? And what is the status of the experiences supposedly captured through such data? From a poststructural position, it is not individuals who have experiences but subjects who are constituted through experience. Identity and experience simultaneously produce each other and cannot be thought about separately, or in some sort of temporal order, as in: experiencing leading to thinking leading to describing. This turns the idea of 'lived experience' on its head. Experience is not the origin of the explanation but that which occurs, that which we seek to describe and explain, at the point when we produce knowledge – when we *do* knowledge through telling, in written or spoken voice. This is made possible through available discourses that 'systematically form the objects of which they speak' (Foucault, 1972), and which always mediate and confound good intentions by locating voices in the shifting relations of discourse, power and desire (Jackson, 2009).

INSTITUTIONAL RESISTANCE TO AUTOETHNOGRAPHIC PRACTICE

Of course, many of the issues, concerns, questions and controversies discussed above may well be resisted at higher education and professional practice institutional levels. Proceeding from onto-epistemological assumptions antithetical to the argument presented so far, institutional resistances relate to well-established tacitly held norms. These are both powerful and insidious, and lead to the thorough and successful socialisation of qualitative scholars and students in higher education to the importance of privileging values such as 'rationality' and 'distanciation', supposedly crucially appropriate rigour sensibilities regarded as foundational and essential rather than socially and culturally constructed and historically contingent.

These normative assumptions around what constitutes good qualitative research are shaped by a hegemonic, global, conservative research agenda (Denzin & Lincoln, 2005). Consequently, emotionality, subjectivity, and related structures of experience are perceived by many in higher education as anathema rather than valuable resource, and are therefore considered a threat to the integrity of their disciplines and associated scholarship (Doloriert & Sambrook, 2011). Such a state of affairs amounts to a kind of professional 'NIMBYism' governed by implicit double standards, where research is always conducted *elsewhere* and *with others*. Conversely, considerable benefits would ensue if autoethnography was pursued as a credible and valuable research agenda. Arguably, academic-, discipline- and profession-based practice based on personal knowledge and experience is more credible, ethical, imbued with integrity, empathic and potentially effective. This marks the difference between implicational and propositional knowledge: between knowing, feeling, connecting and doing, from the heart, based on personal experience, rather than solely on the basis of rationally acquired information.

RISKS OF AUTOETHNOGRAPHY

However, as a cautionary rider, in spite of its benefits and many advantages autoethnography is not for the fainthearted. The accrual of highly reflexive, culturally-related self knowledge can result in a process that is disconcerting and disturbing for the autoethnographer. This relates to the fact that undertaking and publishing autoethnography necessitates a high level of risk taking in relation to personal disclosure and reader reception. Evocative writing by no means guarantees consistent public sympathy or support, and sometimes thick skins, or their speedy growth, are helpful.

ORGANISATION OF THE BOOK

This book is part of a series edited by Ivor Goodson under the banner of educational research in which the interface between professional knowledge and professional lives is interrogated. As such, the chapter authors in this book come from a diverse range of professional cultures. Within their chapters, they may or may not be speaking directly from those professional cultural backgrounds, but the contents of their chapters have a relevance to all undertaking or thinking about undertaking autoethnographic study within or outside of a professional field. Throughout the book you will find professional themes of, Sports, Mental Health, Education, Nursing/Mental Health, Psychotherapy, Tourism/Mental health, and inter-professional themes such as identity and ethics and developing as a professional. There are writings about the dissonance within and between professional and personal selves, the troubling construction of self/relational identity, journeying/travelling and looking back.

The content and themes presented within this book are nomadic. It is a deliberate intention of this collection to describe its territory as it forms and grows. Themes may be both explicit and implicit, and may appear clearly within a chapter, or may wander and fold within the narratives in a fluid non-linear fashion, felted throughout the text of many of the chapters. This book does not lend itself to linear progression. Stories told within the chapters represent fractions of experience which link to other fractions of other experiences, creating a 'relational process ontology' (Stenner, 2008, p.106) of 'variously formed matters and very different dates and speeds' (Deleuze & Guattari, 1987. P.4). As such, experiences of the reader may become intertwined with the reflection of those written experiences within the moment in which they come together.

THE CHAPTERS

To get the book going, in his chapter '*When we got to the top of Elm Grove*', Mike Hayler discusses the idea of sharing stories to develop dialogue around the professional identity of university-based teacher educators. Mike uses analytic autoethnography and narrative self-study writing as a methodological and theoretical basis for his work, alongside life history and illustrative photographs, in exploring how the professional identity of teacher-educators in higher education is both formed and represented by narratives of experience.

In the next chapter, '*Writing teaching and survival in mental health: A discordant quintet for one*', Alec Grant writes from an explicitly poststructural theoretical position. He uses multiple, de-centred voices to represent fragmented experiences. As an academic-mental health survivor and multiple stakeholder, his work critically interrogates the master narratives informing the interface between higher education and mental health practice.

The work of David Carless explores issues around same sex attraction in sport related and cultural settings in his contribution '*Cultural constraints: Experiencing same-sex attraction in sport and dance*'. He uses storied narratives to discuss the lived experience of sexual 'outing' and identity in two contrasting cultures: one (arguably) heterosexual culture, traditionally binaried, exclude same sex attraction and the other a more fluid culture in which same sex attraction permeates throughout.

Jess Moriarty uses multiple voices to reflectively represent fragmented experiences around and through the process of undertaking a doctoral thesis which resists traditional academic writing. '*Leaving the blood in: Experiences with an autoethnographic doctoral thesis*' uses analytical autoethnography together with autoethnodrama and the use of literary tropes to discuss the ways in which personal and professional life(s) are felt through and influence the autoethnographic narrative.

In '*A truth waiting for a telling*', Kitrina Douglas writes about her experience of elite sports research in relation to her life and the demands of working within higher education. She uses messy rather than linear narratives, and literary devices to rhizomatically weave stories of her life, work and academic concerns. This provides the backdrop for her critique of grand narrative realist tales of sporting excellence defined by winning.

In the following chapter, Nigel Short discusses his experiences of tourism and travel alongside those of mental health service consumption. '*An Englishman abroad: an autoethnographic tale*' uses narrative representation to juxtapose his identity as a tourist in a foreign country with that of being a client in an in-patient ward. Nigel moves backwards and forwards between two fixed time positions as he uses these two locations as a vehicle to discuss transforming identity.

Jonathan Wyatt pursues an inquiry into leaving his role as a counsellor, through an exploration of encounters with others in different therapy and non therapy 'spaces' in '*Ash Wednesdays: An autoethnography of (not) counselling*'. Using the methodological and theoretical approach of assemblage/ethnography, he stories and re-stories himself and his encounters with others as he moves through and away from NHS procedural bureaucracy towards becoming a non-counsellor.

In their *'Assemblage/ethnography: troubling constructions of self in the play of materiality and representation chapter'*, Ken Gale and Jonathan Wyatt explore the space(s) constructed within and through their collaborative writing. Jonathan and Ken use diffraction and interference to felt an assemblage in which they attempt to escape what they describe as 'incessant nouning' showing and sharing their 'constructing and construction' as they move away from categorisation through poststructural narrativisation.

In the next chapter, *'Writing forms of fiction: Glimpses on the Essence of Self'*, David Gilbourne and Phil Marshall uses three fictional stories as a medium for an informal reflective analysis of representations of selves. They explore themes of personal interactions within local geographical, sporting and academic culture(s), presenting their selves-in-fiction stories for interpretation and reflective meandering by the reader.

Continuing on the theme of identities, Nigel Short's chapter *'Didn't you used to be...? The role of serendipity and sagaciousness'* provides a reflective and reflexive account of a 31-year career in the English National Health Service the end of which led to disillusionment and retirement. Nigel plays with ideas of transformational change over time, space and person reflecting on those serendipitous moments which influence transformation. He uses metaphors and reflective storying to discuss his self(s) across time and different role(s).

Following this, Brett Smith provides a critique of neo liberalism, power and hierarchy in Higher Education Institutions. In *'Artificial persons and the academy: A story'*, Brett highlights the facade of academic practice which favours the pursuit of quantitative research over education. He presents a critical dialogue which exposes the facilitated rise of the artificial person through an academic grand narrative of applied measurement and subsequent perceived lack of agency for academics.

In the next chapter, *'Autoethnography at the will of the body: reflections on a failure to produce on time'*, Andrew Sparkes seeks to generate a meta-autoethnography in which he reflects on the challenges and ethics of writing autoethnographically 'to order', in the production of a reflective meta autoethnographic narrative of the 'waiting to be told'. Andrew uses an embodied woven narrative and vignettes to discuss issues of masculinity, sport, health, ageing and vulnerability.

In the last autoethnography, Lydia Turner discusses the challenges of undertaking autoethnographic study and writing in an ethical way in *'The evocative autoethnographic I: The Relational Ethics of writing about oneself'*. These challenges are illustrated in and by stories from her life as young girl and later as a grown woman. She uses evocative autoethnography, ethical theories and literary tropes to explore a partial resolution of dissonance using the idea of 'others' as autoethnographically constructed and therefore subject to inevitable re-authoring.

The book ends with a coda chapter, in which the three editors engage with concerns, issues and themes emerging for them from the chapters in the book.

Their trialogue focuses on the use of autoethnography as organisational critique; the role of the approach in transcending traditional arguments and binaries around what is perceived to constitute scholarship in the social and human sciences; and the reflexive ethics of engaging with, reading and writing autoethnography.

REFERENCES

Anderson, L. (2006). Analysing autoethnography. *Journal of Contemporary Ethnography*, *35*(4), 373–395.

Bakhtin, M. (1981). *The dialogic imagination: Four essays by M. M. Bakhtin.* In M. Holquist, C. Emerson, & M. Holquist (Eds.), Austin, Texas: University of Texas Press.

Bakhtin, M. (1984). *Problems of Dostoevsky's poetics.* Minneapolis: University of Minnesota Press.

Berger, L. (2001). Inside out: Narrative autoethnography as a path toward rapport. *Qualitative Inquiry*, *7*(4), 504–518.

Bochner, A. (2001). Narrative's virtues. *Qualitative Inquiry*, *7*(2), 131–157.

Bochner, A., & Ellis, C. (1996). Introduction. Talking over ethnography. In C. Ellis & A. Bochner (Eds.), *Composing ethnography. Alternative forms of qualitative writing.* Walnut Creek, CA: AltaMira Press.

Chaudhry, L. (2009). Forays into the mist: Violences, voices, vignettes. In A. Jackson & L. Mazzei. *Voice in qualitative inquiry: Challenging conventional, interpretive, and critical conceptions in qualitative research.* London and New York: Routledge.

Church, K. (1995). *Forbidden narratives. Critical autobiography as social science.* London, UK: Routledge.

Coffey, A. (1999). *The ethnographic self.* London, UK: Sage Publications Ltd.

Davies B. (2009). Life in Kings cross. A play of voices. In A. Jackson & L. Mazzei. *Voice in qualitative inquiry: Challenging conventional, interpretive, and critical conceptions in qualitative research.* London and New York: Routledge.

Denzin, N. (1989). *Interpretic biography.* Newbury Park, California: Sage Publications, Inc.

Deleuze, G., & Guattari, F. (1987). *A thousand plateaus: Capitalism and schizophrenia* (B. Massumi, Trans.) Minneapolis: University of Minnesota Press.

Denzin, N. (1992). The many faces of emotionality. In C. Ellis & M. Flaherty (Eds.), *Investigating subjectivity: Research on lived experience.* London: Sage Publications Ltd.

Denzin, N. (2006). Analytic autoethnography, or déjà vu all over again. *Journal of Contemporary Ethnography*, *35*(4), 419–428.

Denzin N., & Y. Lincoln Y (2000). *Handbook of qualitative research*, London, Sage Publications.

Denzin N., & Y. Lincoln (2005). Introduction. In N. Denzin & Y. Lincoln (Eds.), *The Sage handbook of qualitative research* (3rd ed.). Thousand Oaks, California: Sage Publications, Inc.

Doloriert, C., & Sambrook, S. (2011). Accommodating an autoethnographic PhD: The Tale of the Thesis, the Viva Voce, and the Traditional Business School. *Journal of Contemporary Ethnography*, *40*, 582–615.

Ellingson, K. (2006). Embodied knowledge: Writing researchers' bodies into qualitative health research. *Qualitative health research*, *16*, 298–310.

Ellis C. (2001). With mother/with child: A true story. *Qualitative inquiry*, *7*(5), 598–616.

Ellis C. (2004). *The ethnographic I: A methodological novel about teaching and doing autoethnography.* Walnut Creek, CA: AltaMira.

Ellis, C. (2007). Telling secrets, revealing lives: Relational ethics in research with intimate others. *Qualitative Inquiry*, *13*(3), 3–29.

Ellis, C., & Bochner, A. (2000). Autoethnography, Personal Narrative, Reflexivity. In N. Denzin & Y. Lincoln (Eds.), *Handbook of qualitative research* (2nd ed.). Thousand Oaks, CA: Sage Publications, Inc.

Ellis, C., & Bochner, A. (2006). Analysing analytic autoethnography. An autopsy. *Journal of Contemporary Ethnography*, *35*(4), 429–449.

Ellis, C., Bochner, A., Denzin, N., Lincoln, Y., Morse, J., Pelias, R., & Richardson, R. (2008). Talking and thinking about qualitative research. *Qualitative Inquiry*, *14*, 254.

Etherington, K. (2004). *Becoming a reflexive researcher. Using our selves in research.* London and Philadelphia: Jessica Kingsley Publishers.

Fine M., & Weis L. (2005). Compositional studies, in two parts. Critical theorizing and analysis on social (in)justice. In N. Denzin & Y. Lincoln (Eds.), *The Sage handbook of qualitative research* (3rd ed.). Thousand Oaks, California: Sage Publications, Inc.

Foucault, M. (1972). *The archaeology of knowledge.* London: Tavistock.

Frank A. (2005). What is dialogical research, and why should we do It? *Qualitative Health Research, 15*(7), 964–974.

Gannon, S. (2006). The (im)possibilities of writing the self-writing: French poststructural theory and autoethnograpy. *Cultural Studies Critical Methodologies, 6*(4), 474–495.

Grant, A. (2010a).Writing the reflexive self: An autoethnography of alcoholism and the impact of psychotherapy culture. *Journal of Psychiatric and Mental Health Nursing, 17*, 577–582.

Grant, A. (2010b). Autoethnographic ethics and re-writing the fragmented self. *Journal of Psychiatric and Mental Health Nursing, 17*, 111–116.

Grant, A. (2011a). Performing the room: Four days on an acute ward. In A. Grant, F. Biley & H. Walker (Eds.), *Our encounters with madness.* Ross-on-Wye: PCCS Books.

Grant, A., & Zeeman, L. (2012). Whose story is it? An autoethnography concerning narrative identity. *The Qualitative Report, 17*(72), 1–12.

Holman Jones, S. (2005). Autoethnography. In N. Denzin & Y. Lincoln (Eds.), *The Sage handbook of qualitative research* (3rd ed.). Thousand Oaks, California: Sage Publications, Inc.

Holquist, M. (2002). *Dialogism* (2nd ed.). London and New York: Routledge.

Jackson, A., & Mazzei L. (2008). Experience and "I" in autoethnography. A deconstruction. *International Review of Qualitative Research, 1*(3), 299–318.

Jackson A. (2009). What am I doing when I speak of this present? Voice, power, and desire in truth-telling. In A. Jackson & L. Mazzei. *Voice in qualitative inquiry: Challenging conventional, interpretive, and critical conceptions in qualitative research.* London and New York: Routledge.

Jackson, A., & Mazzei L. (Eds.). (2009). *Voice in qualitative inquiry. Challenging conventional, interpretive, and critical conceptions in qualitative research.* London and New York: Routledge.

Jones, J. (1996). The self as other: Creating the role of Joni Jones the ethnographer for broken circles. *Text and Performance Quarterly, 16*, 131–145.

Lather, P. (2009). Against empathy, voice and authenticity. In A. Jackson & L. Mazzei (Eds.), *Voice in qualitative inquiry: Challenging conventional, interpretive, and critical conceptions in qualitative research.* London and New York: Routledge.

Lees, J., & Freshwater, D. (Eds.). (2008). *Practitioner-based research. Power, discourse and transformation.* London: Karnac.

Lincoln, Y., & Denzin, N. (2003). *Turning points in qualitative research: Tying knots in a handkerchief.* Walnut Creek, CA: AltaMira Press.

MacLure, M. (2009). Broken voices, dirty words. On the productive insufficiency of voice. In A. Jackson, & L. Mazzei. *Voice in qualitative inquiry: Challenging conventional, interpretive, and critical conceptions in qualitative research.* London and New York: Routledge.

Mazzei, L. (2009). An impossibly full voice. In A. Jackson & L. Mazzei. *Voice in qualitative inquiry: Challenging conventional, interpretive, and critical conceptions in qualitative research.* London and New York: Routledge.

McLeod, J. (2011). *Qualitative research in counselling and psychotherapy.* London: Sage Publications Ltd.

Muncey, T. (2010). *Creating autoethnographies.* London: Sage Publications Ltd.

Park-Fuller, L. (2000). Performing absence: The staged personal narrative as testimony. *Text and Performance Quarterly, 20*, 20–42.

Pelias, R. (2004). *A methodology of the heart.* Walnut Creek, CA: AltaMira Press.

Rambo, C. (2007). Handing IRB an unloaded gun. *Qualitative Inquiry, 13*(3), 353–367.

Rambo Ranoi C. My mother is mentally retarded. In A. Bochner & C. Ellis (Eds.), *Composing ethnography.* Walnut Creek, CA: Altamira Press.

Richardson, L. (2000). Writing: A method of inquiry. In N. Denzin & Y. Lincoln (Eds.), *Handbook of qualitative research* (2nd ed.). Thousand Oaks, CA: Sage Publications, Inc.

15

Richardson L, St. Pierre E. (2005). Writing: A method of inquiry. In N. Denzin & Y. Lincoln (Eds.), *The Sage handbook of qualitative research* (3rd ed.). Thousand Oaks, California: Sage Publications, Inc.

Riemer, J. (1977). Varieties of opportunistic research. *Urban Life, 5*, 467–477.

Riessman, C. (1993). *Narrative analysis.* Newbury Park, California: Sage Publications, Inc.

Riessman C. (2008). *Narrative methods for the human sciences.* Thousand Oaks, California: Sage Publications, Inc.

Rorty, R. (1982). *Consequences of pragmatism (Essays 1972–1980).* Minneapolis: University of Minneapolis Press.

Short, N. (2010). *An evocative autoethnography: A mental health professional's development.* Unpublished doctoral thesis, University of Brighton, United Kingdom.

Short N. (2011). Freeze-frame: Reflections on being in hospital. In A. Grant, F. Biley, & H. Walker (Eds.), *Our encounters with madness.* Ross-on-Wye: PCCS Books.

Short, N., & Grant, A. (2009). Burnard (2007). Autoethnography or a realist account? *Journal of Psychiatric and Mental Health Nursing, 16*, 196–198.

Short, N., Grant, A., & Clarke, L. (2007). Living in the borderlands; writing in the margins: An autoethnographic tale. *Journal of Psychiatric and Mental Health Nursing, 14*, 771–782.

Spry, T. (2001). Performing autoethnography: An embodied methodological praxis. *Qualitative Inquiry. 7*(6), 706–732.

Sparkes, A. (2002). *Telling tales in sport and physical activity. A qualitative journey.* Leeds, UK: Human Kinetics.

St. Pierre, E. (2009). Decentering voice in qualitative inquiry. In A. Jackson & L. Mazzei (Eds.), *Voice in qualitative inquiry: Challenging conventional, interpretive, and critical conceptions in qualitative research.* London and New York: Routledge.

Stenner, P. (2008). A. N. Whitehead and subjectivity. *Subjectivity, 22*, 90–109.

Tilmann-Healy L. A secret life in a culture of thinness. Reflections on body, food, and bulimia. In A. Bochner & C. Ellis (Eds.), *Composing ethnography.* Walnut Creek, CA: Altamira Press.

MIKE HAYLER

WHEN WE GOT TO THE TOP OF ELM GROVE

When we got to the top of Elm Grove, without saying anything and without any sort of sign, we stopped and turned together to look back at the old town where we grew up. Silently and separately we took in the familiar landmarks from our lives. The Pier and the Pavilion and the shape of the coast as it curls out towards Worthing. The various shapes of streets and buildings that we know of old: the flats in Hollingdean, the flaky facades in Roundhill, the car park near St. Barts which used to be several streets of crumbling houses when we were kids. It had taken us a while to get up here.

'Walking really is like writing you know,' said Suzanne. We had been talking about them both earlier in the day.

'A sort of narrative you mean – routes as narrative?' I said.

'Yes, but I mean look at you and me.' She gestured towards me, pointed her thumb at herself and then swept her hand and arm out wide to take in the view. 'We write all the time don't we? We walk everyday. Gets us nowhere most of the time. We don't even call it writing and it's not what we mean when we talk about being a writer. Reports, lesson plans, emails, mapping exercises, memos. The marks we make on a page or a screen to account for ourselves and justify our jobs.'

'Right,' I started to see what she meant as I noticed a new building going up near the centre of town and half-heartedly tried to remember what used to be there, 'and we walk everyday but it's not what we mean by being a walker? From home to work or between the office and the lecture theatre or the seminar room.'

'Between meetings,' she laughed.

'Oh yes, between meetings. The walks we take to justify our lives.'

Writing, walking. They had become something more than the verbs which describe an action for us both. I love to walk, I need to write. Not the emails or the programme outline for faculty scrutiny. We are not talking about the steps we take between the places we work or the rushing around to get to the places we would rather not be.

'So what makes the difference', I asked Suzanne, 'landscape? Is it where we walk? Readership? Is it why we write? Who the writing is for?'

'Presence,' she said, 'presence and nourishment,' without any hesitation.

I knew what she meant by 'nourishment.' There's a writing that, grounds you, makes you bigger. It gives you as much as you put down on the page. It makes you think in a different way. And there's a walking that does the

N. P. Short et al. (Eds.), Contemporary British Autoethnography, 17–31.

same: 'When I stop I cease to think' wrote Rouseau in 1782, 'my mind only works with my legs' (p. 382).

Without saying anything and without any sort of sign, we turned together away from the old town and continued walking towards a different sort of landscape. Neither of us said anything for a couple of miles or so.

This chapter re-explores some examples of shared narratives generated through an autoethnographic research study that considered the professional identity of university-based teacher educators. The research, which emerged from my experience of working as a teacher educator in a university school of education, presented and examined my own narrative of experience alongside those of six other teacher educators.

The original study (Hayler, 2009) offered a perspective of what it means to be a teacher educator in the first decades of the 21st Century through a number of themes which arose from the writing and sharing of self-narratives and conversations. I used a range of methods drawn from narrative self-study writing, life history and autoethnography as a sort of lens with which to examine aspects of the memories, perspectives and experiences of university-based teacher educators. I eventually came to employ a form of what Anderson (2006) calls analytic autoethnography for the study and the subsequent book (Hayler, 2011).

The particular focus of the current chapter is the sharing of stories as a way of developing dialogue with informants beyond the self as part, as well as product, of the research process. I want to consider some of the ways of, and situations in which, this dialogue develops and encourage the reader to further consider how narrative is developed collaboratively in differing contexts.

I use these examples to show aspects of analytic autoethnography as a potentially useful way of framing and employing autoethnography within what Anderson (2006, p. 374) calls 'the analytic ethnographic paradigm'. I do not see the analytic and the evocative as mutually exclusive and I think that by using this method I was able to examine some of the commonalities that arise in the experiences of teacher educators, recognising the individual nature of experience while examining and constructing my own story in collaboration with, and with reference to, others.

In a lecture which he called *Seeing the Blossom*, Dennis Potter once explained that:

You will have to excuse what might at first seem like self-indulgent digression but I need to make this journey to gather up a few things that I want to say. (1994, p. 41)

SATURDAY MORNING 7.08 AM, 9TH NOVEMBER 2002

Finally got to this page! Significant delay of over a week before I've managed to start the journal. My first lesson on the EdD in writing and preparation? . . .

Then a paraphrase from a famous book by Norman Maclean (1990), which I had read not long before:

Sooner or later, all things merge into one and then a river runs through it. Under the water will be the rocks. Under the rocks are the words, and some of the words are mine.

One thing I want from the EdD is the chance to write. Education provides a structure and a spur and an 'excuse'. It legitimises writing for me. You wouldn't think I'd need that by now. Perhaps it's just a way of avoiding reading. I always wrote when I was in trouble, but now I'm not (am I?)Perhaps the EdD is a way of providing a problem – causing 'trouble' for myself which makes me write. Once you've improved upon the blank page and you make the marks which tell the tale of who you are, you're making a sort of poetry and bringing it all together so that the water can wash over it. Then you can know yourself and be yourself. Now that I've started, I could write all day. But I've got things to do.

The aim of the research that I carried out for my thesis in 2009 was to achieve an understanding of how the professional identity of teacher educators is both formed and represented by narratives of experience. A related and equally important purpose of the study for me by then was to contribute towards professional knowledge by using, developing, examining and evaluating a method of inquiry which began from the process of writing (Richardson, 2000). I wanted to develop a research method where my own auto-biographical writing was shared and responded to by other participants as a method of exploring the ways in which professional narratives develop. I'd long given up on the idea of finding incontestable truths or making 'accurate' representations of memory:

There was a big board up at one end of the gallery. We made our way towards it slowly looking at the paintings on the way. I knew the locations in the paintings but I couldn't quite place them. There were some clues like the shape of a hill but then the farm was in the wrong place; a familiar church but the wall and gate looked different from how I remembered it; the local park which looked strangely 'other.' They were unmistakable but seemed different. The paintings captured the feeling of the locations rather than trying to recreate them exactly on the canvas. When we got to the end of the room I read the board about the artist (Harold Mockford) *and his work:*

(By the kind permission of Harold and Margaret Mockford)

That rang a bell with me

Drawing on Polkinghorne's psychological research (1988), and from the philosophical ideas of Paul Ricoeur (1984), the research with teacher educators sat alongside the body of work developed by Connelly and Clandinnin (1988, 1990, 2001) and with the Self Study of Teacher Education Practices (S-STEP) group of practitioner/writers. The focus of this group's work has been largely upon the use

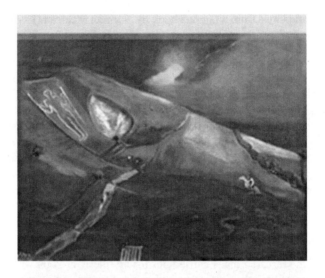

of narrative to support the education and professional development of teachers and teacher educators through reflective self-study (Russell & Munby, 1992; Russell & Loughran, 2007). While this approach could be framed as 'activism' (Hammersley, 2007) since it aims to change practice, I see no inevitable contradiction between the notions of self-study for research purposes and self-study for professional and personal development. Research using S-STEP methodology has included placing teacher educators' own narratives at the centre of the process in order to examine the role of collaboration in self-study (Chryst, Lassonde & Mckay, 2008; Crafton & Smolin, 2008) and exploring the tensions between teaching, methodology and theory in teacher education (Hamilton, 2008).

I had a particular EdD destination to consider at that time and adopted Anderson's (2006) proposals for analytic autoethnography as a way of developing and framing my methodology in relation to more traditional ethnographic qualitative research. This sometimes felt and continues to feel, like an uneasy compromise. 'Writers', as Joan Didion put it, 'are always selling someone out' (1968, p.xiv). I had a go at developing a version of analytic autoethnography that followed Anderson's principles without surrendering my deepening commitment to an interpretive, narrative perspective. The uneasy compromise becomes part of the story:

As the text slips away from me I read through what I've written again and start to think about how I would assess it and respond to it as a tutor if someone had sent it to me. Why? Is that what this is all about? Am I trying to write for an external set of standards and in a particular way? I could take the writing above and chisel and shape it and make it more and more like the chapters and the articles and the books I've been reading for the last year, and less and less like me. Less and less like me. Some of the books and the notes I've written are lying around me on the floor and on my desk. I want to breathe them all in and then breathe them out and onto the page as my own. I reach down and pick up something I copied from Maria Antoniou's (2002) thesis a month ago:

We need to support each other in rejecting the limitations of a tradition – a manner of reading of speaking, of writing, of criticizing – which was never really designed to include us at all.' (Rich, 1987/1981, p.95)

My scribbled note is squashed against the quote: 'we?' 'us?'

Then my notes paraphrase Maria as she writes of how 'this disturbs the myth of the objective academic' (Antoniou, 2002, p.39) and how she took a new turn on her literature chapter from there, how she made a new approach, made a new beginning that was open about the partiality of her reading, that got down to what mattered in her thesis and stopped pretending to be 'complete' or 'objective'.

I look up from my notes. Across the room I can see my reflection in the computer screen. The words I've typed cover my face like a mask. Less and less like me. I think I'd better take a new turn here. I may not be able to be wholly part of the 'we' and 'us' that Rich refers to and Antoniou identifies with but I don't seem to be able to join the tradition they both reject without wearing a mask of words and I'm not sure I've got the skills or the motivation to make one that fits. That's not why I'm doing this thesis. Just the opposite if I remember rightly. This is my attempt to make connections between my past and my future, to understand how identities shift and are used in belief and in practice, and to find my way back to a sense of myself.

I gather up all the notes and put them on the desk. Put the books and the articles in a pile in the corner. That gives me some space. The floor is clear. On the shelves around the room are so many books, all sorts of books that have led me here. There's a story here somewhere:

Lots of stories in fact but what use are they to me now? How can they be part of this story? What sort of story is this? Maybe it's a mystery, a detective story. I go to the shelf and find some old Raymond Chandler books hidden behind a picture of my eldest son. Stories of how the dark 'truth' of human beings emerges the more you look beyond the surface. Left along the shelf I can see the collection of stories by Raymond Carver: 'Where I'm Calling From' (1993). One of the stories inside has that title. The narrator in that story knows it is time to be honest as he prepares to telephone his wife from the drying out clinic:

She'll ask me where I'm calling from, and I'll have to tell her. (p. 242)

That's what I want to do now with the rest of this chapter: tell you where I'm calling from amongst all these words.

My approach was to deliberately focus on individuals and to engage in an intensely personal type of research process. I found experimenting with these methods rewarding, exciting and liberating, but never settling or reassuring. I came to understand and agree with Schon (1971) that all real change and learning involves feelings of 'being at sea, of being lost, of confronting more information than you can handle' (p.12). The discussions illuminated several of the key issues about becoming and being a teacher educator in the 21st Century but it was never their purpose to identify universal processes or generalisations. The feeling of being at sea did not go away but rather I developed some 'sea legs' and learnt to move and think in a way that allowed new types of understanding to emerge. Through this process of research and writing I found new ways of living and working with uncertainty. The sharing of stories illuminates the often hidden and private experiences that give meaning to everyday life, making things more visible without making them simple. In some ways I think this is enough as the reader, the audience, make meaning from the way we tell the story. The stories themselves have an evocative validity as they bring the news of experience and response from one person's world to another.

Rosen (1993) says that stories live off stories and that of all the genres learned through language . . .

narrative is the genre we are most comfortable with. From a very early age we gather a rich experience of stories and learn more and more how they work, their methods and devices. So in our tellings, without our realising it, we use this hidden repertoire. . . We are all story tellers if only we are given the chance. (p. 51)

As soon as I started writing my tale I realised that what really mattered here, was how I remembered and how I constructed my memories and how this narrative shapes my belief and behaviour. I began to explicitly investigate what I had known tacitly for a long time; how the story I make and remake about myself makes me who I am. So

I felt as though consulting the sources such as my diary or other people who were there was no more or less 'reliable' or 'valid' than any other method and that this sort of reliability was not the central issue here. Any attempt to make an 'accurate' history of my learning journey would be firstly in vain and secondly fundamentally miss the point. Bruner (1990) identifies autobiographical narrative as the central phenomena of what he terms as cultural psychology. A particular view of the self is revealed through this window within a culture:

> What all these (reflexive autobiographical) works have in common is the aim and the virtue of locating self not in the fastness of immediate private consciousness but in the cultural-historical situation as well (p. 108).

I knew the story well but found new understandings as I wrote it, then further understanding as I heard others respond to it through stories of their own. I found a story of myself within the stories of becoming and being teacher educators.

IT STARTED LIKE THIS:

It is well into September now and it feels a bit strange. I am at home writing this, trying to make a story about how I came to be here and I keep feeling as though I should be somewhere else. Life stories are to some extent always provisional and they often contain uncertain and contradictory elements. The significance of the myths we live by (Samuel and Thompson, 1990) lies not so much in whether they can be fixed as either true or false expressions of experience but in the ways in which they are constructed and told in an attempt, as Brian Roberts (1998) puts it, 'to make sense of the past and our part in it, and how we have become what we believe we want to be' (p. 103). For many years of my life what I wanted to be was a teacher and then a teacher of teachers. I became a primary school teacher in 1991 and a senior lecturer in a university school of education in 2004, but now, as a song from my past reminds me 'it's late September and I really should be back at school' and I am here writing this. Out 'there' the children are working through the literacy hour, the teachers are sharing their learning intentions with the class and the lecturers are reading emails and attending meetings (the students aren't back yet), and I am writing this and trying to find a voice that sounds like mine and tells my tale.

Perceived success or failure in education often holds a key role in autobiographical texts (Dunn, 1990; Goldman, 1997; Mills, 1978) and it has a central place in my own story of my self. Perhaps like Roberts (1998) I have a mystery to solve: 'in the story of my education and its outcome I see a puzzle: what are the key elements and how do they connect to produce the particular ending?' (p.104).

We can tell our tales in all sorts of ways and never get to an ending but as it is September and this is the story of my education I really should be back at school.

MY TELLING TALE

My parents had faith in education. It worked for them. They gained qualifications at school and trained as nurses. They met in Brighton where they had gone to complete their training in 1950. They liked reading and discussion and going to see plays and they believed that education was the route towards a better life for individuals and a better society for all. They were part of the post-war consensus which supported the welfare state. They voted for the Labour party and described themselves as socialists. I have two brothers who are six and four years older than me. My eldest brother was assessed as having learning difficulties during the early years of school and attended a special school from the age of seven. My other brother did well at primary school, passed the eleven-plus and went to a technical school. I started at a state nursery school at the age of 3 in 1963. There seems to have been a bit of a problem from the start . . .

AND IT ENDED LIKE THIS

When I started a full-time job in the school of education at the university it felt like coming home. And so it was. But coming home is often a mixed experience and in the end it did not work out for me.

At the university I had the unusual experience of becoming less confident the longer I worked there and I felt less and less authentic as the months went by. While I had felt like part of the problem in the education system to some extent as a school teacher and as an advisor I always felt that I was contributing something positive as well; something that some of the children would benefit from at some time. I used to call this 'nourishment': the knowledge that what one is doing is something worthwhile and making a contribution. I got less and less 'nourishment' at the university until it felt as though the scales had tipped and I could not enjoy the parts of the job I had loved at first. There seemed like even less time to think and to reflect upon things although I was in the habit of doing that now. It may well have been better not to in a way but I was committed to finishing something I had started and it seemed like a betrayal of my beliefs about learning to turn away now that I had found a comfortable job. Not that it was very comfortable by the last year when I knew I had to leave, do something else and tell my tale for better or for worse.

SHARING

If writing the story was a method of inquiry in itself, what Richardson (2000) calls *Creative Analytic Practice*, where process and product are displayed as deeply intertwined, then sharing it with the other teacher educators was an invitation for the reader to examine their own narrative after reading the memories of another. While the process of writing a self-narrative invokes memory and brings new understanding within a current context for the writer, it also opens this possibility for the reader; a collaboration that is waiting to happen.

The collaboration that is waiting to happen links closely with Anderson's (2006) principal point of connecting self-narrative with the narrative of others in ethnographic study and emphasises the potential of the relationship between self-narrative and life history interview methods where the self-narrative of the researcher is foregrounded. Such collaborations can bring, as Raymond Carver suggests 'news from one world to another' (Carver, Gentry & Stull, 1990, p. 52) and they can also encourage, expand and develop perspectives and understandings within particular cultures and groups such as that of teacher educators. The engagement with the voices of others became the key vehicle of questioning and developing my own understanding and a way in which to share and compare accounts of experiences so as to extend that understanding further.

I was inspired by Munro (1998) who develops Bakhtins's (1981) notion of the dialogic self and examines how her life history work with women teachers works at the intersection of autobiography, narrative and life history research. This seems to be where I too settled as the discussions proceeded. Ricoeur (1974) shows us that it is narrative that gives the events of the past a meaning they do not otherwise have. Narrative soothes us.

MEETING SUZANNE

We first met at a teacher education conference. The theme was male teachers at Key Stage 1 which was really about the lack of male teachers of children aged three to seven, the old 'infant' age phase. Suzanne and I had both been teachers at infant schools early in our teaching careers; me in the mid 1990s and Suzanne back in the 1970s. We got talking about the changes in educational terminology and how particular ideas come around time and again with a different name.

We had both moved into Higher Education in our late 40s. Suzanne was coming up for retirement in two years. I told her I was a late starter and had a while to go yet:

'Late starter - how come?' She had asked me.

'I didn't get any qualifications until I was 25, and then went to poly when I was 27. So PGCE then started teaching in 1990.'

Her route had been more direct: left school with good grades, went to Teacher Training College then got a job in 1970. She was only 10 years older than me but she had been a teacher twice as long. She wondered why I hadn't taken any exams at school.

'Oh there's a story there,' I said 'I'm writing about it at the moment as part of my Doctorate.'

She was surprised: 'Can you do that? Write about yourself for a PhD?'

'Well it's partly that. It's an EdD. I'm aiming to share the story with colleagues, other teacher educators . . . like you.'

25

There was a pause of some length. She didn't seem keen.

'Then I'll interview them,' I explained, 'gather responses, things in common, things that are different.'

'Will they all work at your place in Brighton?

'No, some from Brighton. All teacher educators based in schools of Ed, but from all over really.'

She was smiling now. She said 'Did you grow up in Brighton?'

'Yes, I did.'

'Me too,' she laughed . . . 'I'll read it if you like.'

London in November. Getting dark at 4pm. The traffic building up. The streets are wet although it doesn't seem to have been raining since I left the station and started walking. I know where I'm going. I came to the Uni where Suzanne works a while ago for a job interview. I need to get a job before March which will be a year since I quit the job at Brighton. I remember being nervous on the train and then relaxing when I started walking. Always helps. Just the movement of walking. Something happens to the mind at 3 miles an hour. Felt Ok by the time I got to the interview. Quite relaxed. I didn't get the job.

Suzanne is waiting in the foyer with her coat on, which makes my heart sink. It looks like she is leaving and won't have time for our meeting.

'Let's walk,' she says. 'We can talk on the way.'

I never did find out where we were on our way to but we walked and talked for two hours. This was the first of three walks we took together while I wrote the thesis, and the first of seven before Suzanne died in 2011. Moving meetings. She wrote to me later that week in November 2007:

Thanks for coming up and having a walk with me. I expect you would have rather met in the office and taped the whole thing but as I said, I really needed to get out. So much easier to talk to someone when you are walking side-by-side. Glad it didn't rain. Anyway, I thought it might help if I wrote about some of the things we talked about. Reading your story made me think about so much in my story. I thought it would be the bits about Brighton but it was more the details of your education and career. These are especially interesting to me now that you've resigned. You said you envied me because I took a direct route to teaching and then to HE but as I told you, I really envy your circuitousness. You learnt so much about teaching by not being a teacher for all those years while I was learning about what teachers were meant to be like.

I wanted to be a teacher since I was about eleven. I think I was also inspired by a couple of teachers at school, but like the one you went to there were enough bad ones in our school to put me off the idea if I'd wanted them to. So I'm not really sure why I swung that way. I enjoyed it most of the time and my parents were so proud of me. They thought I was right posh. In the 26 years that I taught in schools I went from being single to being married, to having two children, to being a single Mum. My kids were at University by the time I left to come into HE. Coming into teacher training felt like a new start for me. I was ready for a change. In the first year, I couldn't believe how easy it seemed and in the second year I couldn't believe how difficult it was.

Like you I come from a fairly poor background. Central Brighton. The house, in fact the whole street has gone now and been replaced by a car park and, rather ironically, a school. My Mother and Father got moved to a council house which was fine really.

I was surprised when I found out where Suzanne had lived as a child. The area and the street she had lived in were well known for their poverty when I was a boy. In the sixties people used to say the houses would fall down before they were knocked down. It was just that, unlike me, Suzanne had no trace of a working class accent by the time I met her when she was 58. There was none of that Brighton accent with the 'Ts' missing. My accent had been modified by adult education and becoming a teacher but Suzanne sounded like someone who might have gone to public school.

The thing that I really connected with in your story was your description of the gap between how you want to be and how you are. Like the gap between pedagogy professed and pedagogy as practiced in teaching and especially in HE. But you know I think that's a common feeling for people from backgrounds like ours.

I had never thought of it like that before although I had written about what you could lose as well as gain in Higher Education in my own story:

I did well at the polytechnic which became a university. I was ready to study and to write and I enjoyed pretty much all of it. I made some good friends. For a while early on I felt as though I was in a sort of social limbo, not part of the younger student group who were fresh out of sixth form and no longer part of the old crowd at the pub. They thought I had lost my mind going 'back to school' and that I ought to at least do something useful like a government training course where I could learn a trade. My wife and my mother were not sure either.

As a lecturer I had felt some resentment towards students from more privileged backgrounds who seemed to be taking their opportunities for granted.
Suzanne wrote:

I have felt some of the resentment that you mention about 'spoilt brats' not knowing how lucky they are but I think you are being harsh. Most of them become thoughtful teachers. I'll be glad to retire in a couple of years but the thing I like best about this job is seeing the students change and grow during the degree. I like being part of that. Some of them are just kids when they arrive and they leave ready to teach a class of children. That's quite a journey they've made.

27

What I hate is this feeling that we are really just a franchise of the Department for Education and the Training and Development Agency. We talk about our vision as a school of education and then a memo arrives telling us what our vision is and what and how to teach our students. One of our managers told us all at a meeting that we had to adapt to changing times and that we couldn't hold onto our principles. If we can't hold onto our principles what can we hold onto?

Davies (1997) says that reflective ethnography should be seen as an interrelationship between researcher and other to inform and change social knowledge, and to some extent Suzanne and I shared the role of researcher and researched. We examined elements of our ethnos through our interactions while reading, writing, talking and walking.

MOVING STORIES

My feet are bigger than Suzanne's but she has longer legs. She sets an early pace which is faster than suits me, but slows as she seems to leave something behind her. She eases up to re-engage during the walk as she gets something out of her system. When we walked in London she hadn't said much for the first two miles which took about 40 minutes: she listened a lot, nodded, and offered short answers to match my short strides. There were lots of gaps when we didn't say anything. We didn't need to fill the gaps because we were walking side by side rather than sitting and talking face to face. Then as we slowed she started talking, responding further to my story which she had read, and then asking questions of her own. Today, on the Downs, the gaps are longer but the conversation more symmetrical and she is talking as much as I am. I realise that you get to know someone in a new way when you walk with them.

It's a simple thing in some ways, an everyday wonder in others. No knowing quite where the movement begins and ends: muscles moving, leg swings, heel down, the weight above the ball of the foot, the big toe pushes off while the balance shifts across the body. There is a step and then another. A word joined by a word that makes a story. The rhythm builds like a story. The rhythm of walk with the pattern of talk.

Thoreau (1862) saw walking as an art and writes of the genius of 'sauntering.' The word derives from people who walked around the countryside in the middle ages asking for charity as they made their way to the Holy Land, (la Sainte Terre), without ever attempting to get there. I love to saunter. To walk without real purpose of destination. I realise that you get to know yourself in a new way when you walk with someone else.

While Rousseau (1782) revived the ancient notion that cognition is motion-sensitive and made it famous in the modern Western world (although it was long established in non-western cultures), Macfarlane (2012) argues that walking is not the action by which one arrives at knowledge; it is itself a means of knowing.

... a foot-worn crevasse into the underlying snow of the chalk - a gap through which one might slip not just to another time, but to another realm or climate (Macfarlane, 2012, p. 24)

I would say the same about writing. In *Notes towards a Supreme Fiction* (1955, p. 336) Wallace Stevens suggested that:

Perhaps
The truth depends upon a walk around a lake.

I go along with that.

Suzanne and I both knew how to go to ground when we needed to. We appreciated the simple gratification of physical movement, what Law (1995, p. 9) calls the 'solidity and certainty of labour':

Suzanne: *I get really sick of the abstract. Thinking all the bloody time. That's not where I come from. Just feeling the ground under my feet as I walk over it feels a bit like coming home*

It had always been like that for me too: moments of clarity when you can measure the distance you cover by looking back at distance done. Solnit (2008) may be right when she says that walking can be an act of resistance to the power of the mainstream (p. 451).

De Creteau (1980) suggests that meaning emerging as narrative is also a means of opposing institutional power. The 'intense singularities' of story telling challenge the scientific discourse as it attempts to eliminate 'time's scandals.'

Nonetheless they return over and over again, noiselessly and surreptitiously, and not least within the scientific activity itself: not merely in the form of the practices of everyday life which go on even without their own discourse, but also in the sly and gossipy practices of everyday storytelling . . . a practical know-how is at work in these stories, where all the features of the 'art of memory' itself can be detected . . . the art of daily life can be witnessed in the tales told about it (p.42).

We told our tales as we walked. The transitory movement of those meetings has come to represent the thing that Suzanne and I had most in common. We had left home and never really arrived at our destination.

'*Nobody tells you what you lose when you get an education do they?' she said.*

She was smiling but seemed sad. She knew the walk would soon be over.

REFERENCES

Anderson, L. (2006). Analytic autoethnography, *Journal of Contemporary Ethnography, 35*, 373–395.
Antoniou, M. (2002). *Writing my body: Exploring methods of articulating embodiment*, unpublished PhD thesis, University of Manchester.
Bakhtin, M. (1981). *The dialogic imagination.* Austin, Texas, University of Texas Press.
Bruner, J. (1990). *Acts of meaning*, Cambridge, Massachusetts, Harvard University Press.
Carver, R., Gentry, M. B., & Stull, W. L. (1990). *Conversations with Raymond Carver*, Univ. Jackson, MS, University Press of Mississippi.
Carver, R. (1993). *Where I'm calling from*, London, Harvill.
Chryst, C., Lassonde, C., & Mckay, Z. (2008). The invisible researcher: New insights into the role of collaboration in self-study. In M. L. Heston, D. L. Tidwell, K. K. East, & L. M. Fitzgerald (Eds.), *The seventh international conference on self-study of teacher education practices. Pathways to change in teacher education: Dialogue, diversity and self-study* (pp. 50–53). Herstmonceux Castle, East Sussex, England, S-Step/University of Northern Iowa.
Connelly, F. M., & Clandinin, D. J. (1988). *Teachers as curriculum planners.* Toronto, ON, OISE Press.
Connelly, F. M., & Clandinin, D. J. (1990). Stories of experience and narrative inquiry, *Educational Researcher, 19*(5), 2–14.
Connelly, F. M., & Clandinin, D. J. (2001). Exploring the landscape of Canadian teacher education, *Asia Pacific Journal of Teacher Education and Development, 4*(1), 1–11.
Crafton, L., & Smolin, L. (2008). The language of collaboration: Moving beyond self and other. In M. L. Heston, D. L. Tidwell, K. K. East, & L. M. Fitzgerald (Eds.), *The seventh international conference on self-study of teacher education practices. Pathways to change in teacher education: Dialogue, diversity and self-study* (pp. 82–86). Herstmonceux Castle, East Sussex, England, S-Step/University of Northern Iowa.
Davies, C. A. (1999). *Reflexive ethnography: A guide to researching selves and others.* London, Routledge.
de Certeau, M. (1980). On the oppositional practice of everyday life. *Social Text, 1*(3).
Didion, J (1968). *Slouching towards Bethlehem.* New York, Farrar.
Dunn, R. (1990). *Moulsecoomb days: Learning and teaching on a Brighton council estate 1922–1947.* Brighton, QueenSpark Books.

Goldman, A. (1993). Is that what she said? The politics of collaborative autobiography, *Cultural Critique*, Fall, 1993, pp. 177–204.

Goldman, L. (1997). *Oh what a lovely shore: Brighton in the twenties through the eyes of a schoolboy*. Brighton, Goldman.

Hamilton, M. L. (2008). Studying my practice: Exploring tensions in my teaching, my methodology and my theory. In M. L. Heston, D. L. Tidwell, K. K. East, & L. M. Fitzgerald (Eds.), *The seventh international conference on self-study of teacher education practices. Pathways to change in teacher education: Dialogue, diversity and self-study* (pp. 163–167). Herstmonceux Castle, East Sussex, England S-Step/University of Northern Iowa.

Hammersley, M. (2007). The issue of quality in qualitative research, *International Journal of Research & Method in Education, 30*(3), 287–305

Hayler, M. (2009). *The self-narrative character of teacher educators' pedagogy*, unpublished EdD thesis, University of Brighton.

Hayler, M. (2011). *Autoethnography, self-narrative and teacher education*. Rotterdam: Sense.

Law, C. L. (1995). Introduction. In C. L. B. Dews & C. L. Law (Eds.), *This fine place so far from home* (pp. 1–11). Philadelphia, Temple University Press.

Maclean, N. (1990). *A river runs through it*. Chicago, Chicago University Press.

Macfarlane, R. (2012). *The old ways: A journey on foot*. London, Hamish Hamilton.

Marcus, L. (1994). *Autobiographical discourses*, Manchester, Manchester University Press.

Mills, R. (1978). *A comprehensive education, 1965–1975*. London, Centerprise.

Munro, P. (1998). *Subject to fiction: Women teachers' life history narratives and the cultural politics of resistance*. Buckingham, Open University Press.

Polkinghorne, D. (1988). *Narrative knowing and human science*. New York, State University of New York Press.

Potter, D. (1994). *Seeing the blossom*. London, Faber and Faber.

Rich, A. (1987/1981). *Toward a more feminist criticism. Blood, bread and poetry: Selected prose 1979–1985*. London, Virago.

Richardson, L. (2000). Writing: A method of inquiry. In N. K Denzin, & Y. S. Lincoln (Eds.), *Handbook of qualitative research* (pp. 923–948). London, Sage.

Ricoeur, P. (1974). *The conflict of interpretations*, Evanston, Ill, Northwestern University Press.

Ricoeur, P. (1984). *Time and narrative (1)*, Chicago, University of Chicago Press.

Roberts, B. (1998). An auto/biographical account of educational experience. In Erben, M. (Ed.) *Biography and education* (pp. 103–115), London, Falmer.

Rosen, H. (1993). *Troublesome boy*, London, English and Media Centre.

Rosen, H. (1998). *Speaking from memory: A guide to autobiographical acts and practices*, London, Trentham Books.

Rousseau, J. J. (1782/1953). *The confessions*. Harmondsworth, Penguin.

Russell, T., & Munby, H. (Eds.). (1992). *Teachers and teaching: From classroom to reflection*. London, Falmer Press.

Russell, T., & Loughran, J. (Eds.). (2007). *Enacting a pedagogy of teacher education*. London, Routledge.

Samuel, R., & Thompson, P. (Eds.). (1990). *The myths we live by*. London, Routledge.

Schon, D. (1971). *Beyond the stable state*. Harmondsworth, Penguin.

Solnit, R. (2001). *Wanderlust: A history of walking*. London, Verso.

Solnit, R (2008). The shape of a walk. In P. C. Hoy, A., Forrest, & R. Martin (Eds.), *Writing the essay, art in the world, the world through art* (pp. 451–461). Boston, McGraw-Hill.

Stevens, W, (1955). *The collected poems of Wallace Stevens*. London, Faber and Faber.

Thoreau, H. D. (1862/1980). Walking. In *The natural history essays* (pp. 93–136). Layton, Utah, Gibbs Smith.

ALEC GRANT

WRITING TEACHING AND SURVIVAL
IN MENTAL HEALTH

A Discordant Quintet for One

*Dr Grant's professional, academic and emotional lives and interests co-exist
and co-evolve. He can't manage his work-life balance very well, or maintain
an appropriately measured, objective and distanced approach to his work. He
gets carried away with his passions to the extent that his ability to teach and
write about academic concerns and issues in a fair and balanced way are often
compromised. He frequently fails to adhere to clear aims and objectives in his
teaching. Most worryingly, we fear that there's a risk he may both indoctrinate
students and portray our partners and us in an unfavourable and inappropriate
light.*

Professor Jim Moir
Director of Quality Standards
in Curricula and Partnership Development

***

I want to tell a story with no real beginning or end, as I'm kind of always in the
middle of it. It's a story about stories, or is it a story with stories in it – something
that's autoethnographic with traces of meta-autoethnography about it? At one level
it's about a trickster self interrogating and troubling culture/s, if 'self' is understood
in poststructural terms and 'culture' as co-performativity and production of meaning
with no essential self behind it. All of this, including analysis, is going to hopefully
happen as 'I' write (Richardson & St.Pierre, 2005; St.Pierre, 2009). The only
experience I'm working with is that which I'm involved in right now, which is
constituting me right now as I write these words, as I create a convenient 'me', 'I',
'us', 'we'. This will be a runway where thoughts can take off; when I-us-we write
with many voices, through 'our' discursive, often unconscious and power-imbued
shaping (Davies, 2009; Jackson, 2009). I hope this will do for our time together.

So, as what follows is read, I'd rather I didn't convey a sense of authentic voices of
coherent individuals (Mazzei & Jackson, 2009). I also don't want to give voice to the
voiceless in evoking empathic identification with universal suffering (Lather, 2009)

N. P. Short et al. (Eds.), Contemporary British Autoethnography, 33–48.

when the story gets emotional, around the idea that 'we're all the same under the skin'. We're not. Neither do I want anyone to think that I'm faithfully representing their-our-my 'lived experiences' (St.Pierre, 2009). The idea of the possibility of a direct transmission from experience, to thinking, to describing, to receiving, in a neat, linear, unproblematic, undistorted, unmediated way by coherent, clear headed, fully conscious folk is a bit of a paradigmatic fairy tale by now.

Although I'll try to at least partially overcome the rhetorical effect of 'me' as central story teller in what I write by taking pains to decentre 'voice' and 'presence' in various ways, as much as I think I should (Jackson & Mazzei, 2008), I will probably fail in this endeavour. However, I will aspire to what has been described as 'distinctive voice'. I will not sanitise or airbrush my-our voice/s, and will display some of the humour, mimicry and expletives delighted that function for several of us as 'strategies of subaltern resistance to disciplinary power' (MacLure 2009, p. 107).

Following St.Pierre (2009), all of what follows below is data. Some of this includes imaginary embellishments, dreams, daydreams, and storied memories of events I was involved in. When I introduce other characters in my story, they are mostly based on real people whose identities have been disguised, including by making them composites or the reverse (several characters as one, or one as several). Sometimes you won't know who's talking: might be me, might not. There are also stories about existing textual data and re-contextualised textual data (procedural ethical approval secured). When I write the latter, I'll make the ownership of particular voices crystal clear.

***

At this early point, you may be wondering what makes 'my' 'voice' possible? There's the usual things people talk of, including: fate, choice, gendered and sexualised embodiment, time-place, circumstance and factors outside my awareness (Jackson & Mazzei, 2012), I'm also, I guess, discursively positioned within several related but often contradictory stories (Varga-Dobai, 2012). These include the 'Grant' (et al., 2008, 2010) who was involved in so-called 'evidence-based' (cognitive behavioural) psychotherapy practice for over a quarter of a century. More recently, there is the 'Grant' who aspires to help mental health workers, including nurses, learn to do better interpersonal care with their patients and clients, while being aware that the organisations in which they work socialise them in exactly the opposite direction (Bach & Grant, 2009, 2011).

Then there's 'survivor' 'Grant', whose reported first hand experience of poor organisationally-mediated interpersonal mental health care flies in the face of much of what he writes about and teaches in the name of 'mental health' (Grant 2006; 2010a,b; 2011; Grant & Zeeman 2012; Grant, Biley & Walker, 2011).

***

As a university teacher in mental healthcare, Alec struggles with having to work within neoliberal higher education. He believes that this culture privileges policy-based training by educational technocrats (Furedi, 2004) rather than critical perspectives by movement intellectuals (Cresswell and Spandler, 2012). He also believes that much of the potentially exciting research related to the latter group is antithetical to what Docherty (2012) describes as a normative 'research by numbers' culture currently prevalent in British universities. Neoliberal 'education' in healthcare assumes rational customer-consumers who are clear about their training needs in fulfilling a progressive, developing, policy-underwritten healthcare agenda. The dream is that these customers of commercialised education work in harmony with their similarly corporately managed educational partners in the academy who facilitate their learning.

This is at odds with Alec's view of what higher education used to be and should be about now. He believes that it should challenge rather than reassure. It should stretch, demand creativity, enable people to think out of the box. It should more often question rather than cohere with local and national practice policies, and place those people and policies in theoretical, historical and political contexts (Mills, 1959). It should recognise that such (locally mediated) policy directives often serve the needs of organisations to the disadvantage of the client and patient groups they purport to serve.

Of course, it is naïve of him to continue to hope that, by definition, policy and risk management-driven healthcare organisations might one day welcome or even tolerate creative, critical thinkers. Equally unsurprisingly, although constantly disappointing for him, not many of his teacher colleagues seem to sign up to his view of what higher education should be about. He believes that one reason for this is that the 'partnership' between universities and mental health services seems characterised by a tacitly held need to avoid asking awkward questions or challenge the organising principles of either group.

Sometimes he becomes very angry about this. It makes his blood boil, given his experiences and those of his associates at the hands of institutional psychiatry, but I guess he believes he can't do much more than write about it.

Dr Roman Imyata, Independent scholar

***

CONSERVING FRUIT

Is good because we can lock the little bastards
in a bottle and
press the unruly sods down so
they don't cause us any trouble.

Then we can keep them for ever and ever
so that we don't need to plant for new ones
whose bastard seeds will burst out
of their skins, spreading around and
mutating,

creating new fruit that we don't understand
which makes us feel and look like fools.
We're supposed to be the people who understand fruit
and teach about it,

to people who know fuck all about fruit
who are our customers.
But they don't know apples from pears.
Neither do we if the truth be told.

We *must* keep the ferment of our ignorance
out of sight in a bottle,
pressed down with the lid on
so that it doesn't cause us any trouble.

***

WHO'S PLATO?

I've recently been awarded my PhD and am teaching on a masters module. The topic is *Reflexivity*. The students are all senior mental health nurses, mostly managers. The focus of my PhD was a specific aspect of the organisational mediation of mental health nurse activity. My thesis broadly was that the state organisations that mental health nurses worked in were socially constructed. I argued that organisational custom and practice about the 'way things are done around here' conspired to maintain trusted, but often ineffective, ways of thinking, behaving and power relations, and that all of this undermined effective nursing interventions.

The group I'm teaching is small, maybe 8 or 9 people. We get off to a bad start when some of them ask me 'what's the minimum number of books from the module reading list that we need to read to pass this module?' (*at this point I want to vomit all over their shoes*). They tell me that they don't like reading books or papers and are only undertaking masters level study for job promotion purposes. I'm also irritated by the consensus among them that the systems and procedures in place in their departments means that mental health nurses are working in a satisfactory way in their work organisations. They can't seem to grasp the concept of the socially constructed organisation, assuming that their organisations are benign, neutral places that simply serve as bricks and mortar backdrops to practice. I try a reflective educational exercise to help them develop some organisational reflexivity, or at least more of an ability to think conceptually (Morgan, 1997).

36

Alec: 'I wonder if we could try an exercise based on the way Morgan uses the Plato's cave metaphor? This exercise, and the reading you've got from it, is grounded in the postmodern idea that it's useful to step back from a literal view and interpretation of organisations, and instead see them through the lens of differently nuanced metaphors. One of the really useful metaphors that Morgan uses is that of the "psychic prison". By this he means that we're often trapped by ways of thinking and related behaviours. These are the product of organisational discourse and may not be the best way to proceed but we invest in them because of our socialisation into organisation beliefs and practices. This socialisation is relatively "silent", tacit, occurring below the radar of our awareness to the extent that we're relatively unaware of this process and simply see what much of what happens in our organisations as simply right and proper "common sense".

We spoke earlier (*well I spoke earlier. They didn't join in*) about Foucault's notion of discourse influencing subjectivity? Well, I think that this complements Morgan's position. In small groups, just imagine for a few minutes the story of a cave with a line of slaves chained up. The slaves are chained to face the back wall of the cave. They have never seen the outside world in their lives, but see the reflection of sunlight on the wall. They think that where they live is reality, but one day one of them escapes. He sees the outside world in all its glory and myriad colours. He come back to tell his fellow slaves that what they had considered to be reality was all along just a pale, dark shadow. They refuse to believe him.

Now, with that information, consider the implications for organisational thinking and behaving. How might someone who was absolutely convinced that organisational custom and practice was right and proper, and the only way it could be, respond to an "outsider" who had a different take on things?'

(A few minutes pass. They don't look terribly enthusiastic about this exercise and I start to feel increasingly irritated with them. I comfort myself with some covert counter-defensive stereotyping: 'How could such a stupid bunch of plonkers be accepted onto a postgraduate degree? This wouldn't have happened in the past.).

Alec: 'Okay, I wonder what you've come up with?'

In response to that question, a large formidable middle-aged woman in the first group turns round to face me with her arms tightly folded around her chest. Speaking on behalf of her group, she bellows 'WELL, WE'RE NOT IN THE CAVE!'

I don't say anything, but think to myself '*you've just demonstrated that you are madam*'.

I get caught up in my anger and barely hear the small bird-like woman in the other group who chirps 'who's Plato?'. Bloody hell! I can't believe that she's asked this.

I want to scream. Everyone knows who Plato is. Worse, she pronounces the first syllable in Plato to rhyme with 'Cat'. '*YOU HAVE SERIOUSLY REACHED YOUR PLATEAU*', I think, loudly.

I go home and get very drunk.

***

THE REFLEXIVITY KOAN

The last thing a fish notices is the water it's swimming in.
What do you think about what you think about?
What do you think about the way you think?
What do you feel about these things?

What do you think about these questions?
What do you feel about these questions?

The knowledge you produce is
produced by the knowledge that's
producing you.

And what do you think about that?
And how does it make you feel?

Reflexivity is not solipsism.
Neither is it self-awareness.
Self awareness seduces humanists. However ,
self awareness makes zero onto-epistemological sense and
a pre-occupation with such naval gazing keeps you at sea;
keeps your eyes off the bigger deal;
stops you from experiencing yourself in the world
and the world in you.
Hold your head up.
Look out, look back, but don't look down.

Humanists assume the truth of
the lone, Romantic, Enlightenment Self,
ontologically prior to
its inscription within
social structure, relationship, dialogue.

Humanists don't get out enough,
or think enough,
or read enough, or, perhaps,
feel enough.

Instead, they float around on the sea
of their own impossibilities.

Reflexivity is postmodern, poststructural, performed, courageous.
Reflexivity is cultural interpretation.
Reflexivity is cultural engagement.
Reflexivity gets you out of the box, out of the cave, onto dry land and into life.

And what do you think about that?
And how does it make you feel?

'IT'S TOO DIFFICULT FOR THEM'

Alec: Oh come on Jim, what do you mean 'too difficult'?

Jim: It's alright for you, with all your interests and reading. What's a bloody koan anyway, when it's at home?

Alec: It's a sodding Zen device to help people let go of their rational minds to achieve a different level of awareness (*no surprises you not knowing this!*). But what are you talking about? They're postgraduate students...

Jim: Yes but...

Alec: Look, all I want to do is help them engage with reflexivity to consider the relationship between the realist-positivist and the interpretivist and poststructuralist paradigms in relation to the politics of representation and how they're caught up in and reproducing discursive positions, all the while thinking they're in 'reality'.

Jim: But they *are* exposed to both quantitative and qualitative approaches.

Alec: Yes, at the level of method, not paradigm. Unless they get the paradigm level and reflexivity they'll never understand the relationship between knowledge and power. They don't even know what the politics of representation means, for fuck's sake, or how that both produces and sidelines the experiences and stories of patients and staff on the shop floor. They need to get hold of reflexivity to begin to question the structures of power that implicate them.

Jim: They're not ready for it.

Alec: Our students are *never* ready for it (*neither are you, Jim, or most of my colleagues*). When will they ever be? Ten years time? When we inhabit fucking Mars?

Jim: Don't be so aggressive.

Alec: Well, it frustrates the hell out of me! Nurses can't do critique! Schools of Nursing *don't* do critique.

Jim: I'll pretend you didn't say that. Look, is there not some scaffolding work, or a bridge if you like, to ease them up to this level of theory and debate.

Alec: Come on Jim! When I was doing my masters in psychotherapy 20 years ago, there was no bridge to Lacan, for example. Now *his* work is bloody difficult and we just had to get on with it.

Jim: I just think you'll alienate and confuse them at this stage in their training. It's not as if they're reticent; they join in discussions.

Alec: Training? I thought they were all on educational programmes! And furthermore, they might not be reticent, but talking shit for six hours isn't quite the same as engaging in critical debate, is it? It's just... irritable fucking vowel syndrome (stomps out of room).

(Phone call to Jim the next day: ...look, I'm sorry about my behaviour. I'll dumb it down. I won't use the reflexivity piece. I'll try to get the information across in a much simpler way.)

***

OUR ENCOUNTERS WITH MADNESS

Roman, I want to talk with you about the expectations we had for the book, *Our Encounters with Madness* (Grant, Biley & Walker, 2011). A collection of user-survivor-carer mental health narratives, some of the autoethnographic data and related discussion that I'm going to introduce below comes from it. In addition to helping the educational development of mental health nurses and other workers in this area, we, or perhaps I (?), thought it might make a small contribution to a much needed paradigm shift. The hegemony of both positivist grand narrative and biomedical and related accounts of human suffering and of counter-colonial humanistic accounts needs to be challenged. These discourses tend to essentialise, romanticise, or otherwise 'fix' people described as in 'recovery' (Stickley and Wright, 2011a,b). In contrast, perhaps rather idealistically, we wanted our book to celebrate stories written by 'unfinalised' people – people whose identities were open, in progress, and who could not be trapped in either qualitative themes or professional, policy or 'evidence-based' discourses (Grant, Biley & Leigh-Phippard, 2012). In this regard, we also thought that it would be helpful for curriculum development to destabilise the exclusivity of biomedical accounts of so-called 'recovery'.

> *But sales of Our Encounters... have been relatively low. I guess that's one reason why you reflexively agonise a lot about the worth and significance of the book?*

Yes Roman, But on the plus side, it arguably contributes new (discursive) stories for people to 'try on' and use (Adams, 2008; Alcoff, 2009; Richardson, 1997). Speaking subjectivities into existence generates possibilities for transgressive and resistance discourse positions, disrupting privileged voice (Burr, 2003; Chaudhry, 2009); for textual performativity (Jackson, 2009; Spry, 2011); for dissolving subject-object dichotomy and for aspiring to postmodern reflexivity (Chaudry, 2009).

But, Our Encounters... might be considered by some as an example of privileged neo-colonialism (Jackson and Mazzei, 2009). There you were – an academically well credentialled 'survivor' – acting as a chaperone; as an advocate for the 'authentic' voice of people presenting real storied experiences, through language assumed as a clear window into their inner lives and pasts. I think you know better now. Doesn't this just signal the great lie of the 'experts by experience' slogan, in accepting the big story of unmediated presence of coherent authentic selves, represented by unproblematic voice (Lather, 2009).

Yeah, okay, but speaking for others can still be politically effective. Sometimes people need a messenger (Alcoff, 2009). Richardson (1997) argues that taking the lead in a project like *Our Encounters...* is a choice that is both ethical and pragmatic. I tried to balance speaking for others with letting them speak for themselves in minimally edited and mediated narratives. And as a scholar-mental health practitioner-survivor I was arguably well suited to take on the role of lead editor/chapter contributor in the interests of social justice. First hand accounts of experiences as a patient in institutional psychiatry are relatively infrequent, and as you well know some of these give the lie to sanitised, sugar coated accounts of what's supposed to be going on, in the research, practice and policy literature.

Right Alec, but supposing your hopes for Our Encounters... was simply a bourgeois fantasy? Counter-discourses have a habit of being marginalised and/or re-absorbed into dominant ones. Some 'survivors' in Our Encounters... rejected the biomedical institutional psychiatric discourse in favour of broader, liberal humanistic ones. This might simply serve to mask oppressive relational and material structures. So, some of your chapter contributors aspire to have the right to happiness and fulfilment in society in terms of their own individual needs and self-actualising possibilities. However, in spite of this, they will continue to be deprived of material resources, debarred from membership of groups and clubs they would otherwise like to join, be the victim of institutionalisms, and be manipulated and exploited by (often unseen) corporate forces who purport to be acting in their best interests (Moore, 2003). All of this might represent 'survivors' re-storying themselves into the substitution of one form of oppression for another, within the dominant moral order (Burr, 2003; Kitzinger, 1989).

Very good points Roman. And there's the critique of Our Encounters (and, by the way, all my other autoethnographic work to date, and this chapter in this book) as neoliberal technology of the self practice. Supposing my/our corpus simply represents the activity of disciplined, docile subjects involved in extended self-projects (Brown and Baker, 2012). Are we fooling ourselves in thinking that what we write is liberating, resistive and counter-discursive? Might it simply represent us demonstrating the management of our own (mental health) risks responsibly through engaging in normative neoliberal practice (Pitts-Taylor, 2010), in what might be described after Giddens as extended reflexivity diary work, reinscribed as 'autoethnography'?

> *Yeah, okay, but back to the social justice thing again: one thing I think Our Encounters did to was highlight the more routine, day-to-day assaults to identity that take place in the name of 'mental health care', expecially in inpatient settings. You know as well as anyone that 'big' emotional, physical and sexual abuses are well documented, but these more routine, day-to-day assaults often go under the radar – at least in the literature.*

Yes, I think you're right. In that context, from a poststructural position, in-patient settings, are both material givens and potential discursive spaces for the production of meaning-experience-performance by staff and patients (Spry, 2011; St.Pierre, 2009). What is produced may run counter to professional, policy or 'evidence-based' stories about 'treatment' or 'intervention' in conferring negative local identities on clients or in enabling clients to create alternative, counter realities.

> *Yep Alec! Our Encounters illustrates how inpatient wards, and the rooms in them, can be places to be verbally assaulted in, let fruit rot in, create alternative, counter-discursive performances, or be disbelieved in such a way as to have your previous taken for granted status as a human being overturned in...*

* * *

SHORT IS AN INPATIENT IN AN ACUTE WARD

Big Ben is chiming 11a.m. across the river. It's wet and miserable. I think it's Thursday...My unwashed matted hair stinks...Sticky discoloured saliva is leaking slowly from the corner of my mouth...I am shivering. I can smell the sweet sickly smell of a rotting banana...on the pillar-box red quarry-tiled window sill... Somebody I do not immediately recognise suddenly bursts into the room. He hasn't knocked... 'Are you getting up?' he shouts. 'You have been in bed all day.' 'I'm tired', I whisper. I feel afraid...He has power. 'Don't you want to get better?...Get up you *cunt*.'

(Short, 2011, p. 131)

GRANT IS AN INPATIENT IN AN ACUTE WARD

He was there to dry out and be medicated. The role of the nurses... wasn't specified, but he began to notice a pattern. Every half hour ...one would pop her or his head through the door, then leave again...Sometimes they pop their heads round and smile, then go away. Sometimes it's a head without a smile. After a while, the man asks one of them why they're doing this... because he's considered a suicide risk.

Fair enough. But he begins to become irritated … that they don't talk with him. Now you see them, now you don't, like a mad and boring Punch and Judy show. The fact that they don't seem to want to talk with him, yet want to look at him at regular intervals, fuels his paranoia. Is there something else going on?...He decides to observe *them* at regular intervals, in between them observing him. So, the next nurse pops her head around at 1pm, and the man opens his door at 1.15pm on his hands and knees (in the interests of subterfuge) and looks up at the nurses' station. He is secure in the knowledge that the nurses can't see him looking at them, and he is initially enthusiastic about keeping up his half hourly observational schedule.

(Grant, 2011, p. 128)

LEIGH-PHIPPARD IS AN INPATIENT IN AN ACUTE WARD

I was already having problems with the medication because the dose had been increased on my admission to hospital, despite my protests, and I was experiencing worsening side effects. By the middle of the evening my arm was burning...I called a nurse and asked for an ice pack to relieve the burning sensation. The nurse left and came back a few minutes later to tell me that I couldn't be experiencing side effects of the meds, because I hadn't taken them. They hadn't been signed off in the medication record book... so I couldn't have had them. I insisted that I had and explained that the alarms had gone off as I was given my meds and that must be why the book hadn't been signed – but no one believed me. Moreover, the nurse wanted me to take a dose of the medication now since she didn't believe that I already had it. I refused and decided that I wasn't prepared to stay there any more. I asked to be discharged but was told... I couldn't leave – I had to stay until a doctor decided I was fit to leave. This was the moment that changed my life forever. As a working professional I had been treated with respect throughout my adult life and as far as I was aware no one had ever doubted the veracity of anything I said. Yet here I was telling the truth but no one would believe me...I was being effectively held against my will. I felt... I had been sent to prison for a crime I hadn't committed.

(Leigh-Phippard, 2011, pp. 104–5)

***

THE PERFORMANCE OF TIME-SPACE

Now, in relation to the above data and the chapter so far Roman, I am interested in Bakhtin's argument that people behave reasonably in relation to the lived circumstances of their lifeworlds at any point in space and time (Bakhtin, 1981; Holquist, 2002). These circumstances include the dialogical relationships people have – of self with self, of self with others and of self with the multitude of cultural and discursive voices available to dialogue with.

I've been thinking about this in relation to what I wrote above about Morgan's psychic prison idea of tacit organisational socialisation of mental health nurses to implicitly held custom and practice rules. According to Bakhtin's 'chronotope' principle, people might occupy the same point in space and time yet talk from radically different cultural and discursive, storied positions. The politics of storytelling mean that some types of narrative are accorded greater respect than others. In mental health wards, 'official' stories of the staff working there will often trump and discredit the individual ones of patents.

This kind of reminds me of Soja's (1989) postmodern geography ideas, Alec. These depart from the traditional view of geographical space as a blank slate or stage with historical events and people impacting on it through time. Instead, Soja argues that class, race, gender, language, subculture, time and sexuality intersect in the social construction of space-time. This results in a continual shifting landscape of cultural politics, with power struggles and resistances played out around cultural diversity, difference and identity. In short, social space cannot be regarded as a mere given or an empty stage waiting to be filled with scripted players. It is more in a constant state of social tension. Thus, in the service of individual and collective cultural meaning production, space, and inevitably time, are always in an active state of rejection, partial acceptance, complete acceptance, production and reproduction.

Bang on Roman! Given their socialisation to broad and local institutional psychiatric discourses, mental health staff will occupy a different cognitive time-space from inpatients and will perform, construct and 'do' the inpatient ward differently. By this means, inpatients can, sometimes unwittingly sometimes not, acquire a negative and unwanted biography for violating the organisational implicit taken-for-granted rules. Moreover, each group – nurses and patients – is likely to judge the other from it's own time-space storied position. One group will find the other's behaviour inappropriate or bizarre and vice versa. This will obviously have emotional consequences.

And when inpatients subsequently find themselves in a different geographical time-space, away from what you're describing as these dominant organisational rules, that can impact positively on the production of their own identity-meaning-experience I guess?

Absolutely!

***

SHORT IS AN INPATIENT IN AN ACUTE WARD

… when I did want to drink, particularly during the night, I was told I couldn't have one. 'If we give you one then everyone will want one. We don't have enough milk'. I would then shuffle back down the long corridor to my room. On the way I would pass several nurses who were sat outside the rooms of people who needed special watching. They would look up from the books they were reading. I saw one nurse reading a book about therapeutic relationships. It felt like they all knew that my request for a drink had been met with refusal. Humiliation and more shame.

(Short, 2011, p. 132)

GRANT IS AN INPATIENT IN AN ACUTE WARD

He decides to observe *them* at regular intervals, in between them observing him... He observes some interesting things...a young African woman is talking about her career development with the other nurses... (he) ... doesn't catch her name, but hears enough to know that she wants to become a community psychiatric nurse. Apparently this will give her more contact time with her clients. The other nurses agree that this is a good thing.... (he) stays in his room for four days. None of the nurses seem particularly bothered about this...

(Grant, 2011, p. 128)

LEIGH-PHIPPARD IS AN INPATIENT IN AN ACUTE WARD

...here I was telling the truth but no one would believe me... I had been told that I could leave when I wanted, but now I was being effectively held against my will...I had to stay for another 36 hours, until... a meeting was held to determine if I should be held under section. I lied throughout the meeting and everyone present knew I was lying. They asked if I was hallucinating and I said no. We all knew that wasn't true but I didn't trust any of the mental health professionals present with the truth any more. Fortunately my husband wouldn't agree to a section and I was allowed to leave... I was transformed completely by my short stay in hospital...in particular by the way I was treated while I was there. I felt angry, frustrated and helpless, but I was determined never to go back. The next five years were devoted to doing what I had to do to survive my mental health problems and... stay in some control of my life. This meant becoming a silent patient, but also often a non-compliant one

(Leigh-Phippard, 2011, p. 105)

***

Alec, I've been thinking... it seems to me that being trapped in mental health stories such as these is perhaps a bit like being on a dreadful coach trip. You get into it innocently enough, but now you find yourself in places you never wanted to visit, and have bad experiences with people you don't want to be with. And all the while you're trying to mind your manners in case you become unpopular with the tour employees, and maybe with some of the other holidaymakers. But this becomes increasingly difficult to sustain so you become unpopular anyway. And while you're in those places you have your photo taken by people in authority, and you find yourself forcing a smile because that's what they seem to want. And then the photo

45

is subsequently placed in an annotated album with other photographs of people with similar forced smiles, labelled and put on public display by the coach company and their cultural masters as an advert for the obvious importance of coach trips for people's leisure, health and wellbeing. This fixes you in a particular space at a particular time, and in a context you'd rather, in retrospect, have avoided. But, in the absence of alternatives, the probability is that you'll find yourself doing it all again next year.

Yep Roman, binaries like freedom-restriction, toxicity-purity, and maybe infantilising-self-determination spring to mind. I looked through Nigel's chapter in *Our Encounters* a few months back and wrote this – it's based on his own description in the book of what he did when he was eventually allowed out of the acute ward in a London hospital for a day pass:

The long street beckons Short as he strolls down it, breathing in sweet fresh air which his body's been aching for. He feels its damp coolness on his skin as he walks. He smells the odours of the street, hears its noises, welcomes the acrid, the loud, the stink of other bodies. His lungs expand with London, the rhythm of his heart in synch with its ancient tune; the syncopated beat of his heart jamming with street rhythms. Footsteps his own, Doc Martens his own, this street his own.

Short merges with the crowd, losing himself in the pulse and cadence of the march of bodies. On a whim, he takes a left into a quiet side road and he's on his own again. Then he takes a right, then another right, and he's back in a crowd. He repeats this pattern for a while as he makes his way through the morning: playing, jamming up front in the crowd, then being quiet off centre stage. Long street, side street, long street again. All the while anonymous. All the while un-noticed. Aware of the difference between his body in the quiet and his body in the crowd. His breathing in time with the rhythm of his feet, matching the convivial progress of the crowd, on his own, in the crowd.

Right now, he doesn't need a nurse to take his emotional temperature or tell him how he's feeling. He buys a CD from a shop. It's his. Belongs to him and him alone. Fuses with him. Is this who he is? Perhaps. He doesn't know. Right now, he's just trying things on for size, as his life needs re-potting. As his life needs re-plotting

His life needs repotting and replotting Alec?

Like a plant that's being held back from developing by a pot that's too small for it Roman. Like the way people are held back by restrictive stories told about them.

***

Dr Grant's course curricula is characterised by both an unnecessary level of theory and unbowdlerized subjective anecdote. Much of this both fails to respond to and undermines the expectations and policy direction of our partners and customers in the NHS Trusts whose contracts we have secured. In order to maintain high standards of excellence in patient care and continually improve on those standards, under- and postgraduate nurses clearly need to engage in curricula that focuses on the necessary skills and competencies they need to fulfil their roles in a rapidly changing mental health service environment.

Professor Jim Moir
Director of Quality Standards
in Curricula and Partnership Development

REFERENCES

Adams, T. E. (2008). A review of narrative ethics. *Qualitative Inquiry, 14*(2), 175–194.

Alcoff, L. M. (2009). The problem of speaking for others. In A. Y. Jackson & L. A. Mazzei (Eds.), *Voice in qualitative inquiry: Challenging conventional, interpretive, and critical conceptions in qualitative research.* London and New York: Routledge.

Bakhtin M. (1981). *The dialogic imagination: Four essays by M. M. Bakhtin* (ed. Holquist, M., trans. Emerson, C., Holquist, M.). Austin, Texas: University of Texas Press.

Bach, S., & Grant, A. (2009). *Communication & interpersonal skills in nursing.* Exeter: Learning Matters.

Bach, S., & Grant, A. (2011). *Communication & Interpersonal skills in nursing* (2nd ed.). Exeter: Learning Matters.

Brown, B. J., & Baker, S (2012). *Responsible citizens: Individuals, health and policy under neoliberalism.* London and New York: Anthem Press.

Burr, V. (2003). *Social constructionism* (2nd ed.). London and New York: Routledge.

Chaudhry, L. N. (2009). Forays into the mist: Violences, voices, vignettes. In A. Y. Jackson & L. A. Mazzei (Eds.) *Voice in qualitative inquiry: Challenging conventional, interpretive, and critical conceptions in qualitative research.* London and New York: Routledge.

Cresswell, M., & Spandler, H. (2012). The engaged academic: Academic intellectuals and the psychiatric survivor movement. *Social Movement Studies: Journal of Social, Cultural and Policitcal Protest, 1,* 1–17.

Davies, B. (2009). Life in Kings Cross: A play of voices. In A. Y. Jackson & L. A. Mazzei (Eds.), *Voice in qualitative inquiry: Challenging conventional, interpretive, and critical conceptions in qualitative research.* London and New York: Routledge.

Docherty, T. (2012). Research by Numbers. *Index on Censorship, 41,* 46–54.

Furedi, F. (2004). *Where have all the intellectuals gone? Confronting 21st century philistinism.* London and New York: Continuum.,

Grant, A. (2006). Testimony: God and planes: My experience of breakdown and recovery. *Journal of Psychiatric and Mental Health Nursing, 13,* 456–457.

Grant, A. (2010a). Autoethnographic ethics and rewriting the fragmented self. *Journal of Psychiatric and Mental Health Nursing. 17,* 111–116.

Grant, A. (2010b). Writing the reflexive self: An autoethnography of alcoholism and the impact of psychotherapy culture. *Journal of Psychiatric and Mental Health Nursing, 17,* 577–582.

Grant, A. (2011). Performing the room: Four days on an acute ward. In A. Grant, F. Biley, & H. Walker. (Eds.), *Our encounters with madness.* Ross-on-Wye: PCCS Books.

Grant, A., & Zeeman, L. (2012). Whose story is it? An autoethnography concerning narrative identity. *The Qualitative Report, 17*(72), 1–12.

Grant, A., Townend, M., Mills, J., & Cockx, A. (2008). *Assessment and case formulation in cognitive behavioural therapy.* London: Sage Publications Ltd.

Grant, A., Townend, M., Mulhern, R., & Short, N. (2010). *Cognitive behavioural therapy in mental health care.* London: Sage Publications Ltd.

Grant, A., Biley, F., & Walker H. (Eds.) (2011). *Our encounters with madness.* Ross-on-Wye: PCCS Books.

47

Grant, A., Biley, F. C., & Leigh-Phippard, H. (2012). The book, the stories, the people: An ongoing dialogic narrative inquiry study combining a practice development project. Part 1: The research context. In press for the *Journal of Psychiatric and Mental Health Nursing.*

Holquist, M. (2002). *Dialogism* (2nd ed.). London and New York: Routledge.

Jackson A. Y. (2009). What am I doing when I speak of this present? Voice, power, and desire in truth-telling. In A. Y. Jackson & L. A. Mazzei (Eds.), *Voice in qualitative inquiry: Challenging conventional, interpretive, and critical conceptions in qualitative research.* London and New York: Routledge.

Jackson, A. Y., & Mazzei, L. A. (2008). Experience and 'I' in autoethnography: A deconstruction. *International Review of Qualitative Research, 1*(3), 299–318.

Jackson, A. Y., & Mazzei, L. A. (Eds.) (2009). *Voice in qualitative inquiry: Challenging conventional, interpretive, and critical conceptions in qualitative research.* London and New York: Routledge.

Jackson, A. Y., & Mazzei, L. A. (2012). *Thinking with theory in qualitative research: Viewing data across multiple perspectives.* London and New York: Routledge.

Kitzinger, C. (1989). The regulation of lesbian identities: Liberal humanism as an ideology of social control. In J. Shotter & K. J. Gergen (Eds.), *Texts of identity.* London: Sage.

Lather P. (2009). Against empathy, voice and authenticity. In A. Y. Jackson & L. A. Mazzei (Eds.), *Voice in qualitative inquiry: Challenging conventional, interpretive, and critical conceptions in qualitative research.* London and New York: Routledge.

Leigh-Phippard H. (2011). Surviving: From silence to speaking out. In A. Grant, F. Biley, & H. Walker. (Eds.), *Our encounters with madness.* Ross-on-Wye: PCCS Books.

MacLure, M. (2009). Broken voices, dirty words: On the productive insufficiency of voice. In A. Y. Jackson & L. A. Mazzei (Eds.), *Voice in Qualitative inquiry: Challenging conventional, interpretive, and critical conceptions in qualitative research.* London and New York: Routledge.

Mazzei, L. A., & Jackson, A. Y. (2009). Introduction: The limit of voice. In A. Y. Jackson & L. A. Mazzei (Eds.), *Voice in qualitative inquiry: Challenging conventional, interpretive, and critical conceptions in qualitative research.* London and New York: Routledge.

Mills, C. W. 1959 (2000). *The sociological imagination. Fortieth Anniversary Edition.* New York: Oxford University Press.

Moore, M. (2003). *Dude, where's my country.* London: Allen Lane.

Morgan, G. (1997). *Images of organization.* Thousand Oaks, California: Sage Publications, Inc.

Pitts-Taylor, V. (2010). The plastic brain: Neoliberalism and the neuronal self. *Health, 14*(6), 635–652.

Richardson, L. (1997). *Fields of play: Constructing an academic life.* New Brunswick, New Jersey: Rutgers University Press.

Richardson L., & St. Pierre, E. A. (2005). Writing: A method of inquiry. In N. K. Denzin, & Y. S. Lincoln. *The Sage handbook of qualitative research,* (3rd ed.). Thousand Oaks, California: Sage Publications, Inc.

Short, N. (2011). Freeze-frame: Reflections on being in hospital. In A. Grant, F. Biley, & H. Walker. (Eds.), *Our encounters with madness.* Ross-on-Wye: PCCS Books.

Soja, E. (1989). *Postmodern geographies. The reassertion of space in critical social theory.* London: Verso.

Spry, T. (2011). *Body, paper, stage: Writing and performing autoethnography.* Walnut Creek, California: Left Coast Press, Inc.

Stickley, T., & Wright, N. (2011a). The British research evidence for recovery, papers published between 2006 and 2009 (inclusive) Part One: A review of the peer reviewed literature using a systematic approach. *Journal of Psychiatric and Mental Health Nursing, 18,* 247–256.

Stickley, T., & Wright, N. (2011b). The British research evidence for recovery, papers published between 2006 and 2009 (inclusive) Part Two: A review of the grey literature using book chapters and policy documents. *Journal of Psychiatric and Mental Health Nursing. 18,* 297–307.

St.Pierre, E. A. (2009). Afterword: Decentering voice in qualitative inquiry. In A. Y. Jackson & L. A. Mazzei (Eds.), *Voice in qualitative inquiry: Challenging conventional, interpretive, and critical conceptions in qualitative research.* London and New York: Routledge.

Varga-Dobai, K. (2012). The relationship of researcher and participant in qualitative inquiry: From "self and other" binaries to the poststructural feminist perspective of subjectivity. *The Qualitative Report, 17*(93), 1–17.

DAVID CARLESS

CULTURAL CONSTRAINTS: EXPERIENCING
SAME-SEX ATTRACTION IN SPORT AND DANCE

Recent years have seen several high profile men in sport publicly identify themselves as gay. The list includes the likes of Mark Tewkesbury (swimming), John Amaechi (basketball), Gareth Thomas (rugby), Stephen Davies (cricket), Anton Hysen (football) and Matthew Mitcham (diving). These announcements are significant given the historical and cultural backdrop of sport, which Eric Anderson (2005, p. 7) suggests, "remains a bastion of hegemonic masculinity, homophobia, and misogyny." The generally positive responses these individuals have reported to their announcements may suggest that prospects of equity and inclusion for same-sex attracted men in sport are improving. This possibility is supported by some recent research (see Anderson, 2009). Yet the numbers – or proportion – of out gay/bisexual men in sport remain remarkably low. At the 2008 Olympics, for example, Mitcham was the *only* out gay male among 10,708 competitors (Buzinski, 2008). Four years later, at the 2012 Olympics, there were just three openly gay men among nearly 10,500 competitors (Briggs, 2012). Mitcham was one of the three.

Bertram Cohler and Phillip Hammack (2009, p. 461) point out that, "like identity more generally, sexual identity is *made* in social practice and in a dynamic engagement with the stories of a cultural surround." This perspective steers away from seeing sexual identity as an essentialist characteristic that is denied, hidden or revealed, towards viewing it as heavily influenced by sociocultural processes. This conception falls in line with narrative theory (e.g., Bruner, 1986; McAdams, 1993; McLeod, 1997), where the stories that circulate within an individual's cultural habitus are understood to shape the identity options and life horizons that are open to that individual. In this way, Arthur Frank (2010) reminds us, stories *act* in human consciousness: "Stories work with people, for people, and always stories work *on* people, affecting what people are able to see as real, as possible, and as worth doing or best avoided" (p. 3). Yet without gay or bisexual men to tell them, how can there *be* stories of same-sex attraction, desire or relationships within sport settings? What effect is this near absence of out gay men likely to have on the identity development of young same-sex attracted men immersed in sport culture? How will these individuals' identities develop if the stories they hear in sport all follow a heterosexual plot?

From my own biographical positioning, I have begun writing and sharing personal stories as a way of exploring the embodied experience of same-sex attraction in a variety of sport-related settings. While not attempting to represent the experiences of all gay or bisexual men in sport, these personal accounts strive instead to engage

N. P. Short et al. (Eds.), Contemporary British Autoethnography, 49–61.

the reader in social and cultural issues through evocative renderings of my own experience. To date, this work has explored how embodied experiences of same-sex attraction intrude upon and derail culturally dominant heterosexual stories (Carless, 2010, 2012a) as well as the ambiguity and paradox that surround same-sex attraction in school sport settings (Carless, 2012b). In this chapter, I use a similar approach to illuminate how two different cultural settings – competitive team sport and contemporary dance – shape not only embodied experience but also identity development among same-sex attracted men. I offer these stories with the intention not to replace, but to augment the currently limited reservoir of stories about gay and bisexual experience in sport. Through the telling, I want to suggest not so much that sport culture is hostile to men who identify as gay or bisexual (although it has historically been so and can still be), but that it can inhibit and even prevent (young) same-sex attracted men from developing a gay or bisexual identity.

THE FIRST TEAM

Not all the team shower after training – Jonesy and Sam are among those who, today at least, choose to use the onsite changing rooms. Jonesy is sat on one of the benches, taking off his socks, when Sam walks in and hangs his clothes directly opposite. By the time Sam turns to sit, Jonesy has stood up and is peeling his shirt off over his head. Sam looks up from his seat, across the small room towards Jonesy. Bodies pass between them, although Sam doesn't notice the movement. His attention is locked on the body before him. For just a second, before Jonesy's head emerges from under his shirt, Sam knows it is safe for him to watch the body in front of him. He watches for what feels like a long second. The thought crosses his mind that Jonesy is taking his time to peel off the shirt, deliberately showing off his stretched torso to maximum effect.

Through the thin fabric, Jonesy can make out Sam's silhouette across the room. Although he can't tell for sure, he thinks Sam is looking in his direction. As Jonesy's head pops out from under his shirt, he sees Sam's eyes drop towards the floor as he starts untying his laces. Sam tries to resist a strong temptation to look up once more – instead something tells him to keep his head down, to look away. On the edges of his field of vision, Sam can just about make out that Jonesy is now unfastening his shorts. Giving in to temptation, Sam raises his head as Jonesy slips both his shorts and Lycra undershorts to the floor in one smooth movement. Breath held, Sam raises his head further still and both men make eye contact for just a split second. Immediately, both look away.

*

Other than the glare of headlights from passing cars it is pitch black outside the bus windows. Onboard, there's a party mood among the established team members after a good win. Beer has been drunk in large quantities by the glass, the jug and the funnel. Sam wonders if he and the driver are the only sober people on the bus as the noise levels at the back escalate. Sam catches glimpses of the flickering screen mounted above his seat near the front of the bus, but can tell by the soundtrack – male-sounding grunts alongside the gasps and occasional expletives of at least one female-sounding voice – that a pornographic video is playing. Sam makes no effort to try to see the screen, happy to let the action roll on above him. He wonders why the driver agreed to play the film.

Every few minutes a name is called out from the back of the bus. Sometimes there's a struggle, but most times the 'victim' goes willingly. This time, the name that is called is *Pap*. The sound of a dozen voices calling "Pap! Pap! Pap!" rises to a crescendo as Ally, one of the few freshers in the 1st team squad, rises and makes his way back down the aisle. Sam leans and looks back, seeing Ally disappear into one of the back rows. *They better not call me*, Sam thinks to himself, deciding not to share this thought with Steve, the second year student sat beside him. They don't 'choose' everyone, Sam has already noticed, although most people seem to get hauled back sooner or later. *What code lies behind this selection process?* Most of the chosen go back willingly. *Why don't they put up a fight? What do they get out of it?*

The voices from the back get louder but Sam can't make out what is said – it's more noise than words. Bits of clothing fly down the bus, landing on the floor and on other players' laps. Heads turn and look back down the bus, smiling, laughing or joining in with random shouts: "Pap! Pap! Let's see what you *gat!*" Sam turns to look too. Leaning out into the aisle, he can just about make out, in the window seat, Ally's head and now-naked shoulders, pressed hard against the seat. There are two pairs of arms around Ally's upper torso and neck. Two faces, red and grimacing from the exertion, peer over the back of Ally's seat. Two further bodies are squashed in beside him. One of these, Sam can see, also has his shirt off. Sam recognises the dishevelled blonde-brown flattop. It's Jonesy.

Sam turns back towards the front. He looks towards Steve and weighs whether or not to speak about the 'ceremonies' unfolding at the back of the bus.

"What the hell are they doing back there?" he eventually asks.

"Ah!" Steve replies, laughing. "Don't even ask! You'd rather not know."

Another burst of cheers prompts Sam to turn to look towards the back of the bus once more. A dozen or so heads further down the bus do the same. Ally is making his way back down the aisle now. He is naked and his penis is semi-erect. He makes no effort to cover himself with his hands, although he looks a bit self-conscious, crouching over forwards and holding onto the headrests as he walks. Various people down the bus throw and hand pieces of Ally's clothing to him. He doesn't make eye contact with anyone. Eventually, he slides back into his seat.

Sam gulps, takes a deep breath and turns back towards the front of the bus. The noise dies down again as he tries to make sense of what he's just seen: a naked and aroused Ally, a half-naked Jonesy, four restraining arms, most of the squad looking on, all played out to a porno film on a bus. *What does all that mean?*

*

Ironically, sport becomes a safe space for those desiring to deeply conceal their same-sex desires. Athletes (particularly in team sports) are shrouded in a cloud of heterosexual assumption, while simultaneously engaging in a highly charged, homoerotic environment. (Anderson, 2005, p. 43)

*

Sam climbs from the back of the car, grabs his bag and follows the others into the hotel reception. One by one, the others check in, collect their keys and head off to their rooms. When it's his turn, he gives his name to the receptionist who replies, "That will be room 116, sharing with Mr Jones." Sam feels a twinge of excitement to be sharing a bedroom with Jonesy for two nights.

Although they've been on the team together for a few weeks now, Sam doesn't feel like he knows Jonesy at all. He's wary of the mixed feelings he's struggling to understand and has a constant battle to resist watching Jonesy's body – something tells him he's not supposed to be looking and that, no matter what, no-one should see him looking. Sam is straight of course – like everyone else on the squad. *Talk of girlfriends and even future wives? Yes, all the time. Talk of boyfriends? Never! You must be joking*! Yes, gay men exist – but *out there*, some*where* else, some*one* else. Never *in here*.

Yet Jonesy's apparent interest in *Sam's* body nags. Jonesy, of course, is straight too. He gets off with women – like Sam does – from time to time. Maybe even has sex with a woman every so often. But why, then, does Jonesy look at Sam that way? And what about the showers and games on the bus – all that nudity and physical contact? From time to time Sam hears other team members joking about Jonesy's enthusiasm for these games, for his tendency to get close to various freshers during 'induction ceremonies'. But at no time is there ever talk of him – or anyone else – actually *being* gay or bisexual. At no time is there any sign that anything ever actually *happens* – a touch, a caress, a kiss, let alone any kind of sex. *Well, it doesn't, does it? This is team sport in the early 1990's – everyone is straight – aren't they?* The interest that Sam feels is felt in silence, shared with no-one, always hidden, always under the surface.

Sam takes a shower in the clean, modern hotel bathroom. He takes his time, enjoying the luxury of a generously heated room, wondering when the car Jonesy is travelling in will arrive. He walks around the room, unpacking, with just a white towel wrapped round him. Sam hears the click of an electronic door card, before hearing the door open. He stops unpacking and turns towards the sound. Jonesy walks in, carrying his bag, dressed in a team tracksuit.

"Hey Jonesy, how's it going?"

"Alright Sam. Not bad." A pause. "Although I'm sorry that you have to share a room with me – probably not what you wanted!"

Sam pauses a beat, not knowing what to say. With hindsight, he might have said: "Don't be daft mate! I'm over the moon to be sharing a bedroom with the hottest man on the team!" But this cheeky – more honest – response would take several years to formulate, and Sam only had a second to respond. Instead, he offers an uncertain: "It's alright, I don't mind."

Jonesy dumps his bag on one of the beds and takes off his tracksuit top. As he turns back from hanging it in the wardrobe, Sam slides out of his towel and, despite now being quite dry, dries himself some more. Facing him now, and just eight feet away, Jonesy finds himself stopping and watching. Sam dries his neck, his hair, as Jonesy looks away and then back once more.

"How is the shower? Is it decent?" Jonesy asks.

"Fantastic – hot and powerful. I'd recommend it," Sam replies. Jonesy is already peeling off his t-shirt and tracksuit trousers. In a moment, he is naked too, the two facing each other. Sam looks on, enjoying this shared intimacy, and the chance to look a little longer than he feels able to in the changing room. Jonesy turns and walks into the bathroom.

*

Sam wakes the next morning to see Jonesy propped up on his elbow and, in the half-light, looking at his watch. He looks over to Sam, nods a "morning," and sinks back onto his pillow. Sam reaches out, turns on the bedside lamp between their two beds, and looks at Jonesy's watch.

"I suppose we better get moving," Sam says. "What time did they say for breakfast?"

"Eight I think," Jonesy replies. "Do you want to use the bathroom first?"

"No, you go mate, I need a minute."

With that, Jonesy pushes back the duvet and sits up on the edge of his bed, facing Sam. His knees are less than two feet from Sam's bed. Jonesy is naked and he has an erection. He sits on his bed for what feels to Sam like some time. Sam cannot stop himself from looking, enjoying the view, so close, just an arms length away. He feels an urge to reach out and touch … but cannot make himself move … he seems frozen. As Jonesy finally stands up, seemingly in slow motion, Sam looks up towards his face. It is only then that Sam understands that Jonesy has been looking at him all along, watching Sam watching him. As Jonesy turns and walks towards the bathroom, Sam, who is naked too, pushes off the covers and follows. He turns the corner to the bathroom and stands in front of the still open door, looking in. Jonesy stands in front of the large mirror. Their eyes meet in the reflection for a couple of seconds, before Jonesy climbs into the shower and pulls the curtain. Sam turns and walks back to his bed.

*

That evening, Sam sits with Jonesy at a table for two for a pub dinner. As the two youngest squad members, and both being students at the university, this probably doesn't seem strange to the rest of the squad who are dotted around the pub. Perhaps this was why they'd been roomed together in the first place. But Sam is aware of a change in his feelings towards this teammate that he can't make sense of. To his surprise, Sam finds himself actually *liking* Jonesy despite the cliques and drinking antics he can't bear. Sam feels a vague urge to get closer – although he has no idea how.

Jonesy is short of cash so Sam pays for his meal. Jonesy is appreciative and says he'll buy Sam dinner sometime. They return to the hotel with the rest of the team and head to their room, talking quietly. Nothing happens between them that night, nor the following morning. They see each other frequently over the next couple of years, sometimes playing on the same team, but never arrange to meet up; not for a beer, not for that dinner, not to explore whether there is – or could be – something between them.

***

The First Team foregrounds experiences of same-sex attraction and desire within the culture of competitive team sport, in a way that stays close to memories of my own embodied experience. The events recounted are permeated by ambiguity, complexity and uncertainty. Was Sam attracted to Jonesy? Was Jonesy attracted to Sam? Did either or both characters desire others, for example during the drinking games on the bus? Tony Adams (2011, p. 88) points out that, "knowledge of others' same-sex attraction is uncertain and fraught with unreliability and error." This seems to be the situation both characters face in the story: an inability to determine whether or not a series of moments and exchanges constitute mutual sexual desire and attraction. It is an uncertainty I still experience when I reflect back on the kinds of moments the story recounts and as I re-read the story.

Sexuality, Anderson (2009, p. 108) suggests, is "an extremely complicated affair that can be described by at least three separate dimensions: sexual behavior (what one does), sexual orientation (what one desires), and sexual identity (how one views one's sexual self)." While both characters might be judged to demonstrate a gay or bisexual *orientation*, signs of gay or bisexual *behaviour* or *identity* are absent. Ironically, however, it is only through an overt behaviour (such as, for example, a kiss) or a declaration of identity (such as saying "I am gay") that each character's uncertainty regarding the other's orientation could be resolved with confidence. Neither of these possibilities occurs. Why might this be the case?

In his groundbreaking book *Telling Sexual Stories*, Ken Plummer (1995, p. 85) explores stories of the experience of 'coming out' – the process of identifying oneself to others as gay or bisexual. He writes:

> *The first step is often the hardest, since it usually has to be taken alone without support from others: the whole weight of cultural indoctrination has to be broken down. This, to engage in understatement, is not easy. At home, at school, with one's peers or confronting the media the message has insidiously been the same: the only story is the heterosexual one.*

In sport contexts, perhaps more so than most other cultural settings, the only (credible, respected) stories among males are, more often than not, heterosexual ones. If homosexual stories have historically been present at all, it has tended to be in sub-narrative forms such as jokes and insults. Developed narrative scripts and credible plots for same-sex relationships are, in my experience, notable by their absence.

For a person to come out, Plummer (1995, p. 58) suggests, "a dim sense of the story must be told to the self. How easy this will be depends on the cultural resources available to support the story and enable it to be assembled." A "dim sense" of untold or silenced stories regarding attraction to another man seems evident in *The First Team*. Attraction and desire is present, but never articulated or acted upon. This account fits pretty closely with my own experiences in sport as a young person. John McLeod (1997, p. 94) says: "Even when a teller is recounting a unique set of individual, personal events, he or she can only do so by drawing upon story structures and genres drawn from the narrative resources of a culture." From the perspective of narrative theory, it is difficult or even impossible to story our own experiences if they are fundamentally at odds with the stories that circulate within our cultural habitus. Because the dominant story is heterosexual, the culture of sport provides little in the way of cultural resources to support the development and telling of embryonic gay/bisexual stories. As a result, it seems likely that (young) same-sex attracted men immersed in sport culture will either be driven to exit the culture or inhibited (perhaps even prevented) from developing this important aspect of their identity.

Frank (2010, p. 14–15) suggests that: "As actors, stories and narrativs are resources for people, and they conduct people, as a conductor conducts an orchestra; they set a tempo, indicate emphases, and instigate performance options." Here, behaviour and actions are understood as legitimated, encouraged or inhibited as a result of the stories that are told and retold within a particular setting. If the public stories are exclusively heterosexual, gay or bisexual stories and actions will be problematic because they transgress the dominant script. It is in this light that the absence of stories of same-sex attraction is perhaps most apparent, constraining not only individuals' ability to create a gay or bisexual identity (through telling stories of one's same-sex attraction) but also their opportunities to enact relationships with others on the basis of that attraction. Moving forward within this cultural setting – in terms of developing a gay/bisexual identity and sharing mutually desired same-sex behaviour – will be difficult, unlikely or impossible. If stories conduct people, as Frank (2010) suggests, then the dominant story in sport 'conducts' (young) men to behave and identify as straight. For same-sex attracted men, this constitutes a profound threat to identity development and mental health. Counter stories with the potential to support and legitimise same-sex experience will need to be found elsewhere.

YOU ARE FAMILY

The theatre is already half full when I walk in. The stage is dimly lit. No music plays, just the muffled buzz of conversation. I look again at the "Company" ticket that Bradley had said would be waiting for me at the box office and read off the seat number. I find my place on the balcony, to the side, at the end of a row. I remove my coat, drape it over the seat beside me and sit. I look around the modern auditorium, taking in the faces, the stylish clothing, the atmosphere. I stand again, take off my sweater, reach over and place it on top of my coat. I sit. I look around the auditorium some more. Maybe I should move my clothing? That seat is probably taken. I reach over again and pull my winter layers onto my lap. I look around again. But I'm going to get too hot like this – maybe I'd be better just putting the clothes on the floor under the seat?

For God's sake David! Relax! You're not the one who's performing! But these nerves are perhaps understandable as it's a string of firsts: My first contemporary dance performance, the first time this solo piece has been toured in the UK and the first time Bradley has invited me to watch him perform. And even he – the consummate professional – told me he'd be nervous knowing his boyfriend was watching.

Bradley's solo is listed in the programme as the second piece that night. He'd told me about the history of the piece, a little about the choreographer and a lot about the music. He loves this solo violin performance and, within seconds of the music beginning, I do too. I can literally *feel* the friction of the bowstring dragging across the strings. After the first few bars, the stage lighting fades in revealing Bradley static and centre-stage, seeming to fill the auditorium. Already, he is drawing and absorbing my attention and, it seems, everyone else's too. As the sound swells, Bradley rises and falls, speeds and slows, in waves of sound and light. Within seconds, I can see his chest heaving with the exertion, the intensity of it all. The whole thing is so *deep*. It's elegant, desperate, hungry, poised, proud and desolate – all at the same time. And it seems like its over in no time.

When the lights come up and Bradley stands to take the applause I realise I've sunken right down into my seat. Suddenly, I'm self-conscious – people can see me now the house lights are on. But I'm too overcome to resume 'normal service.' I wipe my eyes roughly with the back of my hand, unsuccessfully trying to stem the flow. *What on earth has just happened?* I look down at the floor and sit there, lost in emotion, as the audience files out for the interval.

"Are you David?" I half hear the words, spoken with a thick Spanish-sounding accent, but continue looking at the floor. This is not a good moment for me to interact. Anyway, I don't know anyone in this town except Bradley. Whoever it is must be talking to another David – it's a common name after all.

But closer now, clearer: "Excuse me. Are you David?" I look up and nod. *I nod! David! Get with yourself!* I summon the wherewithal to speak.

"Yes, yes I am."

"I am Juan, the company director. Please, come and join us." He raises his arm and gestures, with an open palm and a warm smile, towards a group of people in the centre of the auditorium. "Come on. Do not sit here on your own. You are family."

*

I'm thinking back to a seminar the previous year. Peter – a colleague at that time, but yet to become a friend – presented some of his research. Although it was not an autoethnography, Peter had a personal connection to his research, as is so often the case, and was transparent about this. He talked about the time, just a few years previously, when he was attacked one night on the city streets – a homophobic attack by a gang. Peter was alone. "I nearly died," was all he said. I didn't need any more detail. I didn't need to be any more emotionally engaged. Enough is enough.

*

Ruby Thomas was found guilty of the manslaughter of 62-year-old Ian Baynham, who died 18 days after the drink-fuelled assault in Trafalgar Square, central London, last September. Police later found his blood smeared on her handbag and the ballet pumps she was wearing as she kicked him. The court heard the 18-year-old had smiled as she "put the boot into" Baynham after he had been knocked to the ground by another teenager, Joel Alexander ... The court heard Thomas had screamed "fucking faggots" at the victim and his friend ... Alexander then ran up and knocked him to the ground, causing a severe brain injury as his head struck the pavement ... Brian Altman QC, prosecuting, said: "That did not suffice. There is evidence that the female defendants then began putting the boot into Mr Baynham, who was still on his back, clearly unconscious and in distress ... Shocked onlookers saw repeated stamping to his chest and forceful kicks to his head." (Press Association, 2010)

*

Its only 7.30 pm but already its been inky dark for three hours. Bradley and I walk down a grimy section of one of the city's main streets, heading through the drizzle from café to bar. It's a treacherous stretch – a row of pubs with large screen TV's and posters filling the windows proclaiming "Carling Black Label £1.90 a pint." We walk close to each other, brushing shoulders, staying close to the curb as if we're afraid of being grabbed and hauled into one of the pubs. With just 50 metres to go, the double doors of one pub fly open and – just like in a John Wayne film – a flailing body comes through them at some speed, staggering then falling to the pavement. Impulsively, Bradley and I draw away, and together, recoiling from whatever incident is about to occur. We look down at the figure – a young man, about 19 or 20, now on his hands and knees with his head hung low. After a beat, he raises his head, looking up to meet our gaze. He is wearing an England football shirt, spattered with blood that has dripped from the larger smear that covers his mouth and nose. The three of us freeze for a split second. He seems to snarl, and I find myself staring at his teeth, which look bright white in contrast to the blood that surrounds them. I wait for whatever obscenities are to come. But instead he picks himself up, turns and immediately rushes, with gusto, through the double doors and back into the pub.

*

The all-white Christmas lights create a pleasant misty glow now the shops have finally shut and the last of the late-night shoppers head to car parks and buses. We are ready to go home too, with work the next morning. At the next intersection, not far from the football-pub incident, Daniel and Paulo can turn left and walk home, Bradley and I can go straight on for our bus.

I never quite know how to say goodbye to gay friends in public, out on the street. This time, Daniel makes the decision for me. Always elegant, always the dancer, he gently holds the back of Bradley's head as he kisses him goodnight. Somewhat less elegantly, I imagine, I follow suit with Paulo, who, as usual, shares a wide toothy grin in return. I sense shoppers watching us – heads turning and eyebrows raised, as men and women, boys and girls, scurry home with their Debenhams carrier bags. I try to put my self-consciousness aside. Times have changed haven't they? Next, Daniel turns towards me, reaching for the back of my neck with his hand, sharing a tender and generous kiss. I put my arm round his torso, leaving it there for a few seconds.

Later, I speak with a friend in Cornwall about that moment. Or, at least, moments like it. I also write around it in song. *Why do I still feel self-conscious at these times? Why do I, in public places, still sometimes feel a sense of fear? Why do I not see men kiss on British streets? Why have I never seen two men kissing or holding hands on my university's campus?* University – a supposedly liberal place full of open-minded young people. *Are we being "too gay," too "in your face" by sharing a kiss? Are we even – through a kiss – placing each other in danger?*

"Dave, look," my friend says. "If I walked out onto the streets around this village, grabbed *my wife* and we started kissing and hugging, people would look. It's not just with two men! A lot of people round here don't seem able to deal with a public expression of love between a man and a woman either."

*

It's the dance company's Christmas party and Bradley has invited me to come along. It's not an extravagant affair – a few drinks at the studio after the day's rehearsals. The company members have organised a "Secret Santa" and Bradley hasn't been able to stop chuckling for a week, knowing the gift he has bought for Juan, the sometimes flamboyant and always irreverent director. I haven't spoken with Juan since the night of that first performance a couple of months previously. And I don't know the other dancers, with the exception of Daniel. Well, that's not entirely true: *part* of me feels like I know them intimately, particularly the men whose performing, exposed and sometimes near-naked bodies I watched intently for two hours that evening at the theatre.

Slightly nervous again now, I encourage myself by putting on my favourite leather jacket and trying to do something with my hair. When I arrive, Bradley rushes across the crowded and lively room to greet me with a hug, a kiss and a smile. "Everyone's *desperate* to meet you, baby!" he says, arm round my shoulders. "They can't wait!" He laughs and beams a theatrical grin. His enthusiasm and delight makes me feel welcome, at home. He takes me to where Daniel and Paulo are stood, and I'm smothered in hugs and kisses again. Bradley introduces me to the two women Daniel and Paulo are talking to, who also greet me with extravagant hugs and kisses. *Wow! I wish it were like this at the university!*

The talk is of boys with boyfriends, girls with "partners," who in the company has done what with whom, the pressure for men in the ballet world to "try it with a man at least once," enthusiastically endorsed rumours about one of the (currently) straight male dancer's taste for muscled men, and edgy banter about how Juan's recent break up has left him supposedly feeling – at 46 – too old find a new man.

For me, it is a different world. Different to suburban towns and villages, different to the Southwest's beaches and coast, different to playing in school sport teams, different to being a schoolteacher, different to the university campus, different to the 1980's, the 1990's ... and different to the streets of this city that lie just the other side of the studio door.

***

Many differences might be noted between *The First Team* and *You Are Family*. One is the passing of time – roughly sixteen years elapsed between the events of the two stories. During this time, significant sociopolitical change occurred: Section 28 (the discriminatory British law banning discussion of homosexuality with young people) was repealed, civil partnership was introduced (allowing gay couples similar rights to heterosexual married couples) and lesbian and gay persons were granted the right to adopt children. Many agree that social attitudes towards lesbian, gay and bisexual people changed for the better over this period, moving towards greater acceptance, equity and inclusivity. Perhaps the most significant difference between the two stories, however, is the differing cultures of competitive team sports and contemporary dance.

Plummer (1995) suggests that within cultures characterised by heterosexism and homophobia,

> *those who may later 'go gay' will initially be socialised to believe that they are heterosexual; nagging feelings of being different may emerge very early in childhood or adolescence, but a clear sense of being gay will only unfold later. Gays and lesbians typically feel that they have been given all the wrong stories and that they are living a lie. (p. 84)*

While this description closely fits the events recounted in *The First Team*, a very different environment is evident in sections of *You Are Family* (sections 1 and 6 particularly), where the culture is neither heterosexist nor homophobic. Instead, the actions and interactions portrayed here embrace, welcome and support gay stories, identity and behaviour. In these sections of the story, sexuality is not assumed to be this way or that way, rigid and fixed. Instead, several characters demonstrate signs of an open playfulness towards a range of possibilities. Under the cultural conditions portrayed in these story sections, what Adams (2011) describes as an *existential need for acknowledgment* is likely to be met. Adams writes: "One thing I realized from my experiences of same-sex attraction is that positive forms of acknowledgment, of confirmation, for this attraction (and my intimate, same-sex relationships) make me feel good and worthy" (p. 145). My experiences in the culture of contemporary dance echo this sentiment. Under these cultural conditions, there is much more than acceptance; instead a sense of genuine inclusion, belonging, connection and, yes, *family* is apparent.

The cultural conditions portrayed in *The First Team* differ markedly. Here, the heterosexist and (arguably) homophobic culture conspires to deny the possibility of positive existential acknowledgment. The consequences of this, Adams (2011, p. 145) suggests, can be severe:

> *the lack of positive acknowledgment, of making legitimate time and space for others in our lives, can contribute to feelings of anxiety, despair, and unworthiness – it can expose a person to "social death". This may be one reason why suicide rates for LGBQ persons are high – they may have experienced too much disconfirmation about whom they like. Their existence is not confirmed, explicitly, and, if it is, it is not confirmed in affirming ways.*

The cultural conditions and experiences portrayed in *The First Team* might be interpreted as illustrating this kind of process, as Sam and Jonesy limit their interactions and stories to remain within the contours of the dominant heterosexual narrative. Their lives, over time, come to be shaped by a singular monologue that is at odds with their personal experience. This, McLeod (1997) suggests, threatens long-term wellbeing and mental health as one's life story is falsely narrowed or, in Mark Freeman's (2010) terms, *foreclosed*. Freeman identifies *demystification* as the way that we can move beyond the constraints imposed by our cultural habitus: "The first step of demystification," he suggests, involves "acknowledging one's own mystification, one's own condition of being inhabited by scripts and storylines so pervasive as to be mistaken for the natural order of things. Upon doing so, one can begin to undo them, loosen their hold" (p. 139). Cultures such as the one portrayed during certain sections of *You Are Family* allow this to occur, showing heterosexuality itself to be a pervasive storyline rather than the natural order of things.

Despite these differences, there remain some troubling cultural similarities across the two stories. While positive sociocultural change has indeed occurred in recent years, many things remain the same: heterosexism and homophobia continue to be evident within particular cultural settings, in the UK and elsewhere. The cultural conditions I have been fortunate enough to experience through contemporary dance have felt, to me, like stepping into the sunshine. Straying outside this culture has, at times, led to a return to cold and closed experiences characterised by difference, vulnerability and threat (as other sections of *You Are Family* portray). Writing and re-reading these stories reminds me of the powerful interdependence of self and culture, and of the need to continually nurture and develop those precious cultural spaces that provide opportunities to expand, multiply and diversify stories of what it is to be human.

REFERENCES

Adams, T. (2011). *Narrating the closet: An autoethnography of same-sex attraction.* Walnut Creek, CA: Left Coast Press.

Anderson, E. (2005). *In the game.* Albany, NY: SUNY Press.

Anderson, E. (2009). *Inclusive masculinity.* Abingdon, UK: Routledge.

Briggs, S. (2012). *London 2012 Olympics: Gay role models in short supply.* (Online) retrieved 4 December from 2012http://www.telegraph.co.uk/sport/olympics/9461941/London-2012-Olympics-gay-role-models-in-short-supply.html

Buzinski, J. (2008). In Beijing Olympics, only 10 openly gay athletes. (Online). Retrieved 4 June 2010 from http://www.outsports.com/os/index2.php?option=com_content&task=view&id=111&pop=1&page

Bruner, J. S. (1986). *Actual minds, possible worlds.* Cambridge, MA: Harvard University Press.

Carless, D. (2010). Who the hell was *that*? Stories, bodies and actions in the world. *Qualitative Research in Psychology, 7*(4), 332–344.

Carless, D. (2012a). Young men, sport and sexuality: A poetic exploration. In Dowling, F., Fitzgerald, H., & A. Flintoff (Eds.), *Equity and difference in physical education, youth sport and health: A narrative approach* (pp. 67–71) London: Routledge.

Carless, D. (2012b). Negotiating sexuality and masculinity in school sport: An autoethnography. *Sport, Education and Society, 17*(5), 607–625.

Cohler, B., & Hammack, P. (2009). Lives, times and narrative engagement. In P. Hammack & B. Cohler (Eds.), *The story of sexual identity: Narrative perspectives on the gay and lesbian life course* (pp. 453–465). New York, NY: Oxford University Press.

Frank, A. W. (2010). *Letting stories breathe: A socio-narratology.* Chicago, IL: University of Chicago Press.

Freeman, M. (2010). *Hindsight: The pomise and peril of looking backward.* New York: Oxford University Press.

McAdams, D. (1993). *The stories we live by.* New York, NY: The Guildford Press.

McLeod, J. (1997). *Narrative and psychotherapy.* London: Sage.

Plummer, K. (1995). *Telling sexual stories: Power, change and social worlds.* London: Routledge.

Press Association (2010). *Ex-private schoolgirl found guilty of manslaughter in homophobic attack.* (Online) http://www.guardian.co.uk/uk/2010/dec/16/ex-public-schoolgirl-guilty-manslaughter-homophobic (Accessed 28, November 2012).

JESS MORIARTY

LEAVING THE BLOOD IN: EXPERIENCES WITH AN AUTOETHNOGRAPHIC DOCTORAL THESIS

This chapter explores my own experiences of using analytical autoethnography (Anderson, 2006) as a methodology in my thesis and of how my research and my experience of completing the doctorate interspersed and overlapped. Autoethnographies tend to tell stories of pain and suffering which any doctoral student will agree is applicable when detailing the process of completing a thesis. I have attempted to represent the fracturing and splintering of my own life via an evocative and messy text that aims to empower the reader with an enlightened reading, facilitating meaning making that is not determined by an omnipotent author telling them how and what to think. Instead the text interweaves, overlaps, stops and starts and reflects and represents the splintered narratives of my real life.

JUMPING IN

I started toying with the idea of a doctorate in 2007 but it was a toe in, toe out kind of beginning and I wondered what I had to say that would be of any interest to anyone and how I would write it. I was standing on the edge, self-conscious and goose-bumped, watching other academics I perceived to be floating effortlessly, powering up and down and all dismissive of the newbie gripping the side with her toes, sure she was going to cough and splutter in her own snot and phlegm if she dared to jump in. At the same time I was doing the 'should I, shouldn't I' dance, I found myself comforted and inspired by comments from academics on a series of writing retreats I was co-facilitating where it seemed that, regardless of role or experience within Higher Education (HE), all of the participants had experienced feelings of stress and/or vulnerability with academic culture and specifically the academic writing process. They had all felt or were feeling as unsure and out of their depth as me.

> *In one* (academic writing) *there is still very largely...it's highly controlled fantasy where people have no emotion and where writing is a highly genre-ed and sort of yeah, academic writing is Halal the blood is taken out of it whereas writing* (creative writing), *the blood is left in. (laughs)"* **Giovanni (Professor)**

The idea that academic work had to be drained in order to be deemed worthy was a powerful idea that also reflected how I was feeling: academia was bleeding me dry. When I came to write my proposal for the thesis, Giovanni's comment served as a

N. P. Short et al. (Eds.), Contemporary British Autoethnography, 63
© 2013 Sense Publishers. All rights reserved.

working title and formed the basis for my research question: how could I leave the blood in?

Participants who came on the residential and non-residential retreats were looking for time out from the plate spinning of their daily academic lives and a safe and supported space where they could discuss issues with academic writing and where they would also have time to write. The retreats recruited academics from across the UK to engage in writing tasks and often highly personal conversations on the individual and sometimes shared barriers and motivators with the writing process. Other comments from retreat participants described this unnatural sensation of having to pretend to be somebody they didn't feel they actually were in their academic writing and discussed why this was difficult – professionally but also personally:

> *"'the voice that I use in academic mode, is it mine, or is the voice of my profession, my 'ought to' voice, the voice that I've been taught to use? The voice I use today, it is my own; I recognise in it myself, the person who is really me. To find again that voice restores to me myself, it makes me whole, it wake me up. Oh that I could reconcile those two voices to be me, myself in every situation'. And I suppose that's how I felt."* **Dee (Senior Lecturer – Late Career)**

> *"I suppose this is a development from your retreat which was really good and it was great to be there but there was a thing about for me about being real erm versus being I don't know being pretend, you have to make so many compromises don't you?"* **Miles (Principal Lecturer – Mid Career)**

My subsequent research and interviews with academics from one Higher Education Institute (HEI) on the south coast suggested that the burgeoning role of an academic and the pressure (wanted and unwanted) to write for academic publication in order to be recognised as 'successful' and/or 'expert' can cause anxiety which can permeate their professional work and even overspill into their personal lives.

The trigger for my thesis was to legitimise my experiences and the experiences of my interviewees as cultural insights on academic life in one HEI and to use these insights to suggest strategies for supporting academic writing processes at that particular university. This was with the intention of developing support strategies that would potentially increase confidence with academic writing and offer a more holistic and inclusive approach to research that might enhance the working environment and culture. My hope was these recommendations might (and should) have resonance outside of the university where the research took place. At this point however I was still drowning in possible theories and styles of writing up that didn't seem to fit. Despite this, I decided to jump in and just write (Elbow, 1988). I told myself that I would discover the story I wanted to tell only once I had let go of the side.

Whilst carrying out my research, I simultaneously experienced a personal trauma that was a result of the pressure I was experiencing at work impacting on my personal life. My relationship hit a crisis point and I also had a cancer scare that caused me to question the emphasis I placed on work and re-evaluate my goals and desires. The image of me lying on my deathbed contemplating the number of e-mails I had sent and the journal articles that I had failed to get published seemed so ridiculous that my desperation to have a baby was suddenly magnified ten million percent and this caused me to feel even more miserable and unfulfilled meaning that my personal and professional life was ultimately blurred and blurry.

IMPACT – SCENE 1

Jess is in her early thirties

JESS: My dad ended up going with me, mum was at work and Pete said he couldn't get the time off but I think he just couldn't face it. He wouldn't have known what to say in the car and he just isn't much good when I'm having a wobble. Just wants me to get it together so he can stop worrying about me I suppose. We got parked easy enough. We had to go to the waiting room next to the STI clinic where you can have a HIV test and stuff like that and dad said, 'Hope I don't see anyone I know,' and then we were both giggling when we walked in which made the other women look at us like we were mental.

The chairs in the waiting area were like the ones you find in an old people's home and it was like the coffee had sent us mad or something cos we just kept laughing and being silly, like this was all a big joke and we didn't even know what we were doing there. *(Pause)* And then this young woman came out of one of the little rooms, and she must have been younger than me, and she came out and saw her friend sitting next to us and she just burst into tears. Just sat there holding her mate and sobbing. And that shut us both up.

And they called my name, 'Jessica Moriarty?' and dad gave me a kiss and squeezed my arm very tight, 'It'll be fine,' he promised and off I went. They told me to strip off below the waist and lay down in that chair with the stirrups; the one that looks like it should be in one of those horror films where they just torture people for two hours while you're eating your popcorn. And the first thing I noticed when I lay back is the mural on the ceiling that had this polar bear and its cub sort of nuzzling together beneath a rainbow which I thought was pretty funny as the doctor I was seeing introduced himself as Dr Panda. 'It's a like a zoo in here!' I remember thinking, 'I bet loads of other women have pointed that out,' but then I had a panic, I mean, what if I was the first and he found it raucously amusing and ended up making a mistake with the laser, burnt off the wrong bloody bit. So I left it and went back to watching his handiwork on the TV beside me. I could see everything magnified which was weird because I didn't actually feel that it was my body on the screen; it just didn't seem possible that this was actually happening to me. It was like someone was playing a big joke, maybe an ex or someone I'd really pissed off at work, and the idea that someone somewhere was laughing at me made me start to tense up and my left leg started twitching so Dr Panda couldn't see properly.

'Don't worry Mrs Moriarty, it won't take long.' He said, he was really nice, 'It's Ms Moriarty,' I said, 'I'm not married.' It was silent then for a bit, which I thought was a good thing, I wanted him to concentrate. But then the nurse on my left asked,
"Do you smoke?"
"I don't now but I did, I used to smoke a lot." And I suddenly catch sight of the 18 year old me, and I remember how much I used to love smoking and I felt really guilty, as if it's something I needed to confess. Like I wanted to repent and be saved.
"Well that's it then." she says happily, as if we have come up with the answer to the universe between us. "Now just you try and relax."

I sighed a little and went back to the polar bear cub and its mother. And then a thought got into my head and it wouldn't go, it drones on and on and on: *What if I can't have children? What if I can't have children?* And that's it then, because the thought of death has never really scared me, I fell off a balcony when I was seventeen and all I could think when they told me that I might have died was, 'Poor mum and dad. They must be really upset.' Cos if you're gone, you're gone aren't you? And I'm not religious or anything so...but out of nowhere, the idea that I might not have children really frightened me. And I wondered: *where has that come from?*

WHEN REAL LIFE GETS IN THE WAY

When I fell pregnant at the same time as starting work for my thesis, it tended to prompt one of two responses: "You're an idiot." One of my best friends told me, "There is no way you are going to get this done and have a baby. Do yourself a favour and shelve it." I could take this from her because she knew how desperate I had been to have a baby and how miserable I had become focusing on my career in Higher Education (HE), losing all sense of work/life balance. Despite enjoying working with students on their creative processes and feeling predominantly positive about my role at the university where I worked, the pressure of academic life and my determination to convince my colleagues that I was coping with it effortlessly caused me to experience extreme anxiety that almost resulted in the collapse of my relationship with my long-time partner and was also detrimental to my health. My friend had watched me unravel, cancelling social events, abandoning my family for work commitments and blaming my often bewildered partner for my increasing stress levels. I could take it from her because I knew she'd be there telling me I could do it when I doubted myself (whilst simultaneously reminding me that she told me so).

The second response to my pregnancy in relation to my doctoral work was the more common and more infuriating one. When I told colleagues of my intention to persevere with the thesis in parallel with the experience of having my first child, they would exchange glances and say, "Well we'll see." in a tone that suggested this was highly improbable and that I had no concept of the commitment and hard work either role - mother or student – was going to take. To be fair and honest, I didn't but the gift of hindsight makes their doubtful looks no less aggravating. In a meeting where contributions to the Research Excellence Framework (REF) were being discussed, a senior colleague told me in front of colleagues from my school that they wouldn't be interested in me. "We understand that people having babies won't have anything to submit." He said as if he was doing me a favour and some of my colleagues laughed as if in support of his dismissal of my contribution and ability. It was like the real me who would have asked him what he was talking about had left the building. It was like I wasn't really there.

I can remember being furious with myself for simpering and smiling and offering no resistance to what he was saying and what some of the others were thinking. I can remember the feeling of disgust, like heartburn, as I complied with the version of me he was projecting. In this version I had children and didn't matter in the world of HE and specifically to academic writing. I had nothing to say, nothing to offer. I can remember thinking - *I'll show them.* I can remember thinking – *I'm still here.*

SMALL BANG

It started
with tiny perfect explosions
near the surface of my skin,
your Luke Skywalker to my Death Star.

In the mornings
I stroke and prod my new moon
not sure where you have folded yourself,
if you're playing Sleeping Lions.

On the screen
you point your E.T. finger, singling me out,
you are slightly sinister,
you make me laugh.

You stretch
to your full length of a king-size Mars bar
you poke my sides, checking for a weak point,
a potential means of escape.

More and more
I feel you make your statement with your hand or heel,
and I want to call back -
I'm here,
I'm here.

For me, the fracturing of work, career, of being perceived to be in control from my *real* life, the personal and vulnerable, increased once I became pregnant and desperately wanted and needed to become more than just a careerist. It was the start of a new identity where pretending that I was one sure, clear entity became unachievable and also undesirable. I wanted the necessary and not unpleasant messiness and complication I was facing to be open at work and at home as pretending to be certain, expert and in control by day and vulnerable, stressed and unsure by night meant that I was complying with the very discourses I wanted to actively resist and change. I decided to use my own doctoral journey as my own resistance to the academic voices telling me to conceal this messiness and remain expert, objective, or as I saw it: unreal.

On re-reading Barthes, I became interested in his challenge to conventional discourse. Barthes identified that all writing, even his own, should be regarded as a product of codes, and subsequently, there is no single truth or representation of truth, "This 'I' which approaches the text is already itself a plurality of other texts, of codes which are infinite or, more precisely, lost...Yet reading is not a parasitical act... To read is to find meanings, and to find meanings is to name them" (Barthes, 1974, pp. 10–11). In this case, a function of the writer is to produce text to which readers will ascribe their own individual meaning(s). In traditional academic writing this plurality can be resisted, as academics conventionally write in an objective style, devoid of personal utterances, in an attempt to avoid bias and to represent a convincing form of certainty and truth in their work.

Barthes was consistently frustrated by the "vulgar rules of system-builder, authority, mentor, expert" (Barthes, 1982b, p.x) that were imposed by the existing writing culture in HE instead seeking something untried, untested and new (Barthes, 1982b). He scorned traditional approaches, saying that the point of writing "is to make us bold, agile, subtle, intelligent, detached. And to give us pleasure" (Barthes, 1982b, p. xvii) In his discussion of genres of writing, Barthes disavows conventional academic writing as it is enforced and regulated by authoritarian regimes, policed by journal editors and review panels, meaning that the writers of academic work are essentially repressed and controlled and therefore their work cannot inform freely as good writing should (Barthes, 1982b). He suggested that not only is "the line between autobiography and fiction... muted, but that between essay and fiction as well" (Barthes, 1982b, p. xv), and that the lines between genres of writing were ultimately and positively blurry and blurring, providing potential for new modes of writing that would challenge, inform and entertain. Barthes favoured split narratives and splintered texts that better represented the writer saying,

The best way to conceive the classical plural is then to listen to the text as an iridescent exchange carried on by multiple voices, on different wavelengths and subject to a sudden dissolve, leaving a gap which enables the utterance to shift from one point of view to another, without warning: the writing is set up across this tonal instability, which makes it a glistening texture of ephemeral origins. (Barthes, 1974, p. 41–42)

By giving voice to these multiple voices instead of presenting my research as one sure, certain and expert voice, I began to think it might be possible to maintain some sort of authenticity that better reflected the fragments of my experience and offered some kind of mirror on what the process of the research had really been like.

When I finally started work on the thesis in 2009, I had become disillusioned with academic writing and the master narratives which I felt were often impersonal and lacking in creativity, even in qualitative research. Initially the thesis was driven by a Utopian ideal that the sharing of lived experiences can provide opportunities for a process of co-creation on the part of the reader and writer. The production of necessarily vulnerable and evocative texts that offer an insight into how life is (or was) for the writer and foster empathy, understanding and meaning making on the part of the reader offer a potential method for resisting traditional academic writing (Grant, 2010a,b). It is through this process that we can then begin to re-imagine, recover and reinvent the world as we know/knew it (Denzin, 2003), and this instability, this messiness is real to me in a way that traditional academic writing never has been. It moves me, inspires me, it makes me think and perhaps come to know a little better. It helps me to think, 'yes, that is what life really can be like'. In addition, I was in need of recovery and reinvention myself and I saw the doctorate as a way of rediscovering the person my friends, family and partner kept telling me they had lost. The person I knew was still there but had disappeared under relentless e-mails and deadlines and an inability to say 'no' to more work and increased pressure. The person I hoped my child would come to know. The circumstances in my personal life were intrinsic to what was happening in my professional life and I hoped that the writing process would enable me to feel more sure about both.

Instead of a thesis that claimed to be 'expert' and hold unshakeable and immovable truths, my thesis would be an evocative, creative and personal text that shed some light on the publish or perish culture and encouraged readers of the research to think *with* rather than about the text. Writing in 1794, Kant (2009) suggested that an enlightened reading can take place when the text empowers the reader to evolve past a self-/imposed immaturity and have confidence in their own understanding, appreciation and/or criticism without explicit guidance from another (in this case, the author). But this enlightened approach is potentially problematic when producing a thesis which is meant to explicitly state what it is it has helped the reader to understand. Despite this possible tension between my aspirational aims for the thesis and the aims as set out by my doctoral college, I was optimistic that the evolution of knowledge and dissemination were worthy intentions and that I would sail through my doctoral journey.

THE POWER OF DRAMA IN DOCTORAL WORK

I remember: The tube from Edgware Road to Waterloo, young men living under cardboard sheets in concrete caves. Summer 1983, me and my brother in shorts, him shivering in the interval, his tiny legs and his feet that don't quite fit. I remember laughing when dad first comes out, my dad in white robes, being lifted twenty feet up on a forklift truck, that shakes and moans as if it might not make it all the way. I am seven years old and he is God (Harrison, 1985). He splits the audience in two and the music is loud and me and Matt and mum make it into heaven with some of the audience and the man who played Noah who has tea at our house and as we move onto the side of the stage that is covered in hot white lights, the rest of the audience and the man with the beard move off, into the dark, where we can't see them. And we don't even know if they are there or if they have gone and my brother, my brother looks up at my dad and his tiny legs begin to bend and give and he asks my mum in a small voice that everyone can still hear, "Mummy, is this what it will be like when you die?'

The potential of performance texts to move, entertain, educate and inspire has never left me, and as a means of social and cultural critique, the power of drama is an exciting and valuable tool. I was drawn to autoethnography, and specifically autoethnodrama (Bagley, 2008; Conquergood, 1985; Denzin, 1997, 2003; Gray & Sinding, 2002; Saldana, 2003; Sinding, Gray, Fitch, & Greenberg, 2002), as I identify it as a methodology that synthesises autobiography and social critique in order to resist, and also change, dominant authoritative discourse. The author of an autoethnodrama should ideally be able to resist positivist-informed 'master' narratives, instead offering a highly charged, creatively written text that explicitly links autobiographical experiences with the social/cultural group under study without claiming objectivity. Autoethnodrama also fulfilled my intention to produce a creative and innovative text as part of my doctoral work.

IMPACT – SCENE 2

Office at the university. JESS sits at her desk with her back to the door, typing furiously. Her e-mail pings and she stops work to look at whatever has arrived in her inbox.

JESS: *(laughs)* Oh that's a good one!

JAN enters the office. JAN is also in her 30s and head of the school that JESS is in; she grimaces as she sees JESS laughing and not working.

JAN: Something funny?
JESS: *(turning round)* Oh, hello Jan, I didn't hear you knock?
JAN: I didn't. We run an open door policy.
JESS: Of course.
JAN: I've just come from a strategy meeting…
JESS: …another one?

JAN: Yes, it seems you're on the radar.

JESS: The radar?

JAN: *(leans against the desk)* People know who you are.

JESS: And that's good is it?

JAN: It's good for you, not so good for your colleagues who don't appear to have done any research for the last 5 years.

JESS: Everyone knows that our teaching load is higher than in other schools, there are only so many hours in the week!

JAN: Then how have you managed it?

JESS: I don't know. No life I guess!

JAN: And you did have to go to counselling last year didn't you?

JESS: CBT.

JAN: Yes…for stress?

JESS: It's all in my file.

JAN: I'm not here to talk about that now; I just want you to know Jess that the department is in a very vulnerable position at the moment. I have to save 5% on staffing costs this year alone, and that's just the start, anyone not seen to be making an impact is at risk.

JESS: Doesn't good teaching and feedback from the students count as 'impact'?

JAN: It does, of course it does, but funding and research, they count too. Not that you need to worry, you carry on as you are! A real high flyer aren't you?

Uncomfortable silence.

JAN: There is one thing; a lot of your work doesn't have anything in the title that can directly tie you to the school.

JESS: It's mainly about creativity and personal development.

JAN: That's what I mean. It isn't always relevant is it?

JESS: Oh?

JAN: I just wanted to ask you if you could put the word 'Literature' in some of your titles.

JESS: I could…

JAN: …after all, you don't want it all to be meaningless when it comes to the REF?

JESS: Meaningless?

JAN: Not meaningless! It must mean something to someone, but from our point of view, well, we're worried if it will count.

JESS: Even my thesis?

JAN: Yes, that too. *(pause, puts her hand on JESS's arm)* You understand? I'm just thinking of your profile? I can really see you going somewhere at the university and I want to do all I can to support you.

JESS: Of course, no, no, that's great Jan, thanks. I'll er, I'll have a think and see what I can do.

With all the very best of intentions and invigorated by the views of colleagues that I couldn't have it all, I couldn't become a mother and doctor in the same push, I set to work. I identified colleagues from across the university to interview and successfully recruited early career academics, mid-career academics and professors who were willing to discuss their experiences. At the same time, I made notes about my own experiences and researched evolving methodologies that encouraged creative and personal writing in academic research.

Autoethnodramas use tales of pain, suffering, hope and loss that seek to move audiences/readers on an emotional level but also encourage them to have an enlightened connection that is reflective and critical (Denzin, 1997). In autoethnodrama, the writer represents their lived experience and invites the audience/reader to interrogate that experience and take a moral stand on what is presented and what it might mean (Conquergood, 1985). The text offers an interpretative process of the social world or group under study without enforcing meaning on what is being researched. The combination of aesthetic practice and depictions of cultural experience can provoke audiences and readers to form critical social realizations that potentially resist dominant structures and also (and perhaps more usually) help them to consider themselves in relation to others (Alexander, 2005). In this way, work intended for performance is a useful and powerful tool of developing cultural awareness and facilitating social change. Such work can illuminate cultural politics, develop understanding, inspire change and enhance the lives of those in and readers of the research (Alexander, 2005).

Creative writing plays an important role in self- and social-understanding and determination. We tell stories to make sense of ourselves and our experiences over the course of time, and to help us seek meanings to cope with our changing circumstances. Such narratives are existential, in that they reflect our desire to grasp or seize the possibilities of meaning and to imbue life with imagination and creativity. To imagine and re-imagine the world and what it is and can be like.

MY BEAUTIFUL GIRL, MY BEAUTIFUL BOY

Your father is sure you are a little girl,
brown, blonde or maybe red hair,
tights and wellies on your rocking horse,
me begging you to slow down.

I've always said you are a boy,
with ears you'll grow into,
stripes and smudges, webs of drool.
Eyes I know but can't give a colour to.

We have imagined
bathing you in a bucket,
deciding whose nose you ended up with,
blaming each other for your stubborn streak.

When you arrive
it will be like everything and nothing
we've been dreaming of.
You're already better than our every wish.

Before I went on maternity leave in September 2009, I handed 70,000 words of what I hoped would be a penultimate draft of my thesis to my supervisor. Prior to that meeting our tutorial sessions had been informal and positive and I assumed this stood me in good stead for skipping through to the viva. We met every couple of months and the professor would tell me about his family and latest work and I would bring him a latte and tell him that it was all going fine. When other colleagues told me about their frustrations with supervisors it only increased my smugness and enhanced my new and piously joyful take on life. In our last tutorial before I went off to have Reilly, my physically and mentally inflated self were somewhat needled by the unforgettable line: "What's all this creative stuff doing in your thesis?" As he thumbed the pages of what I thought was my life's work, his face started to fall as if the muscles around his eyes and mouth had prolapsed and the weight of what I had done dragged his whole expression into an unrelenting state of depression. "What have you done?" he asked, "What exactly is this?"

IMPACT – SCENE 3

Office at the university. GERALD sits at his desk facing JESS who is sat in a chair across the room. GERALD is in his early 60s.

GERALD: I don't know why you're surprised. The woman eats babies.

JESS: She isn't that bad.

GERALD: Jess, Jess, Jess…

JESS: If you're going to make some patronising comment then just stop right there.

GERALD: I was just going to say, that if you want my opinion…

JESS: Do I have a choice Professor?

GERALD: …as soon as she finds out you're pregnant, you'll be written off.

JESS: Don't be ridiculous.

GERLAD: I'm serious Jess.

JESS: You're just trying to frighten me.

GERALD: You can be an academic or you can be a mum. But both? *(shakes head)*

JESS: And is that what you think?

GERALD: (looks wounded) I may have been here since the dawn of time but I like to think I've managed to remain outside that male, hierarchical culture.

JESS: A maverick?

GERALD: If you like.

JESS: Haven't you heard? 'Mavericks and free thinkers no longer required'.

GERALD: Must be why they want me to retire.

JESS: Don't you want to?

GERALD shrugs.

JESS: What? No more e-mails? No more meetings? No more pissing REF?

GERALD: No more students hanging on my every word? No more standing ovations at conferences? No more doctoral students begging me for advice?

JESS: I promise I'll still beg you for advice.

GERALD: Just whiling away the days watching Countdown until the inevitable happens and I'm weeing into a bag and struggling with the crossword in *The Guardian.*

JESS: You do that now.

GERALD: Not the peeing in the bag…

JESS: You'll be fine. Just stop feeling sorry for yourself and start enjoying the prospect of retirement? You're not in God's Waiting Room! Why don't you book a holiday? Do some writing? Spend some time with your grandchildren?

GERALD shudders.

JESS: Besides. I still hang on your every word don't I? Now what did you think of the chapter?

GERALD: I have always wanted to travel and Agnes has been going on about it…

JESS: Gerald. The chapter?

GERALD: Yes! Quite. Honestly?

JESS: Of course.

GERALD: I thought it was boring.

JESS: Oh. That honest.

GERALD: I'm sorry. It's just…

JESS: What?

GERALD: It doesn't feel like you. It doesn't feel like you care.

JESS: Oh God.

GERALD: I mean it's alright but…

JESS: …it sounds like I'm trying to sound like someone else?

GERALD: Exactly!

JESS: I wanted to sound like an academic.

GERALD: You are an academic.

JESS: But I wanted to sound like a real one.

GERALD: Oh Jess!

JESS: Don't.

GERALD: You've really let them get to you?

JESS: I just want to be taken seriously.

GERALD: Then write in your own voice?

JESS: What if it isn't good enough?

GERALD: It will never be good enough for some of these morons, but so what? To thine own self be true?

JESS: Even if it's meaningless?

GERALD: It is not meaningless. Stop letting Jan ruin your confidence with her own issues and insecurities and rewrite this chapter.

JESS: Was it really that bad?

GERALD: I stopped reading it to listen to what they were saying in a budget meeting.

JESS: I hope you do have to wee in a bag.

GERALD: Charming.

BLACKOUT.

Whilst on maternity leave I forgot about the thesis almost entirely. Infatuated with my son and sleep deprived, I discovered a sense of calm in my personal life that made the prospect of returning to work and the doctorate almost unbearable. When I did return to full time work six months after Reilly was born I hoped to apply this new found somewhat convoluted peace to my academic work and continue "the process of 'undisciplining' my academic life." (Richardson, 1997, p. ix) via my doctoral work, which I now knew would need to be reframed, rewritten and revived. If I'm honest, I think I was still pretending that I was a fully-engaged and motivated doctoral student, reading articles, making notes, thinking about the reshaping and all the time wondering if I had the motivation, time or drive to remake what I had already done.

At this point I came across an article by a colleague on autoethnography and contacted him to ask if he would consider co-supervising me. I look back and see now that this was the defining moment on my doctoral journey. The difference between almost certain failure and possible success. Finding someone who got what I was doing, had confidence in my work and also in me was critical in terms of galvanising me and helping me to fall back in love with my thesis. Now that I have handed it in, people ask me if the final stage was the hardest but it wasn't, not for me. The hardest bit was when I stopped caring and I am forever grateful to the person who helped me find the bits of my thesis I still felt something for and guided me on how to stitch them back together to produce something that might eventually pass but has also managed to retain a sense of me. He also kept me sane when I was told that the original title, which I was able to recycle for this chapter, wasn't academic enough. That it was too creative and not authoritative. And he joined me in a sage grin when I received the same response to my abstract. I suppose he helped me to believe that I could do it on my own terms but that I had to be realistic about what those terms were in relation to a dominant and oppressive discourse that had thrived for hundreds of years. Let me make it clear: I did not knock down any walls when I completed my thesis but I tried to take part in helping those already at work building the tunnel through, the bridge over and the road around the concrete mass that is conventional academic research. The result is that academic work is no longer as alien and frightening to me as it was when I started the doctoral journey. It can be personal and creative and inspiring and life-affirming and it feels positive to aspire to create work that is framed by these ideals.

MY DARK MATERIAL

3:35 York to King's Cross,
going home to Brighton and you.
I am an alien in the North,
exhausted, sweaty from the effort
of being so cut off.
Heart muscles stretch,
sinew and tendon reaching out,
not quite getting through.
You are everywhere –
your face in the £1.80 cup of tea,
your laugh in the chugging and clacking
of train on track,
racing the wires linking pylon to pylon,
all pointing South, all leading back
cross country to you.
I will the train on, navigating past
Doncaster, Peterborough, Potter's Bar,
needing the dent of you on my chest,
needing more than just love
to join us through the air.

Four years and two children later with my thesis on its way to the printers, I know I didn't win any battles over conventional academic discourse. In the end, I got my head down, I jumped through the hoops and I did whatever it took to get my thesis to the Viva Voce. I am still evangelical about autoethnography; I'm just not convinced that (at present) any doctoral student can ultimately resist the discourses permeating academic life and complete a thesis on their own terms and perhaps this is how it should be. I'm not sure. It has been hard and I am proud of the final edit but I still ticked the boxes and complied with certain traditions of academic research in order to get to the final stage. In the end, I left a little bit of the blood out because it felt like that was what I had to do to get past the gatekeepers in my doctoral college. I'm not even sure that I mind. What I hope is that what happens next via the dissemination of my doctoral work will form part of the resistance to the neo-Liberalist ideals that threaten academic freedom and attempt to reframe study and research in the humanities as superfluous to the requirements of a government who values students as customers and academics as civil servants (Doherty, 2012). Furthering resistance is crucial, not just in terms of our freedom of speech but also our freedom to think, to learn, to evolve.

> *The point of research is not to rehearse what we know, but to explore and extend the boundaries of our ignorance and, by thus disturbing our idea of ourselves, to prise open those human possibilities that were previously undreamt of. Such ideals sit uneasily alongside the now normative corporatist ideas of accountable efficiency. (Doherty, 2012).*

Whilst waiting for the dust of political fallout to settle on a potentially diminished HE Academy, I am comforted by the knowledge that resistances exist and that working with autoethnodrama enables me to begin post-doctorate life politically aware and with my social consciousness better informed and angrier. Autoethnography and completing the thesis changed me. It made me think about the kind of academic I am and the kind of academic I hope to be and it turns out that she is completely entwined with the kind of mother, sister, daughter, lover, friend I already am. I've started to think she might be ok.

I suppose then that this is a cautionary tale of how it was for me that I hope will be useful to other doctoral students seeking to take up arms against traditional approaches to doctoral work. Like Laurel Richardson in *Fields of Play* (1997), I hope "that by hearing about my intellectual and emotional struggles with "authority" and with "my place" in my texts, academic department, discipline – my life – will be of value to others who are struggling with their "place"." (Richardson, 1997, p. 2). I hope it furthers the resistance. I hope it changes where HE is at and where I fear we might be heading. I hope we get to leave the blood in.

NOTE FROM THE AUTHOR

The names of all the interviewees have been altered to ensure anonymity. With the exception of 'Jess', any similarities between characters in the autoethnodrama 'Impact' and any persons living or dead is entirely coincidental.

REFERENCES

Alexander, B. (2005). Performance ethnography: The re-enacting and inciting of culture. In N. Denzin & Y. Lincoln (Eds.), *Handbook of qualitative research* (Vol. 3rd). London: Sage.

Anderson, A. (2006). Analytic autoethnography. *Journal of Contemporary Ethnography, 35*, 373–395.

Bagley, C. (2008). Educational ethnography as performance art: Towards a sensuous feeling and knowing. *Qualitative Research, 8*(1).

Barthes, R. (1974). *S/Z* (S. a. G. Farrar, Inc., Trans.). Oxford: Blackwell Publishers.

Barthes, R. (1982). *Barthes: Selected Writings*. Oxford: Jonathan Cape Ltd.

Canagarajah, A. S. (2002). *A geopolitics of academic writing*. Pittsburgh: University of Pittsburgh Press

Conquergood, D. (1985). Performing as a moral act: Ethical dimenstions of the ethnography of performance. *Literature in Performance, 5*, 1–13.

Denzin, N. K. (1997). Performance Texts. In W. G. Tierney & Y. S. Lincoln (Eds.), *Representation and the text: Reframing the narrative voice*. New York: State University of New York University Press.

Denzin, N. K. (2003). Reading and writing performance. *Qualitative Research, 3*(2).

Doherty, T (2012). Research by numbers. *Index on Censorship, Sage, 41*,(3).

Doloriet, C., & Sambrook, S. (2011). Accomodating and Autoethnographic PhD: The tale of the thesis, the Viva Voce and the Traditional Business School. *Journal of Contemporary Ethnography, XX*(X), 1–34.

Elbow, P. (1988). *The power of writing*. New York: Oxford University Press.

Grant, A. (2010a). Autoethnographic ethics and rewriting the fragmented self. *Journal of Psychiatric and Mental Health Nursing, 17*, 111–116.

Grant, A. (2010b). Writing the reflexive self: An autoethnography of alcoholism and the impact of psychotherapy culture. *Journal of Psychiatric and Mental Health Nursing, 17*, 577–582.

Gray, R., & Sinding, G. (2002). *Standing ovation: Performing social science research about cancer*. Walnut Creek, CA: AltaMira Press.

Harrison, T. (1985). *The mysteries*. London: The National Theatre.

Kant, I. (2009). *An answer to the question: 'What is enlightenment?'*. London: Penguin.

Richardson, L. (1997). *Fields of play: Constructing an academic life*. New Jersey: Rutgers University Press.

Saldana, J. (2003). Dramatizing data: A primer. *Qualitative Inquiry, 9*, 218–236.

Sinding, C., Gray, R., Fitch, M., & Greenberg, M. (2002). Staging breast cancer, rehearsing metastatic disease. *Qualitative Health Research, 12*, 61–73.

KITRINA DOUGLAS

A TRUTH WAITING FOR A TELLING

be gentle with my stories
they come on angel's breath
tiptoe down the high wire
fragile precious things

Some people get excited when they are asked to do something. Others see work piling up in the in-tray, and a mound of obligations, commitments, expectations. She was, she thought, in the former category, almost always ready and excited to say, "*Yes*," without really considering drawbacks. Her best friend, she thought, was in the latter category. His first reaction, especially if it concerned work, was almost always opposite to hers. Although most times they ended up in the same place, their journeys charted a different course. Overall, it seemed to be a good thing that they often responded differently to things because it kept them both open, sensitive-to and aware-of alternative ways of being.

She'd first considered the importance of alternative ways of being when they started applying narrative theory to their research which explored motivation and persistence among women professional tournament golfers (Douglas, 2004) and '*PING*!' Suddenly, narrative theory, as explained by John McLeod (1997), made sense of her life in sport too. Up to that point, according to mainstream psychological theories, she, along with all the other professional sports men and women, had, or *must* have had, such a narrow focus on winning, such that "it is *impossible*... to be much else" (Werthner & Orlick, 1986, p. 337). "*Thanks!*" she thought, "*nothing like finalising me in the middle of my life.*"

It wasn't until she and her friend followed Arthur Frank (1995) and conducted a narrative analysis that they came to see how this dominant *performance narrative* type of story could silence and de-legitimise alternative ways of being in sport (Douglas & Carless, 2008 a,b,c, 2009, 2012; Carless & Douglas, 2012a, b, 2008). It was a narrative script where sporting excellence was defined solely through winning. '*All* of us' Georgi had said, 'it becomes our whole life. Because I don't think that you can possibly be successful without it being the most important thing.' (Douglas & Carless, 2006, p.20). Yet, despite Georgi and others who told this type of story, believing *all* athletes had to be this way, other women shared alternative types of stories. The '*Discovery narrative*,' for example, showed how some women embraced life in a multidimensional way while the '*Relational narrative*,' provided stories about women valuing relationships above winning (Douglas & Carless,

N. P. Short et al. (Eds.), Contemporary British Autoethnography, 79–95.

2006). These alternatives suggested it was *possible* for an athlete not to solely focus on winning. The problem was though, as she looked across the sporting landscape, systematically alternative ways of 'being in' and 'making sense' of life in sport, at the elite and professional level, were being eradicated by the way sport was funded, researched and policed (Carless & Douglas, 2013; Denison, 2007, 2010). It was this awareness that gave her the impetus to continue to write about her experiences in professional golf as a way to challenge the totalitarian assumptions about what a sport person is and what she had to become in order to win. One route to achieve this aim was to write stories about her golf, taking the reader with her on that journey.

As a researcher, however, the inculcating culture of elite sport was not the only issue that troubled her. While writing about her experiences in sport was important, she became aware that academic convention was also problematic in terms of considering alternative ways of being a student or taking an academic journey. How she was expected to write, for example, via realist tales, shaped how others understood her participants lives. Worryingly for her, in Mikhail Bakhtin's (1984) terms, she wondered, had she too, like those who she had been critical of, written about women in ways that cemented 'who' or 'what' her participants were or might become. Was her analysis or thinking framed in a monologue she was unaware of? She had a growing unease with what may be missing from the way she wrote academic texts in her march to tick academic boxes. She became aware that in her first published reports her connection to the women in her research was mostly absent, she was a detached observer – at least in the way she wrote. These ideas were swimming around in her sea when she wrote, in her diary,

"My body is my witness, it feels, it responds, and like the stories hidden within the folds and lines of my skin, I feel fractures and fault lines that provoke me to consider what we know and how we present that knowledge."

What does that mean she asked herself?

It was about this time she received an invitation to contribute to the handbook of, "*Contemporary British Autoethnography.*" She was delighted, excited even, "*Oooooh British*," she thought. She made a British move with her British body, like that! A raise of her eyebrows, a tilt of her head to the left, her shoulder brought forward, very dramatically Othello like. She had been invited, included, it was a privilege, a reward, and a challenge. But what exactly she ought to contribute was more vexing. She had found autoethnography to be useful methodology that allowed her, of late at least, to show her reflexivity (Etherington, 2004, 2007) and to present her research in ways that suited her body, her writing style, her way of thinking, her way of theorising, her way of blurring them and us, problem and answer, participant and researcher, theory and practice, praxis, then and now (Douglas, 2009, 2012; Douglas & Carless, 2008). Autoethnography allowed her to trespass.

"If I had my way," her friend had said, the one who was more cautious, "You'd stop doing all the other work and just write stories." He made her laugh, she loved writing with him. She liked the actual process of sharing. Their communal construction that was the anti-thesis of the lone writing strategies so many others talked about. Chunking sections of science reportage through e mail exchanges, notching up scalps in high impact journals, jumbled together political giants, a plethora of names that perhaps never sat *physically* with each other eating toasted crumpets with butter dripping down their chins.

Although *he* liked *her* writing stories, she felt that *only* writing stories would restrict her to yet another monological script. Although she liked writing stories, she couldn't help be excited and drawn into the nitty-gritty of theoretical insights – they allowed her to understand her own life and the actions of people around. She also liked methodological discussions and learning that helped her conduct research more reflexively, not trampling over people unaware of the damage, or so she hoped.

As she reflected on the handbook, and what her contribution might contain, she wondered if storying her life, and scenes from it, would allow her to show her strands of thought, about playing professional golf, her research and her life more broadly. *"OK- This time"* she thought, as if speaking to her friend, *"I'll take your advice, if you think my stories are so good lets see!"* she was challenging him.

She thought back to when she had first encountered narrative theory and it was right at the end of her PhD, when 80,000 words had already been written, approved, signed off. She'd been trying to use theories that made no sense in the context of her life, such as Deci and Ryan's, (1985) *Intrinsic Motivation and Self-Determination in human Behaviour* and Maehr and Braskamp's (1986) *Motivation Factor, The Theory of Personal Investment.* Yes, there were genuine insights in these concepts – but they didn't help make sense of her life, and therefore, she had little confidence applying these theories to other women's lives, motivation, or experiences.

"Aligning stories within narratives," Frank had suggested, "Is ultimately aligning decisions about how to live" because they illuminate when "normal guidance systems fail". (Frank, 2010, p. 62)

She liked that concept, that she had a 'guidance system' and it may fail her and identifying the types of stories she was embedded within might help her make more ethical choices in the future, they were a way to reorient her moral compass (Denzin, 2003). In contrast to other theories Frank's work made absolute sense to her, and seemed to capture in a nutshell a narrative thread she was trying to explore.

"Dialogical narrative ethics," Frank went on to say, "addresses how stories connect," they "make our actions recognisable," (p.159) "depict characters who acknowledge mistakes." *"Exactly,"* she said to herself, and began to write about some of the tensions, contradictions and reflections that were hidden in her body, waiting perhaps, to share their truths. She found the playwright and academic Jonny Saldana's writing helpful in this regard as it articulated something she hoped for when she wrote, "should you somehow insure that a theme of some sort is woven into your play? My answer is no. If you write with a message, moral or lesson in mind, the result is most often a heavy-handed, theme-driven fable rather than a character-inspired and story-driven drama" (Saldana, 2011, p.121). And so it was with the way she wrote, she didn't attempt to capture a moral or message, she just described a scene. And that's how she began the project.

**

PRELUDE: VOICE

> The race is not to the swift, nor the battle to the strong…time
> and chance happen to all.
>
> Ecclesiastes 9.1

She put the book down and considered its teaching. She liked *that* verse because she knew she didn't hit the ball a long way, and all the others girls did. She was a plodder, and couldn't help it. The problem was, in this world, everyone wanted to watch the '*big hitters*.' The golf courses were set up for - and talk on tour was - '*who could hit the ball the furthest*.' But, according to Ecclesiastes, big hitters, fast runners, the strong and mighty, didn't always win, and she was glad of that, it made her laugh a little. The thought was comforting. She knew the next day would settle it, and that the saying was a good thing for her to remember. She was in the lead of the biggest event on the women's tour, and the next day was the final day.

Then, while lying in her bed, she committed the cardinal sin. She started writing her speech – well writing is too strong a word - she started running through, in her head, what she would say, *if* she won.

"I'd like to thank," she began.

She loved the power that winning gave her, it meant that everyone would shut up and listened to her. For those few minutes she could say anything she wanted –they even gave her a microphone. During play, she was mute, she had no voice, her body was supposed to speak for her. The crowd watched her body, commented on her body: the way she dressed, the way she walked, the flower in her hair. Journalists commented on the way she swung the club, the way she caressed the ball, the length of her swing, the length of her stride, the length of her legs and yes, the length – or lack of it, from her shots. They said she, "*Didn't punch her weight*," whatever that meant. But if she won, she was allowed to speak, to *say* whatever she wanted. The script was her own.

MR PREDICTABLE

She was tired, glad she was booked on a flight home and couldn't wait to get off the golf course. Her playing partner, fortunately, wanted to get the 3:40pm flight too, so they almost ran round the course completing their round in a stunning, 2hrs 49 minutes. "*So much for pro's playing slowly*" she thought.

Were they concentrating? Were they giving it everything? Were they being sport*man*like? No. Well, yes. They were concentrating on getting round the golf course as quickly as possible, focussed fully on getting to the airport on time, playing carefully enough not to lose a ball and have to walk back to the tee or do anything which would waste precious moments and jeopardise catching the 3:40 pm flight. What they both wanted, was home.

She'd started the week quite well scoring 69 in the first round and was two behind the leader. The next day she had a late tee time and was one of 20 players caught in thunder, lightning and storm force winds. The weather arrived from nowhere after the morning had been clear sunny skies and no wind. It meant she had to endure a rain delay, a waterlogged course, a ball lost in a puddle in the middle of the fairway, and a penalty stroke in a sand trap at the last hole when she grounded her club after being buffeted by the wind. The upshot was she scored 76 and slipped down the field. Although she made the cut[1] her poor scores meant she had an early start time on the third day when it seemed neither she - or the golf course - had dried out at all. To rub salt in to the wound, it rained while she was playing in the morning but the sun arrived later in the day and players with afternoon tee times enjoyed perfect conditions; unsurprisingly the scores in the afternoon were better. Hey ho. It goes with the territory. But, it was the backdrop to why she didn't care whether she finished 40th or 50th. Where she finished wasn't going to make much difference to how much money she won that week. There was only one flight out on Sunday and that was the 3:40 pm flight which, if they finished in less than 3 hours, even with the two hour drive to the airport, she would make. Then, she would be home on Sunday: That was a big deal.

They signed their cards speed walking to the scorer's tent and didn't wait to check if the details were correct. Their taxi was waiting and each player threw their huge tournament bags into even bigger covers and the taxi zoomed away. At the airport, life improved, they not only made the flight but were offered an upgrade and as she sank into her club class seat, she finally felt relieved.

Hannah, the other pro she'd played and travelled to the airport with, had taken the window seat and she found herself, not by preference, sandwiched between Hannah and a rather large man with sweaty hands. He seemed to be rubbing his hands continually down his thighs, so she decided his hands must either be very dirty or very sweaty. As the nuts, food and drinks trolley hadn't arrived, and as the man was wearing pristine white shirt and this was club class, she decided he was a sweat – er, and hoped he wouldn't be a stinker too.

"You been on holiday?" the man said, after the cabin crew had been through with the beverage trolley.

She shook her head, "No, I've been working." She knew exactly what was coming next.

He threw a few nuts in the direction of his mouth, most missed, and then as he gathered the strays from the crevasses in his shirt he asked, "What do you do?" Curious, most probably, she decided, about what two English girls were doing working in Copenhagen.

"I play golf," she said. Very matter of fact-ly, and then gulped her orange juice. Aware suddenly that she was feeling sticky, wanting a bath and was still wearing her sweaty golf shirt, socks and shorts. She was tired, and didn't want to talk work.

"You any good?" He came back after sipping his gin, and turning slightly toward her in his seat. She observed his actions wondering, "*Aren't you going to put a little more tonic in that?*" and then "*Why are they always so predictable.*"

She could answer his question truthfully by saying, "*Yes I'm brilliant,*" or she could be a little more humble, perhaps not so truthful and say, "*Not bad.*" But you see, whichever way she played it, however she answered, brilliant or bad, *they* would always ask, "*Oh, so have you won anything?*" and then "*What have you won?*" then, "*Do I know you?*" then, "*What's your name?*" then, "*I can't wait to tell my mate.*"

What have you won, how much money, what's your name?
What have you won, how much money, what's your name?
What have you won, how much money, what's your name?
drip drip drip
imagine the ones
drip drip drip
those who can't say
I'm soooo good
Who can't say
yes, I've done it all
who say
no, no money, I'm skint,
those who sweat blood
who long, just
to finish 50th
Desperately,
need a sponsor
miss the cut
again
they have to answer
again and again
F***ed the queen
We call it
Those players, who return and enter the clubhouse
Greeted by a member, with scissors
and they snip snip snip snip
Right in front of her eyes
Missed the cut did you?
Why do they gloat?

***

"Did that happen to you," her nephew asked, sitting next to her with only a towel separating her from his manhood as she read him the start of her chapter.

"No, it happened to a friend of mine," she said.

"That's so," he couldn't find the adjective so he paused and she agreed with him in her mind, *"Shit!"*

"I can't believe it!" he continued, still unable to describe what it was he was trying to convey.

"No, I couldn't either!" They paused. Both lost in their own thoughts, then James carried on.

"I really like those stories," he said, his eyes dancing, "It's like," he paused again and she finished the sentence for him, thinking back to the stories she read him in the summer.

"Those other ones I read you."

"Yea," he agreed.

"Andrew's father and the false teeth," she reminded him. James started laughing,

"And him watching his son play rugby! Yes, I remember!" he sat up. "He's a legend that man, he's my hero."

How funny, she thought, making a mental note of his exact words, *"how can Andrew Sparkes be your hero?"* Her nephew hadn't even met Andrew Sparkes, and yet he had used to term, *'legend.'*

She wanted to call Andrew up immediately, she thought he'd find it funny, she also hoped he'd find it validating; his work had found a 17year old lad in depths of Cornwall, he had read it, understood it, remembered it and valued it (Sparkes, 2012). She thought back to Hilary Dixon who she saw briefly in the department while she was waiting excitedly to pick up a copy of a book she'd written a chapter in.

"Oh Hello," Hilary had said, "What brings you in?"

"I've come in to collect a book - I can't wait to read my chapter," she's said, honestly, anticipating the shapes of words crafted on the page.

"Oh, I never read mine," Hilary responded breezing past.

"Why would anyone else then?" she wondered *"What are you writing?"* Well, not only did she read everything she wrote when it was published, her family did too. Well actually, most times, they had to sit while she read her research to them, and most times, like James at that moment, they seemed to be hooked by something and asked for more. Perhaps she was being unfair to Hilary. But, she had found that it was only through reading her stories to the people who were characters in the stories, or other people like the characters in her stories, and then to colleagues and friends, that the truth of the stories was made known to her, their response was her touchstone, she needed their feedback, she wanted to watch their eyes, their bodies, she valued their voice. James disturbed her contemplation.

"What's next," he asked.

"Well," she paused, thinking how to frame what it was she wanted to read to him, "It's a story about our relationship."

"Is there a context?" he asked frankly.

She laughed, "Yes, but I'm not going to tell you, I'm just going to read the story. It's called

James." And I hoping to put it in a book chapter I'm writing.

***

JAMES

James hadn't said goodnight to her, and so she popped along to his room where he and his dad were in the last throws of readying themselves for sleep. She tapped the door gentle and went in without waiting to be invited. James, as usual, was bare chested, smooth and white, skinny and fresh. His dad, in contrast, had the shadow of a days growth on his face, was already in bed, pyjama'd up, but still had an air of the naughty kid at prep school,

"Ahhhh….hello Tig," His father murmured lying back as she entered the bedroom, and then, "Com'on Jamsie," encouraging his son, and then pulling the duvet up to his chest.

"I've just got to…," James continued pulling something from his bag.

"You didn't come and say good night," she said looking straight at James as she picked her way across the room through the abandoned clothes, shoes and neatly piled clutter, ready for a hug, to feel his pat on her back and a good night.

"Well Tigga," James said, turning from his previous chores and smiling. He couldn't pronounce her name as a toddler, so he came up with *his* version of who *she* was and "*Tigger*" was born and stuck. It tied them together in some special way she couldn't really fathom. It went beyond being asked to attend his birth, a task that she hadn't really relished - but went along with in order to support her sister, placing her body by the hospital bed, along with her brother-in-law, out of the way, up the '*head*' end, joking and eating sandwiches. She performing one duty while her sister, lying on her back, was performing another: One she wasn't prepared to do. She trying to fulfil some role, to give support, she didn't know quite what, feeling awkward, unsure, fake.

"Ah-sister," said the Sri Lankan midwife from down there – the other end, "Com'n see the baby's head!"

WHAT! She thought. It was the most ridiculous invitation she's ever had. Nurse Fernando, however, had beckoned with such authority any refusal was unthinkable. So, she obeyed the call. While her body obeyed, some part of her resisted becoming an on-looker. At that point her academic head took over, so, of course, looking with the academic filter with a distanced and unemotional lens it was all "*very interesting.*" Surreal, but a view she had never seen before.

Sister Fernando was the guide, "There's baby's head," "*Oh yes, there was the head.*"

But, it was stuck.

Whoa, episiotomy,
A CUT TO FEAR
So much better
Then a lingering tear
For who
you wonder
The cutter with the cure
Scissors
Incision
Cut to the core
No rush of excitement
A little Relief? No joy in the feeling
sowing up be-neath, Look! a boy

She stayed at her sisters and slept in James' room, listening to him sleep, but she couldn't sleep. His irregular breath scared her, what if he...? He was their first born, after two miscarriages, after two of James' older siblings didn't make it this far, they left their mothers womb after only a few months. They never breathed. So much sorrow, so many changes in her sister's body, mind, emotions, expectations.

So she didn't sleep. She lay awake all night when she stayed next to James, just listening, making sure he didn't stop breathing, not on her watch.

"Do you promise," the pastor asked from his lofty platform, "Before God." And if that wasn't scary enough, "And everyone here." The pastor turned and cast his long arm toward the mass of faces, sitting in silence, acknowledging the weight of the pledge that she and the others were about to make.

"That you will protect him, guide him in his ways, nurture him," the gathered family and close friends listened respectfully, as did the very large mainly Afro-Caribbean congregation at her sisters church, huge in number, huge in size, huge in their lungs, huge with their voices, huge hugs, huge love, laughter. Whoah, huge pledge she just made. She glanced around at the colourful clothes, hats, lips,

do i?
do we?
wot do I do?
can I refuse?
Refuse, can I choose?
not to be
GOD MOTHER
shhhhh
expectation
resistance,
surrender,
a sister
in need,

a baby to feed,
kindness and hope,

responsibility, freed,
but here I go
another I do

Then came James' sister, two years later at 13lb, THIRTEEN POUNDS and a caesarean,

emergency op
you thought she was free
came home from the hospital
went up just to be
all had gone well
came home duty free
but late in the night
a body cut twice
replace and repair,
did the hospital care?

"Watch out for his pooh!" Her sister warned, "If you don't get it quick, it'll go everywhere." Her sister was right, James, '*Poohed for England*,' and if his nappy wasn't changed within ten minutes it would be all over! Over the bedding, over his body, over the bed, over his toys, over everything, everywhere!

But, she was juggling the first year of her degree, working away from home doing commentary for Eurosport in Paris and the BBC all over the UK, the kitchen floor was being installed. Her sister slept in her bed, the new baby at the end, while her sister's husband worked in London during the week and came down at weekends. James had the spare room. She slept on the floor in the sitting room, and her partner went along with it all, both sleeping on cushions for months. But, she didn't want to be nurse, she didn't want to change nappies, feed a family, organise a rota if she was away. She hated it, in every part of her body,

A flood
A wave
An unmentionable feel
Decay
Death
A vice like grip

It rose, made her feel angry, want to erupt.

"You failed your psychology," said the professor on the telephone.

"*Typical,*" she thought, "*the one subject I am really interested in I fail the first exam and the thing I'm not bothered about, stuff like metabolic calculations in physiology I come in the top 3, ironic.*"

"You can retake it tomorrow,' he carried on.

"Tomorrow," she thought, *"but my sister nearly died and I'm looking after her, her baby, her two year old son, and I'm working and I don't have time to revise tonight, and I."* He didn't want to know.

Of course, she'd been playing roulette with her degree, focussing on the areas she was weakest in and making choices about what she thought may come up in the exam. She got it wrong. It wasn't a difficult exam, she just remembered the wrong thing.

"So, either you take it again or we have to fail you," he finished – her choice.

> Hope drains when fairness wanes
> Fellows
> undergraduates
> Form a distance she watched
> sleepy eyes
> late night parties
> pasties and pies
> Fussing with grants, always ready for a game
> Not bothering to make it in, lies so lame

She replaced the receiver, and allowed her frustration to seep quietly out, it just wasn't fair. Then at six the next morning, after not very much sleep, too tired to take in her psychology notes, she went in to check on James and more specifically his body motions. He was stood up in his cot, barred from escaping, nappy hanging under a heavy load. This was one big baby. Out he came happy for underwear renewal. Then she popped him back and went to get ready herself. Before leaving, she came back to say goodbye to James.

Pausing, she stood a while, leaning her elbows on the side of the cot and just looked at her nephew, so happy playing in the confined space, murmuring away to himself. He always stood up when she came in. She wanted to cry. She feared she was about to drive for two hours and re-take an exam that she hadn't prepared for, then she would get expelled from the degree, she was tired, annoyed at herself, annoyed at a system, so uncaring and rigid, she was drained by looking after family members who she felt tied to, bonded with, loved, but hated doing what she'd been called to do. She gave James a hug, and he hugged her back. Then she paused again, close to his face, and looked into his eyes. James placed his small hand on her cheek, gently, calmly, concerned, and then, he looked into her eyes and said,

"Don't worry Tigga."

> Was it the feel of his palm on her cheek
> Was it the stare and the words he could speak
> Was it a moment unlocked and so rare
> In the mist of disaster, two year old care

After releasing her from the hug, which now he was 16 came without her bending over, he patted her on the back with his palm three times and she was brought back to the present.

"You were in your room." He tilted his head forward and raised his eyebrows as he said the words *your room*, "That's why I didn't like to come in to say goodnight."

She took up the bate, "What difference does that make?" she asked, "*my room?*" Stepping back and glancing at James' dad, who was also waiting for the punch line he'd come to expect from his son.

"I didn't like to disturb you," James paused, "Because, you're a lady."

She didn't think she had ever heard James call her *that*, but went along with it, shrugging her shoulder, "And? That makes a difference because?"

"You've got a vagina" James said, without laughing, blinking, or taking a pause.

She'd never said the V word, she didn't even want to acknowledge that it existed, but, here she was, with her 16 year old nephew, talking about something she had never talked about in public before, never even talked about to herself before, acting a coolness that wasn't her own. She giggled at herself, at the part of her that was coy and embarrassed by V things, and the other part of her, that academic feminist who wouldn't be put off by an old chestnut of a taboo.

"Yes, I know I have a vagina," she continued, as if talking about a shopping list. Acting was a role she could play too, so she played along, intrigued to see where *he* was taking *them*. "But I didn't have it out!"

Did he know he'd been rumbled, did he think she knew he'd been pushing the boundaries and did he see she was prepared to push too? Were they dancing, jousting, passing the batten, juggling, playing dares?

"Yes, well" James continued, a huge smile spreading across his face, "I wasn't sure."

***

James lay back smiling and thinking about the story she'd just read him, "I forgot we lived at your house when I was small," he said, then, "Any more?"

She paused. She wasn't sure if this other story she was holding in her hands was going to be included in the chapter or not. She wasn't sure, yet, if they would all hang together, 'as a set' or be split up, or if it was going to be too many words to include. She didn't know if it showed the right things, and she was slightly uneasy about what it would reveal about her to her nephew.

"I was considering putting this one in the chapter, but," She paused, "I wasn't sure, do you want to hear it?"

"Yes."

***

THE COFFIN

She sat outside the room waiting. She wasn't nervous, her heart rate told her so, a steady 42 beats per minute, a sign, she knew, of how fit she was, a sign that her body was in control, as ease and at rest. While she wasn't nervous, and didn't fear failing, she didn't want to go through with it. There was something else she was wrestling with, something far more dangerous to her than a viva. She was wrestling with who she was, or was it, who she was becoming. If she stepped over the threshold, she feared she would lose the self she wanted to claim.

"You have to go through with it, don't be silly" said a chirpy Dr Bradley-Cook. Bradley-Cook, a professor at Eastern Star University, had contacted her along with 100 other professional female golfers inviting them to fill in her questionnaire. When she read the survey she couldn't do it, it didn't ask the right questions, it assumed too much about female professional golfers, but, following the lessons she'd learned from the feminists' literature, her plan was not to slag the research off, but to contact the researcher, and explain her own "problems" with the questionnaire. Dr Bradley-Cook had been really gracious, interested in her observations about the questionnaire, said her comments were invaluable and they had become friends. They didn't only talk about Bradley-Cook's research, Bradley-Cook showed an interest in what she was doing and offered support to *her*. It was the first time in her PhD that she felt she'd anyone cared about her. But, when she said she was considering not taking her viva Bradley-Cook also said, "If you decide not to go through with it, you will never have that stamp of approval on your work, your research won't be taken seriously, you need that stamp."

So what did that mean? Did it mean she should be prepared to exploit the women in her research in order to gain a qualification, in order to gain glory and esteem. Did it meant she would be hailed as 'the expert', and have name on the thesis. The problem was, she didn't want to exploit other women, and the more she read the feminist literature the more concerned she became about her research methods and ethics. Several times, when she had asked for more time to complete her doctoral studies she had been refused, the department, it seemed, had goals, four years, it was only a PhD.

"It's the women in your research and others like them who'll lose out, if you don't go through with it," Dr Bradley-Cook had reasoned. Fine, but it wouldn't be Bradley-Cook who was letting these women down. Nor was it Bradley-Cook who'd sat through their tears as one-by-one multiple winning wealthy female professional athletes confided in her. She listened to stories about sexual abuse, self harm, trauma, rape, depression, bullying, pain. For some of her participants words would fail, "I've…" was as far it went, for others, she was the only one to hear, "I've never… told anyone…but." One-by-one these women deposited secrets in her bank. Did they think she was solid, secure, safe, an impenetrable stronghold? But now she was confused - *You have to speak out for them – Don't drive a wedge between you and them, you have to include yourself, where are you on the page?*

Eventually the examiners called her in.

You are an exploiter then, you are a scam, you say you care? Seems like you don't! If you did, you wouldn't be here! Just like the rest then, saving yourself, getting the stamp of approval for your actions, where are your lofty morals now?

She felt cool air drifting in through open window and sat down at the head of the table. The first examiner, to her right, was dressed, as she'd always seen him, in black, ready for a funeral, his head reflected the light as he moved, she loved him, his work, what he stood for, how he wrote.

He began with a preamble. She wasn't really aware of what his words meant, they came and went. The second examiner piped up, saying other words, those words had little meaning either. In front of her, on the table, the black coffin, her PhD thesis. Closed. Aligned perfectly with the edge of the table. She looked down at it. Its lid tightly shut holding those bodies inside. The bodies she'd put there. The chief examiner asked a question.

"On page....," she turned to the page and the decay of death seeped out. As she tried to scan, her vision clouded, the black print disappeared.

There is a point, when you bear grief, that you can hold on and be tough. Act tough or be tough. She was a good actor, perhaps the best. There is also a point where the acting must stop, and she knew she wasn't tough, nor did she did want to become any tougher or harder than she had already become. It meant that they would have to know, the performance, for her, had to end. At that moment she showed herself, naked, broken, and unable to speak. *Let them see me as I am.*

Before she let go, in that briefest of seconds, time slowed down in order that she could walk through this choice, and ask herself, one final time "W*hat do you want to do?"* She stared at the page, *"I can't do this,"* she said, *"I can't do this, and, yes, I am prepared for them to see me as I am."*

Have you heard a wolf howl at night? Its voice tears the silence, and so did she: while more words were coming at her, the tears that clouded her eyes, and the grief that had been clouding her soul and raining a torrent on the inside, began to flood out.

But these weren't ordinary tears of grief. Like watching a soldier dying from incurable wounds her examiners looked on helpless, their expressions told her much about her injuries. In their eyes she saw fear. Their faces saddened and cut her more. But she was helpless to reach out, to say: *"Please don't be upset by what you see."* She tried to clear her vision: *"Please don't be upset at my pain,"* but it was too late, she was mute and they felt her grief.

"Did I say something wrong?"

"Was I too hard?"

Two examiners were in shock that day.

Of course a psychologist would be able to explain it all, she was anxious because she wanted to pass and was worried her work wasn't good enough. She knew their theories, but could find no right way out of this maze.

Her life had been privileged, she saw this now, that coffin on the table had made it all clear. She'd despised some of those bodies when she played the tour, she knew she did. She joined in with the boys at her club, trying to fit in and joking when they asked her to identify the lesbians from the tour handbook, so she distanced herself from her fellow professionals and stood with the homophobic males. That information wasn't in the coffin, she wasn't allowed to put that in, only participants bodies, not your own, not other students and certainly not the professors, but that information, and lots more, was lodged in her soul.

"They confided in you," she said to herself some time later, "Perhaps because you were the first one to listen, and you were gentle and caring with their stories, open enough to hear. But perhaps, because you think about how you *should* have been, you are aware of your hard, vitriolic side too, and this grief is too much, just now. You need just a little more time."

***

"That was heavy," James said when the story came to the end. She agreed, but whatever she feared before sharing the last story with her nephew, she needn't have worried. He seemed to value being with her and talking about issues raised by the story.

As she reflected, some time later, about what she liked about the stories, it was that they crystallised a number of theoretical issues she'd been trying to understand and explore in her research more generally.

Firstly, each story made more obvious how life can be *interpellated*, a term coined by Louis Althusser (1971) to describe how an individual, because he or she has been shaped to act in certain ways by the ideology they are embedded within, responds when he or she is called or 'hailed.' Mark Freeman and Alistair MacIntyre extended the concept, of an individual's actions being shaped by forces outside the individual, suggesting that personal history begins even before birth, "The story of my life" MacIntyre (1981, p. 205) wrote, "is always embedded in those communities from which I derive my identity. I am born with a past; and to try to cut myself off from that past, in the individualist mode, is to deform my present relationship." Arthur Frank's (2010) work to her complemented these ideas from a narrative perspective by describing the way stories have the capacity to illuminate the process of interpellation. In her stories she could see how, playing professional sport, as a member of a family and studying for a doctorate, she had acted according to others' expectations of her because of the 'rituals' and 'practices' that she had learned through her family, community, culture.

Secondly, she liked the way the stories also showed some of the tensions that arise during the process of interpellation. That is, although Althusser had presented interpellations as "virtually nonrefusable," Arthur Frank had suggested that people *do* refuse to be hailed. The stories provided examples of different situations where she had been hailed and then responded - by making a 'nice' after winning, by giving a non-controversial response of 'who she was' on the flight, to answer the call of her sister to attend her nephew's birth, to walk into her PhD viva - but the stories also revealed some of the tensions and dilemmas behind these actions.

As she considered what lay behind her experience of dilemma, one narrative theoretical answer was that opposing narratives were vying for supremacy, and each calling her to act in a different way. One of these, perhaps learned from the faith of her family, was the call to be 'good' where good would be judged by acts of care, support, encouragement, submission. The counter narrative was where 'good' was a story about being strong, competitive, powerful, individualistic, winning, beating others, and achieving success. The stories suggested a step toward one ideological good was a step away from other.

A third element of the stories she liked was the way the stories showed how, at times, an individual resists being hailed. For example, even though the distance she hit her shots proved she wasn't 'strong' by drawing on the counter-narrative 'the race isn't to the swift or battle to the strong' *perhaps* it made it possible for her to believe she could win, despite the courses and 'game' being centred on strength skills. At other times, it was her body that provided a counter experience to the interpellation process – she didn't *feel* what was 'expected' to feel as a 'female' when she attended the birth of her nephew, and when she provided child care. These insights she thought, made it easier to understand some of the tensions, and moral and ethical dimension to her life and perhaps this would be useful to reorient her moral compass.

Finally, she liked telling a story about stories because by doing not only were multiple interpretations possible, but she had remained faithful to how she experienced her research and life. Not as separated, but informing, connected to, and embedded within complex relationships. She liked that, and for now at least, that seemed *good* enough.

NOTE

[1] In most four day professional golf events the number of players is reduced for the last two rounds, the players with the 60 best scores continue, the others are 'cut' from the event.

REFERENCES

Althusser, L. (1971). Lenin and philosophy, and other essays. *Monthly Review Press*. Trans. Ben Brewster. London: New Left Books.

Bakhtin, M. (1984). *Problems of dostoevsky's poetics*. Minneapolis: University of Minnesota Press.

Carless, D., & Douglas, K. (2009). "We haven't got a seat on the bus for you" or "All the seats are mine": Narratives and career transition in professional golf. *Qualitative Research in Sport and Exercise, 1*(1), 51–66.

Carless, D., & Douglas, K. (2012a). "In the boat" but "selling myself short": Stories, narratives, and identity development in elite sport. *The Sport Psychologist*.

Carless, D., & Douglas, K. (2012b). Stories of success: Cultural narratives and personal stories of elite and professional athletes. *Reflective Practice, 13*(3), 387–398.

Carless, D., & Douglas, K. (2013). "In the boat" but "selling myself short": Stories, narratives, and identity development in elite sport. *The Sport Psychologist, 27*, 27–39.

Deci, E., & Ryan, R. (1985). *Intrinsic motivation and self-determination*. In *Human behaviour*. New York: Plenum.

Denison, J. (2007). Social theory for coaches: A foucauldian reading of one athlete's poor performance. *International Journal of Sport Science and Coaching, 2*(4), 369–383.

Denison, J. (2010). "Messy texts," or the unexplained performance. *International Review of Qualitative Research, 3*(1), 149–160.

Denzin, N. (2003). *Performance ethnography*. Thousand Oaks, CA: Sage.

Douglas, K., & Carless, D. (2009). Exploring taboo issues in high performance sport through a fictional approach. *Reflective Practice, 10*(3), 311–323.

Douglas, K. (2004). *What's the drive in golf? Motivation and persistence in women professional tournament golfers*. Doctoral Dissertation, University of Bristol.

Douglas, K. (2009). Storying my self: Negotiating a relational identity in professional sport. *Qualitative Research in Sport and Exercise, 1*(2), 176–190

Douglas, K. (2012). Signals and Signs. *Qualitative Inquiry, 18*(6), 525–532.

Douglas, K., & Carless, D. (2006). Performance, discovery, and relational narratives among women professional tournament golfers. *Women in Sport and Physical Activity Journal, 15*(2), 14–27.

Douglas, K., & Carless, D. (2008a). The team are off: Getting inside women's experiences in professional sport. *Aethlon: The Journal of Sport Literature, XXV*(1), 241–251.

Douglas, K., & Carless, D. (2008b). Using stories in coach education. *International Journal of Sports Science and Coaching, 3*(1), 33–49.

Douglas, K., & Carless, D. (2009a). Abandoning the performance narrative: Two women's stories of transition from professional golf. *Journal of Applied Sport Psychology, 21*(2), 213–230.

Douglas, K., & Carless, D. (2012). Taboo tales in elite sport: Relationships, ethics, and witnessing. *Psychology of Women Section Review, 14*(2), 50–56.

Ecclesiasties, 9(1), (1984). *New International Version*.

Etherington, K. (2004). *Becoming a reflexive researcher*. London: Jessica-Kingsley.

Etherington, K. (2007). Ethical research in reflexive relationships. *Qualitative Inquiry, 13*, 599

Frank, A (2010). *Letting stories breathe, a socio-narratology*. University of Chicago Press, London.

Frank, A. (1995). *The wounded storyteller*. Chicago, IL: University of Chicago Press.

Frank, A. (2000a). The standpoint of the storyteller. *Qualitative health research, 10*(3), 354–365.

Frank, A. (2000b). *Illness and autobiographical work: Dialogue as narrative destabilization*.

Freeman, M. (2010). *Hindsight*. Oxford University Press. New York.

MacIntyre, A. (1984). *After virtue: A study in moral theory* (2nd ed.). Notre Dame, IN: University of Notre Dame Press.

Maehr, M., & Braskamp, L. (1986). *The motivation factor: A theory of personal investment*, Lexington Books.

McAdams, D. (1993). *The stories we live by: Personal myth and the making of the self*. New York & London, Guilford Press.

McLeod, J. (1997). *Narrative and psychotherapy*. London: Sage.

Saldana, J. (2011). *Ethnotheatre: Research from page to stage*, Left Coast Press, Walnut Creek, California.

Sparkes, A. (2012). Fathers and sons in bits and pieces. *Qualitative Inquiry, 18*(2), 174–185.

Werthner, P., & Orlick, T. (1986). Retirement experiences of successful Olympic athletes.

NIGEL P. SHORT

AN ENGLISHMAN ABROAD:
AN AUTOETHNOGRAPHIC TALE

Cities are to be judged by their welcome
(Kahn 1987, 12)

*****

Life's trajectories are unpredictable despite our well-intended plans. It is only when we look back that life attracts an incremental, linear and chronological continuum. The anthropologist Anthony P Cohen (1995) says that who a person is at any given time depends upon who is being asked and who is doing the asking.

*****

Whilst there have been many detailed and often uniquely courageous, compelling accounts about being a 'client', 'patient' or 'user' of English Mental Health Services (see for example Grant, Biley & Walker, 2011; Hardcastle, Kennard, Grandison & Fagin, 2007), many of these representations are frequently delivered as being the 'truth' about events.

'The fact of the matter is.....'
'Let's look at the facts'
'That story is untrue, this is really what happened'.
'That's not what he told the psychiatrist; he is manipulating us'.

I am suggesting that what is reported is but one account of an event and consequently representations are unable to be 'the truth'. The 'selves' animated by stories, animate further stories: revising old stories and creating new ones-though whether any story is ever truly new is contestable' (Frank, 2010, p.15). Despite the best intentions of writers to be accurate and authentic, from a post structural perspective our narratives are insufficient. The 'present' is clearly influenced by pasts and futures. What we report however, a work of reassembling, may be thought of as *trustworthy* accounts, accounts that help towards our continuing *'in progress reflexive project'* (Giddens, 1991; Adams, 2007). One difficulty for the user narrative representation is conveying what it is really like in serendipitous moments to experience mental health services.

N. P. Short et al. (Eds.), Contemporary British Autoethnography, 97–126.
© *2013 Sense Publishers. All rights reserved.*

How can we help people experience these 'moments'? I have used *'being a tourist'* as a possible vehicle for developing and conveying new insights and understandings of *'being a client'*; interesting to note that people are not routinely described as ex-tourists when they return 'home'.

*****

Ruth Behar (1997) says that what happens within the observer must be made known if the nature of what has been observed is to be understood. In autoethnographic, writing the researcher's own epistemology is at the very heart of the researcher's tale.

*****

This is a story about journeys, some actual, some imaginary some caught in the ambiguity between the two. Although the story jumps, loses itself and digresses, it does have themes of tourism and mental health. I may repeat things. Similar to the old woman at the beginning of Franz Kafka's *The Trial*, there may be characters you are introduced to that may not be mentioned again. They may seem irrelevant to the story but I am keen to develop an idea that if we gather up what appears to be discarded scraps we can take many different types of paths. To help the readers 'embed' themselves in the stories of the characters, I have benefited from Virginia Woolf's (1882–1941) writings. She often moved away from the 'plot' and 'structure' to employ streams of consciousness, with limited chronology.

*****

January 2000-Hospital

> *By the time, I got to hospital I had used up all my narratives. I had run out of things to say and had so far been unsuccessful in trying to explain what I was thinking and feeling. I had resorted to self-damaging ways of communicating. My difficulties had separated me from people; people I knew and loved. Now I was in a hospital about 60 miles from home; even further separation. The friends who visited me would have seen a very quiet withdrawn person. I wanted to see them but felt ashamed. I thought I had a personality disorder and this perception was confirmed by my clinical nursing notes (I was shown my nursing notes by a nurse). In spite of what seemed like reasonable internal dialogues I felt like a failure. Like Church (1995, p. 153), I knew that I did not want:*
>
> *'to psychologize my breakdown but' 'to socialize it'*

*****

Unlike 'being a mental health client', 'being a tourist' is something that most people will experience in their lives. It has been argued that tourism and holiday experiences are not just important but are a 'necessary' part of people's lives' (Gibson & Yiannakis, 2002).

*****

His shiny leather shoes clicked as he made his way towards my bed. His bright patterned tie was in stark contrast to his dark blue pin striped suit. He introduced himself. He was the Senior Registrar. He seemed to know who I was. He asked me questions, many questions. I liked him.

*****

I hope that by comparing and contrasting a trip to Albania with an admission to an acute psychiatric ward; both 'foreign' places, will 'capture' recognisable moments and offer a different perspective with accompanying insight and awareness. I make no claims to reveal completeness of understanding; however, it highlights previously neglected aspects of social lives and contributes to our understanding of the role of culture in social formations. I inhabit marginalised spaces, taking 'my' voices into 'contested spaces'. It is an account of some moments in time, space and circumstances understood as an 'ethnographic present' (Douglas & Isherwood, 1979, p. 10).

*****

He would take off his false leg, which he called Doug, and then pour his tea into the empty vessel. He would drink the tea, and then wipe his mouth and finish of his trick by replacing his artificial limb. A sort of re-purposing.

*****

I often wonder what happened to the female nurse who gave me time and would regularly play chess with me. We were evenly matched. I wonder if she ever thinks about me.

*****

Although the two accounts are separated by a decade, there are many connections; they both involve my multiple selves. There is an affinity between the episodes, which reaches beyond the obvious and non-obvious associations.

As Spivak (1993, p. 53) suggests 'there can be no universalist claims in the human sciences'. In deconstructing two experiences, I do so from within; it is from within these structures that I am able to critique.

*****

The butcher came out of his shop pulling a cow. He stood tall on the corrugated concrete pad outside. The cow's eyes looked sad. Large trucks rolled by, a caravan of horse drawn carts painted a medieval scene as they slowly made their way towards Tirana. The butcher's long leather apron shone in the morning sun; a knife appeared from his back trouser pocket, the beasts' throat was swiftly cut with one slick movement; the lifeless ox slumped slowly to the floor. The oozing pulsating bright red blood drained into a deep gutter. I wanted to take a photo. 'No' said the butcher.

*****

Both experiences broke from established routines, the often-troubled practices of everyday life; many often-unused senses were stimulated in contrast to the often-repetitive ordinariness of everyday life (Lefebure, 2002). During both situations, I entered a psychologically and spiritually intense period, where every experience seemed to be demanding the closest possible attention.

*****

Thursday 6th January 2000

I travel to the hospital in a volunteer's car. I tell myself on the way to London 'Now Nigel I want you to take note of all you are about to experience'. (Notes from my diary) The car driver owned a handmade brick company. I use my brickie experiences to join in some conversations. I eventually pretend to be asleep.

*****

These experiences offered opportunities to go somewhere foreign where nobody knew me (apart from details that were sent to the hotel and a referral letter sent to the hospital); I suspect that my respective hosts was already beginning to build a picture of me. Time and spaces were organised differently; both experiences involved travelling to my destination. There was arguably at the time an intention to return to somewhere. I experienced fresh landscapes, new prospects and vistas with unaccustomed opportunities; I saw new surroundings, saw things from different and pristine perspectives. I became aware of the unknown and unseen. MacCannell (2001) suggests that people are conscious of something 'beyond', something 'hidden', he continues 'that for everything that is said or seen, there is unsaid and not seen' (MacCannell, 2001, p.31, 36).

*****

I was born in 1954. I have four siblings. I was educated in a secondary modern school in my home town of Brighton. I have been employed as a barman,

*factory worker, kitchen porter and nurse, both general and mental health.
I retired from the NHS after 31 years in January 2011.*

*****

In addition, it is worth noting *that if* communities are constituted by their past stories (Hinchman & Hinchman, 2001) then hotel staff and ward staff are influenced by *their* pasts.

I have combined different 'gazes' into a plural representation. Tourism has the 'Tourist Gaze (Urry, 1992), where tourists may gaze at the 'mad' locals behind bars (Maoz, 2006) and medicine has the Medical Gaze (Foucault, 1975), where the gaze of a Doctor was supported and justified by the institution. Maoz (2006) develops these ideas by adding the new concept of the 'Local Gaze' (Maoz, 2006, p. 221) where tourists can become the 'mad' behind bars closely being watched by the locals. I would see these 'gazes' as cyclic, where one groups' concepts are made up of stereotypes about each group; the tourist would influence the local and the local influences the tourist. A 'mutual gaze' may help to appreciate new understandings. I have attempted this mutual gaze in a previously published work:

*****

Short N *(2005) Vocal Heroes: the views of two people who experienced a cognitive behavioural approach for their difficulties. Their narratives are accompanied by a commentary from the therapist. Journal of Psychiatric and Mental Health Nursing, 12, 574–581*

Although I do 'gaze' at others, I often feel distanced from the people I am gazing at. I often feel like an observer in an elevated hot air balloon; not part of what is going on.

*****

6ᵗʰ January 2000. Admitted to a hospital in London. I am 46. Father of two children, a brother to three sisters and one brother. A long-term relationship had ended. I initially dealt OK with this event, however, over a period of several months my mental health slowly incrementally deteriorated. I needed help.

I sit motionless on top of the hospital bed. I am staring at the cold grey linoleum flooring. Two nurses are looking through my backpack checking my belongings; rather like people's possessions on top of a table at a boot fair, I feel my life is being sifted over. They are talking to each other. I seem invisible to them. As Noble (2005, p.115) suggests, if other people do not acknowledge an individual 'as a legitimate participant in a given setting', then it is likely to introduce a sense of discomfort and leads to what Giddens (1990) deems to be a source of ontological insecurity. I do not think they need me. I feel flat as a pancake. In addition, I experience what Breakwell (1986) describes as a 'threatened identity'; there was a conflict between different personal needs and as often happens, between personal needs and social expectations (Brygoła, 2011).

I can smell the hospital linen, clean yet harsh, their fresh smell. The red NHS laundry mark spells out the local Health Authority's name. The 'material geographies' (Blunt, 2005, p. 506) of what I call home, are absent. No photos, no books, no pictures of my family. I do not know what to expect. The scenery was familiar; I had seen a bed before, I knew what a window was, yet their collective presentation was new and I felt insecure. I feel like a foreigner. Big Ben is chiming away in the background.

The world outside our own 'borders' often places additional demands on us. We try to comprehend alternative systems and the accompanying social practices. Common cultural features, for example similar language, recognisable symbols, may appear only superficially consistent (Edensor, 2002).

*****

*****

Sunday 3rd October 2010.

Reading a National Geographic Traveller supplement: The Western Balkans; Land of Discovery. I was fascinated by what I was reading. I wanted to visit the Balkans

*****

Some of my 'encounters' from both experiences are described; my entanglements with the people I met and places I visited. I focus on how I attempted to 'join in' with established social lives and consider specifically, some of the social interactions that occurred, in relation to the sensuous, social, dimensions of embodiment. I believe that humans create their social and spatial worlds through processes that are socially constructed and thus made meaningful.

*****

January 2000-London. Hospital

*It was early morning, seven o'clock maybe. The ward domestic comes in the room unannounced and begins the hover the carpet. How dirty can a room become overnight? The nursing staff had the unenviable **task** of getting me to* *eat and drink. Hearing their different tactics was interesting. I tried to imagine what each one would say as they came into the room.*

'You won't be able to go home if you don't eat and drink'.

'C'mon it will make you feel better'

*****

I went for about ten days without eating.

I had been making small marks on the wall behind the small wooden locker in the side room with a pencil to help me keep track of the days. I had seen Gene Hackman do this in the film 'The French Connection 2'.

I had no appetite. I was able to drink however; I had remembered liking cold Ovaltine when I had been in hospital at the age of ten. I was offered this drink several times a day. I was also drinking the warm cold water from the sink in the room, making a cup with my hands like Marlon Brando does when we first see him in the in the film Apocalypse Now.

I often shuffled down the long corridor to my room. On the way, I would pass several nurses who were sat outside the rooms of people who needed special watching. I saw one nurse reading a book about therapeutic relationships.

*****

February 2000-London. Hospital

My enthusiasm for life has drained away. I am unmotivated and I lack energy. The prospect of work is daunting and I am aware at the end of each day how much I am confabulating. I seem to be permanently hot, sweaty and cold. My creative edge has abandoned me and I feel worthless and hopeless. Now I am unable to see a way through the sticky treacle path that lies ahead of me. (Short, 2010)

*****

Through enacting these meaningful processes, human agents reproduce and question macrological structures in the everyday of place-bound action. Autoethnography provides insight into these processes and meanings; it can vividly illuminate the relationships between an individual and the different cultures they inhabit. This writing enterprise could be described as 'faction' (Geertz, 1988): an imaginative reflection on real events; a 'making out' of a particular meaningful scenario but *not* a 'making up'.

*****

While it has been argued that reflexivity and indeed autoethnography can result in 'navel-gazing' (Delamont, 2007), I do not believe that being reflexive about one's own positionality is to self-indulge but to reflect on how one is inserted in many matrixes of power relations and how that influences methods, interpretations, and knowledge production (Kobayashi, 2003). The tension in autoethnography reminds me of the tension with the 'green agenda'. If we keep objects, we may be accused of 'hoarding', or creating our own landfill, yet if we take our 'rubbish to the tip we are accused of not fulfilling the green agenda by filling landfill sites. If we disclose we are accused of being self-indulgent. Yet if we store our experiences and keep to ourselves this stance reduces any opportunities for furthering communication and dialogue.

*****

Both experiences had many similarities; for example, I packed the same backpack, I had to travel to get to the destinations. I was unsure what the rooms might look like; as well as many differences for example different languages or codes, different ways of greeting people (in Albania nodding the head up and down means no and shaking the head from side to side means yes). I entered both encounters with some innocence, unsure of hidden rules and expectations. I was open to possible exploitation. I was open to 'objectification'. I was an 'outsider' and had to trust the people I met.

*****

March 2000

One of the nurses on the ward tells me that I am going to be given some time off the ward unaccompanied. I make my way up to Soho in the west end of London. There is a take away cafe in Charing Cross Road that sells what I think are the best Falafels in the city. (A falafel is a fried ball or patty made from ground chickpeas and or fava beans). I first tried Falafels on a visit to Jerusalem in 1976. I brought a Falafel and some pita bread and made my way to Tower records in Piccadilly. On the walk I munched my way thought my snack. For a short period, all seemed well. I was anonymous and content. At Tower records, I brought myself two compact discs.

1. *Pieces in a Modern Style (2000) by William Orbit*
2. *Painted From Memory (1998) by Elvis Costello and Burt Bacharach*

*****

I also brought a small personal compact disc player. Interesting how songs seemed to fit into where we are at that time. A crystallising! One of the songs on the Costello and Bacharach compact disc 'This house is empty now' was particularly poignant and painful. It is a song about a couple breaking up. The protagonist is sat in their empty house. The partner has taken their belongings. I interpreted this song literally and metaphorically.. Where did I belong? I also thought that my life, my brain, my whole being was 'empty now'.

I had moved away from 'home'. As Case (1996, p.1) says 'by being away from home, the things, places, activities and people associated with home become more apparent (and perhaps valued) through their absence'. Saunders (1990, p.361) continues this theme by noting that being at home makes people 'feel in control of the environment, free from surveillance, free to be themselves and at ease, in the deepest psychological sense'.

*****

*I was captain of the school football and basketballs teams. I represented Sussex in the shot put and discus. I left home at the age of 16; job opportunities in Brighton were limited. I moved to South Wales. Our stories are therefore about the past and **not the past itself**.*

*****

Unlike most hospital experiences, tourists generally take holidays for pleasure and when doing so, they implicitly assume that going on holiday makes them feel happier. Recent research reveals that individuals indeed benefit from vacationing in terms of happiness (Nawijn, 2011).

*****

How is one meant to know about the hidden rules of different social norms? For example, during the fifth week of my hospital stay the medical and nursing staff considered Nigel' safe enough' to be allowed off the ward for a few hours unaccompanied. I walked a distance of a few miles in to London's west end. I became so immersed in my 'freedom' that I forgot about the time. I walked briskly back to the hospital. There are many internal phones in the main corridors. I rang the ward and explained that I was going to be a few minutes later that agreed. (I remembered what is was like to be a nurse on a ward and worrying if a patient did not return at the agreed time). The nurse I spoke with 'thanked me' for letting informing her. When I eventually got back to the ward, I was summoned to the ward office. The Charge Nurse reprimanded me and told me to 'never use' the hospitals internal phone; they were not for the patients or public.

I thought the phone call demonstrated that my mental health was improving; I was taking responsibility, problem solving and being an adult. The charge nurse's response infantilised me, humiliated me. I had clearly broken an unwritten rule.

*****

Albania has a tourist environment set within the wider context of transformation in post-communism development. Owing to the impoverishment, relative isolation and austere ideological circumstances that Albania endured for half a century, the country's subsequent experience of 'transition' has been characterised by mass emigration, civil unrest, violent destruction and administrative dysfunction (Hall, 2000). These elements add to the element of continuing instability in the region.

*****

The hospital ward had landmarks: bedrooms, bathrooms, toilets and the often-comforting external phone. My experiences were influenced by my internal landmarks. The linen cupboard was immediately on the right hand side then the kitchen. On either side of the long corridor were individual rooms. Ten on each side I think. In between rooms, four and five were the toilets and bathrooms. At the far end of the corridor was the lounge, the nurses' office and the medication room.

*****

*****

The warm grey speckled marble hall and stairwells were interrupted with soft patterned wool carpets. The white clean walls were punctuated with paintings; paintings of scenes I assumed were the Albanian countryside. My room was occupied by a double bed, a chest of drawers and a small table with a television on top. There was a separate shower and toilet. Two large glass doors opened up onto a balcony. I could see miles of countryside. I could receive three stations on the television. I chose to watch Al Jazeera English, a 24-hour English-language news and current affairs channel.

*****

I perceived myself as being 'unusual' for many of the people I met in Albania. I was often asked 'what are you doing her?' More, I thought out of curiosity than suspicion. Some people asked me 'Why on earth would you come here?' Interestingly part of my internal dialogue in hospital was very similar. I wanted to know why I was in there; I was a therapist, why couldn't I sort out myself. During my stay in hospital, I discovered that none of the staff I met had met a nurse cognitive behaviour therapist before. I was again 'unusual'.

*****

My family consider me unusual and eccentric; often accusing me of 'doing things differently to the crowd'.

*****

Both tourism and 'being a client' are often regulated by conventions and sets of activities. I suggest that both activities can be seen alternatively as 'stages' for improvisation and liberation; a removal from traditional straitjackets. Both activities can be destabilised by rebellious performances. As Harrison (2000) says 'in the everyday enactment of the world there is always immanent potential for new possibilities of life' (Harrison 2000, p. 498). Our narratives become distinct episodes in our oral histories (Haldrup & Larsen, 2003). Episodes of personal narratives, both tourist moments and client moments, are socially and semiotically constructed. Narratives are constructions.

I believe that we need to communicate our experiences in such a way that offers the reader an insight into 'our worlds'. The way we all interpret the world is influenced by our own unique ways of knowing, hence what I might feel in a situation and what I might conclude and construct from a situation may be different to the original observations and interpretations that I had. Van Maanen (1988, p.103) supports this idea by suggesting that:

> 'The idea is to draw an audience into an unfamiliar story world and allow it **as far as possible** (my bold) to see, hear and feel as the fieldworker saw, heard and felt'.

He continues (p.105):

> 'The audience cannot be concerned with the story's correctness, since they were not there and cannot know if it is correct. The standards are largely those of interest (does it attract?), coherence (does it hang together?) and fidelity (does it seem true?)'.

I was going to become a tourist; an activity that is often conventionally understood to be motivated by a desire to escape 'normal' life (Rojek, 1993). People usually have a choice in their destination. Tourists are often exposed to the unfamiliar. Something I have enjoyed for many years, in particularly when I experience a temporary suspension of time and movement.

*****

In her book The Enchantment of Modern Life (2001), Jane Bennett discusses how enchantment has been lost. Her book seeks to reintroduce enchantment, to experience genuine wonder. To help us reconsider a world where 'cultural and natural sites have the power to enchant' (p. 3), Furthermore to be enchanted is to participate in a 'momentarily immobilising encounter; is to be transfixed and spellbound' (p. 5).

*****

I visit the Da le Warr Pavilion and see an exhibition about secrets. 'A Secret Service: Art, Compulsion and Concealment'. The first pieces of work I saw was a collection of photographs by an artist named Kurt Scwitters, an artist who lived in Hanover. Over a period of twenty years, he secretly concealed images and objects in his house. Some of these 'hidden' objects and their 'hiding places' had been photographed for this exhibition; they were now not secrets anymore! For many years, I have 'hidden' objects. For example when I visit churchyards, I will place a stick or some other object somewhere, and unless I am being watched this location will only be known by me.

*As I was reading the information about each photo at the De La Warr, I suddenly felt very alone and yet part of something as well. I was frightened, yet very liberated. I started crying. It 'felt' like I had caught a butterfly and harnessed some mercury. I described it to my friend as best I could. It felt like a window to **me** had been opened up.*

I was enchanted by this vision. Everything seemed relevant to me at that particular moment. I thought momentarily, that I was going mad! I had not told too many people that I hide objects. There are two reasons for this. Firstly, that it may be considered odd and secondly it would not be a secret anymore. Another way of interpreting the above experience is to see it as a Transformational moment for me, this experience was troublesome knowledge – knowledge that is alien or counter intuitive, or even intellectually absurd at face value (Short, 2010).

*****

Social encounters provide tourists particularly, with the opportunity to gain new information about and to confirm congruent understandings of shared social and cultural landscapes (Harrison, 2003). Association is seen as fundamental to the process of giving meaning to our expeditions (White & White, 2008).

*****

Tuesday 18th January 2011

> *I have arrived. I am sat in Tirana International Airport. There are more people here than I expected. The airport is very busy. Many of the men are carrying Kompoloi beads. I do not understand many of the information signs. Some have pictographs, which makes it easier.*

Need to get some Albanian Lek, unable to buy any in England. I approach a foreign exchange booth. I communicate with smiles and the occasional English word. We laugh with each other. The airport smells dry. I can feel the crunch of sand under my Dr Marten boots; my reliable walking companions. I am alone but not lonely.

I get in a Taxi; a journey of about 15 miles. I enjoy not knowing where I am going. The Bradt travel guide recommended 3000Lek (about £19.00), that is what I am charged. The taxi driver tells me about his devotion to Manchester United football club. I can see another set of **kompoloi** *beads swaying from the rear view mirror. The car smells of Jasmine. It is very clean. The driver's leather jacket squeaks as we negotiate roundabouts and junctions. He has rings on all of his fingers. I feel nourished by this new place already. We drive through the city of Tirana, the driver points out the main University.*

There is the Enver Hoxha's memorial. Hoxha was leader of Albania from the end World war two until his death in 1985. He was the first secretary of the Party of Labour of Albania.

The roads are filthy. I can smell and taste the dust. I make a mental note to make myself a bandana from a neckerchief, like the cowboys, I watched when I was a youngster. Protect my lungs. I later read when I got home (Bon, 2008) that rubbish is a common feature of Albania; I see enough rubbish to evidence the literature.

*****

Hospital

In the months leading up to my hospital admission, I had been living in a one room flat. It was near the old house. I could continue to see my children. I was also spending most evenings in The Clown, a local public house. It was usually full up with people like me; people who were disenfranchised for some reason or other. The jukebox contained many of my favourites and the Guinness was good.

I often think of the irony of the pubs name. Perhaps all along I was being a clown.

*****

The hotel is in the outskirts of Tirana. I make a mental note of the roads we drive along; this will help me later when I walk back into town; great names, the Rruga Ismail Qemali and the Rruga Elbasanit. We pass the American Embassy. The local buses look very crowded; people's faces squashed against the windows. I see a Mosque, a Catholic Church and a Greek orthodox cathedral. A secular place. Did Enver Hoxha really tolerate this?

I enter the Hotel Baron.

http://www.hotelbaron.al/template.php?pag=37250

I am greeted with a handshake by the hotel manageress. She has a badge pinned on her red waistcoat 'Manageress: Hotel Baron'. She sounds German. This is confirmed when she greets me with Guten Tag. She tells me in English that her Grandparents were originally from Germany.

The reception area is bright and shiny. The tables look ready for the evening meal. Beautiful crisp white tablecloths. Each table has a bottle of olive oil, a bottle of vinegar and a small white cup with some tooth picks. I feel very comfortable.

I am given a key to my room and a young man hailed by the manageress escorts me in silence to my room. I ask where I can get a bus into Tirana.

Ku mund të gjej një autobus në Tiranë, ju lutem? (Where can I get a bus into Tirana please?)

He points to a bus stop on the opposite side of the road. '30 Lek' he says.

I unpack my large backpack; search for my small rucksack, put in my small bottle of water, my diary, my notebook and head out for Tirana.

*****

Goffman (1983) talks about the 'interaction order', he says that this sphere of life demonstrates that intervening successfully in daily life requires a high degree of competence in controlling expressions, movements and communications of the body. He considers the body as central in the structure of encounters. Body management (Shilling, 2003) is seen as central to the smooth flow of encounters, to influence our acceptance as a member of the 'interaction order'. In Goffman's (1983) work, this 'acceptance' is vital to our self-identity and our sense of worth. If we are unable to achieve this acceptance we are often categorises as a 'failure', what he terms a 'spoiled identity'.

*****

I am walking behind another patient down the corridor in the hospital. I change my style, pace and length of stride to 'copy' them. I want to see and feel what it might be like to be them for a moment.

*****

This is my first encounter with an Albanian. Crouch (2010) says that *encounters* are at the heart of tourism, a defining and distinguishing feature. These encounters are 'immediate, embodied and geographical' (Crouch 2010, p. 521). Interestingly there is the paradox that if tourism is a desire for distraction from the demands and drudgery of everyday routines (Britton, 1991) , the flip side of the coin is that we are displaced and immersed in the unfamiliar environments (unless we go back to the same place each year in order to seek the familiar).

*****

6ᵗʰ January 2000

The room is warm. I can hear Big Ben again. I have not slept successfully for about two weeks. Any sleep I have had has been influenced by alcohol; too much alcohol. I am tired and want to sleep. It is about 10.00 pm. One of the nurses leaves the room. The remaining nurse begins to talk to me; he is asking many questions. 'Where are you from?' What do you do for a living?' I do not feel like talking. I am alone and feel lonely. I tell him, politely, that I do not want to talk; he keeps 'keeping on'.

*****

The member of staff was trying to gather information, trying to engage and presumably begin to piece together information about me. Through interactions, we develop understandings; I understand that. Unfortunately, I was unable at this time to 'join in' verbally. I was now at the mercy of his interpretation of me.

*****

6th January 2000

I am awoken by the sound of Big Ben chiming 5.00 am. I could hear breathing; it was not mine. I open my eyes, there is a man sat in chair about two feet away from my bed. His eyes are closed. Is he asleep? I can smell his breath; it is horrible, he has halitosis. I assume he is a nurse. I roll away and face the opposite wall. I do not want him to know I am awake or that I have seen him asleep.

I am awake, I hear the nurse 'hand me over' to his colleague. 'This is Nigel; he has been asleep since 10.00pm last night' (No I had not!)

June 2010

My Mother has recently been admitted to a nursing home in Brighton; she refers to the 'hand over 'as 'pass over', we laugh.

The white cotton blanket is hard against my skin. The room feels warm, yet I am cold. The lumpy pillows are uncomfortable. I have started scratching the bridge of my nose and twiddling my hair between my right index and middle fingers; I have never done either of these activities before.

*****

Drawing on wider literature, Valentine (2008, p. 325) talks about 'meaningful contact'. By this she means contact that actually changes values and has the possibility of translating beyond the specifics of an individual moment into a more general positive respect for–rather than just merely tolerance of- others.

The one thought I took away from this to reflect upon was: Let us move from a position of being tolerant of another to a position of acceptance; try being more accepting of each and NOT just tolerant.

*****

7th January 2000

> *In my hospital room*

> *I can smell the sweet sickly smell of a rotting banana. Its decomposing shape rests on the pillar-box red quarry tiled windowsill.*

> *The unwanted*

> *White bread coronation chicken sandwich sits motionless on top of a cheap paper plate: another reminder that I am worthless. I am off my food. A white plastic cup is full of tea. I did not want it when it was warm. I do not want it now it is cold.*

> *Near the ward day room/television room*

> *The evening 'rush' to the small kitchen adjacent to the ward lounge takes place about 9.30 pm. Sandwiches wrapped in cellophane. Small, attached pieces of white paper detail the ingredients. Teaspoons covered in sugar from the previous user. Some of the paper cups have cigarette butts in them.*

*****

Eating and drinking spaces break up the routine of the typical hospital day. Eating venues provide opportunities for interaction; alas, there was little verbal interaction with the nurses. The staff stood guard as we picked over the food. As Gergen (1991) indicates, the self does not operate independently of the social; the self is understood as a social account.

*****

March 2000-Hospital

> *I am lying flat in my bed. I am feeling anxious again. Seems like a permanent experience. I think I am improving however. I have not cared about my feelings for weeks. I want to relax. I am tired of feeling agitated. I am usually a relaxed type of person. I remember the Jacobson (1938) progressive muscle (PMR) relaxation method. Progressive relaxation involves alternately tensing and relaxing the muscles. PMR may start by sitting or lying down in a comfortable position. With the eyes closed, the muscles are tensed (10 seconds) and relaxed (20 seconds) in sequence. I try it. I start at my toes and slowly working my way up to my head, I relax the major muscle groups in my body. It works. I am just left with my mind. I hold this experience for what seems like just a few seconds. The clock tells me is has been several minutes. I become very frightened. I cannot feel my body. I have to move my hands. How else do I know I exist? I gingerly touch my left thigh with my left hand. I have to, I need to. What a wonderful sense of relief. I am still here. Whom can I tell? I go the nurses'*

office. I tell one of the two nurses what I have just experienced. The nurse I have spoken to looks towards the other nurse. She looks bored.

The more I try to explain my experience to the nurses the more bored

they both appear to become with my story and me. I apologise to them, retire to my room, and feel worthless and vulnerable again. (Short, 2010)

*****

The non-verbal interaction with staff helped to maintain the 'invisible' wall between both staff and patients. Like tourists the clients would speak with each other; seeking out the familiar. Social interactions with significant others are integral to the process of negotiating a tourist identity (Moore, 2002), and I would argue client identity. Through interactions with others, we acquire common understandings that guide our actions.

*****

Most of my verbal interactions took place in the corridor of the hospital and the most meaningful conversations for me were with other patients. I shared my newly brought CD player with many people; Elvis Costello and William Orbit's new releases.

That bloody corridor. Sticky linoleum underfoot. Uninviting hard red Lloyd Loom chairs positioned infrequently on either side of the unwelcomed corridor. The atmosphere punctuated with chaos, a landscape of noises; the noise of music, the noise of people in distress; an assault on the ears. The abnegation of ambition.

*****

*****

My first breakfast in the hotel.

Mirëmëngjesi. A e keni gjumë të mirë? Çfarë do të dëshironit për mëngjes?

(Good morning. Did you sleep well? What would you like for breakfast?)

Mirëmëngjesi. (Good morning) I say. I had read some helpful words in a little tourist book I had been given. I am welcomed and invited to sit at a large round table.

Dëshironi një omëletë dhe tomotoes? Unë mund të bëj disa bukë dhe reçel dhe gjalpë (Would you like an omelette? I can give you some tomatoes, toast, and jam)

Shumë falemnderit. Kjo ishte e shijshme (Thank you very much. That was delicious)

*****

The internal decorations of the dining area create a visual impression of wealth. There are musical instruments hung on the wall. There are several scenic paintings showing places in Albania that I recognise; views over Lake Ohrid and the port of Duress. Through the clean windows, I can see over an adjacent valley.

116

Cuthill (2007) suggests that eating and drinking cultures are created thought the following features:

*****

'The visual appeal of the material environment, the multiple complex and mixed personal sensations of that environment and through performances in a multitude of possible scenarios between customers and staff. Together these factors create an ambience specific to each venue but specific also to the geographical place in which it is located' (Cuthill 2007, p. 67)

*****

The large silver trolley rattles as it enters the ward kitchen. The lids that cover the hot food are unsettled and jostle for their rightful positions. A Buddy Rich composition. I am sat at a table with four other people. Our plastic cutlery is wrapped in a paper tissue; the knife, fork and spoon looks like they are tucked inside a sleeping bag. The walls are bare. There are no windows. I can see members of staff collecting clean laundry from the room next door. There is very little talking in this room. Some of the staff watch us eating and occasionally try to encourage us to eat.

*****

*****

I take of my shoes and walk into the main Mosque in Tirana.

I am greeted with many smiles from the men preparing for their prayers. I wanted to get away from what Sibley (1988) calls 'purified spaces', these are spaces that are strongly circumscribed, where conformity is important and required. I respect this space; this new space.

I decide that each time I walk back to the hotel, a journey of about four miles, that I will walk a different way: another opportunity to get away from the 'usual' route. I like getting off the 'beaten track'. I walk down alleyways; dark labyrinths. Wander down narrow serpentine streets. The warm smell of bakeries; I buy some local handmade bread rolls. Busy backstreets. Groups of people stop and chat; stray dogs barking loudly and relentlessly. The gutters are steep; take away the winter rains I suspect. I am wonderfully lost and feel very safe. I cross several rivers; gushing dirty coloured water. Like jetsam, the riverbanks are covered in unwanted objects. The snow is melting in the mountains high up above the city.

*****

*****

Since childhood, I have enjoyed entering busy thoroughfares from a side street. Joining established pedestrians then leaving them when the next side street becomes available. I join the patterns of activity, the sounds of the street, influenced by the time of day, what day of the week. I like how crowds conform to patterns. I feel alone and anonymous in crowds. An observer. As Lowry says, 'I am interested in the flow of people, the rhythm rather than the individual; I am the individual' (Lowry, 2012). I enjoy watching groups of people rather than individuals'. Do crowds have a collective imagination?

*****

Like Vergunst (2010) who writes about the Rhythms of Walking, I enjoy the temporality of walking; how my temporary presence might affect people I am walking with. The ways that people walk becomes part of our social relations.

*****

Somebody I do not immediately recognise suddenly bursts into the room. He has not knocked on the door. He is now standing at the foot of the bed. His sudden appearance startles me. My heart rate increases.
'Are you getting up?' he shouts. 'You have been in bed all day'.
'I'm tired' I whisper. I feel afraid again, He has power.
'Don't you want to get better? He says.
He finishes his verbal interaction aggressively by saying, through gritted teeth

'Get up you **cunt**'.

I am worried about saying anything. I eventually get up. I make my way to the nurse's office. The walk down the corridor is long and deliberate. I am walking in slow motion. I join the pace of other people already walking. I seem to have no control over the speed of my movement. Other people are staring at me. There are two nurses in the office.

I had no appetite. I was able to drink however; I had remembered liking cold Ovaltine when I had been in hospital at the age of ten. I asked the staff and was offered this drink several times a day. I was also drinking the warm cold water from the sink in the room, making a cup with my hands like Marlon Brando does when we first see him in the in the film Apocalypse Now.

I shuffle back down the long corridor to my room. On the way, I would pass several nurses who were sat outside the rooms of people who needed special watching. They would look up from the books they were reading. I saw one nurse reading a book about therapeutic relationships. It felt like they all knew that my request for a drink had been met with refusal. More humiliation and more shame.

*****

*****

I leave the peace and quiet of tree lined Rruga Fatmir Haxha and enter the noise of Bulevardi Deshmoret e Kombit. I hear the mullah calling people to prayer at the Mosque. Fruit sellers are shouting; their stalls provide wonderful beautiful colours. Some people sit begging on the pavement, rattling plastic cups in a gentle rhythm. Young children holding small pieces of corrugated cardboard with messages written in black ink. Words I do not understand. Lots of makeshift tables; wooden fruit boxes, young men selling mobile phones and plastic cigarette lighters. The Bulevardi is noisy. Police, stand in the middle of the road blowing their whistles, waving and pointing at cars. Filthy, oversubscribed buses thunder past, taxi drivers beep their horns and I hear conversations; conversations that overlap with the sounds of traffic and pedestrians. Their noises offer a rhythmical flow. I would love to record this wonderful cacophony.

*****

*****

The bloke in the side room on the opposite side of the corridor is an African. He tells me he is a King. I do not immediately recognise the name of his

Kingdom. He is a large man; possibly twenty stone. His personal hygiene has been neglected; I can smell his unwashed body.

During one afternoon, I hear the male staff encouraging the King to take a bath. He tells them he does not need one. As the afternoon progresses, the voices of the staff get louder and I can hear more men arriving. A fight breaks out, there is much screaming and scuffling. The King is taken to the bathroom.

*****

*****

I take a mini bus trip to the town of Elbasan. Elbasan lies about 20 miles southeast of Tirana. The driver spends most of the journey either talking-to someone on his mobile phone or turning his head to talk to some of the passengers. I can see the deep valley below me about three feet away from my window.

I spend few hours in the town and then return to Tirana. The pace of the town is noticeably slower that Tirana. An old industrial town; reminds me of mining towns in England that have shut down. I post several letters home. (As of time of writing, these letters have still not arrived).

When I arrive back in Tirana, I see plumes of black smoke near The Government buildings. As I make my way towards the thick dark smoke, I see hundreds of people throwing missiles, pieces of wood, stones and rock at the police.

I am in the middle of a riot. There are riot police and several water cannons. The air is thick with clouds of gas; tear gas. I learn later that three people had been shot! I stand next to an older man who tells me what is happening. He suddenly shouts out 'run'. The riot police are making another baton charge.

121

I run as fast as I can. I trip over a chair in the garden of a café. I am on the floor on all fours. I am frightened.

I make my way to the tree-lined boulevard near the cities large hotels and walk, very very slowly. The riot police run pass me and I assume that they do not think I am anything to do with the rioters. I chat with an Italian Anthropology student. He is in Albania to study a particular village in the north of the country. He writes down his email address on a cigarette pack.

*****

6th January 2012. A year later, I am tidying my house and I find the cigarette pack. I write to him and he replies.

It is nearly a year since we met on the streets of Tirana, the day of the riots. I have only just found your email address again. You wrote it on a piece of a cigarette pack.

I am back home in England, unharmed. I often wonder what happened to you on that day. I ran away when the riot police charged and made my way back to the hotel, where I was staying in. I only stayed in Albania for another couple of days. I visited Shkoder the day after the riots and had a fantastic time; Albania is certainly a land of diversity and variety.

Hope all ok with you

His reply:

alò alò
it's nice to hear from you, ehehe,
who no died write!!!

im safe too, i survived that day fortunaty thanks god., but i see the hell in this moment. police charged and i escaped in the hotel behinde.
remember you and when you say me: you speak in english how i speak in albanish.

now my english is little better.
albanian is very variety land, and i wont to return.
im very interesting to see the photo of the riot.

whishing to hear from you very soon, and i'm very happy you stay good.
now i.m in italy, in sicily.
when you come call me.
best regarders

*****

The riot was scary. My heart rate increased and my breathing was intermittently shallow and quick. I briefly entertained the idea that I would be OK; I was English for heaven's sake. A strange fleeting sensation that I was omnipotent. I was worried how I might explain my presence in the riot. A tourist with a camera. At one point I was accosted by a person who started shouting at me; I could not understand what they were saying. Fortunately for me another person came along and explained that I was an innocent tourist and NOT as the first person thought, a government agent.

Interestingly, I text my sister and told them what had happened in Tirana and should they see it reported on the television for her to tell MUM I was OK. The riot was NOT reported at all on English television, despite three people being shot dead in a European capital. A friend of mine who works for Reuters sent a comforting text. H had seen the riot on the television in London where he works.

*****

CODA

Post trip/hospital recollections are often considered to be unreliable (Braun-LaTour, Grinley & Loftus, 2006; Kemp, Burt, & Furneaux, 2008). Although the memories in themselves are 'real', they are not necessarily an accurate summary of the actual experiences; much "reconstruction" takes place (Geertz, 1988; Rapport, 2003; Kemp, Burt & Furneaux, 2008). The accounts presented here can be considered as are trustworthy; after all they are just stories. I present a dialogical work that

123

contains many voices, as Frank (2010, p. 16) puts it 'every voice contains multiple voices and that in the interpretation of a story, as in the telling of stories, no speaker should ever be FINALISED'.

*****

'As in all battles, the eyewitnesses at Trafalgar did not record minute by minute details during the fighting, but set down what they remembered afterwards. Together with the confusion of the battle and the fact that no one could see more than a small part of the action, this led to large differences between individual accounts. The greatest discrepancies are in the precise times of various incidents, where records may differ not just by minutes but by hours' *(Adkins, 2004, p. 3)*

*****

'Given the distortions of memory and the mediation of language, narrative is always a story about the past and not the past itself' (Ellis & Bochner, 2000, p. 745)

REFERENCES

Adams, M. (2007). *Self and social change*. London: Sage Publications.

Adkins, R. (2004). *Trafalgar: The biography of a battle*. London: Abacus.

Behar, R. (1997). *The vulnerable observer: Anthropology that breaks your heart*. Boston, Mass: Beacon

Bennett, J. (2001). *The enchantment of modern life: Attachments, crossings and ethics*. Princeton; Princeton University Press.

Bloom, B. (Ed.). (1956). *Taxonomy of educational objectives, the classification of educational goals. Handbook I: Cognitive Domain*. New York: McKay

Blunt, A. (2005). Cultural geography: Cultural geographies of home. *Progress in human geography*, *29*(4), 245–268.

Bon, N. (2008). Negotiating rubbish in Dhermi/Drimades of Southern Albania. *Tourism, Culture and Communication*, *8*, 123–134.

Braun-LaTour, K., M. Grinley, & E. Loftus. (2006). Tourist memory distortion. *Journal of Travel Research*, *44*(4), 360–67.

Breakwell, G. (1986). *Coping with threatened identities*. London: Methuen.

Britton, S. (1991). Tourism, capital and place: Towards a critical geography of tourism. *Environment and Planning D: Society and Space*, *9*, 451–478.

Brygoła, E. (2011). The threatened identity: An empirical study. *Psychology of Language and Communication*, *15*(1).

Case, D. (1996). Contributions of journeys away to the definition of home: An empirical study of a dialectical process. *Journal of Environmental Psychology*, *16*, 1–15.

Cohen, A. (1995). Self-conscious anthropology. In J. Oakley & H. Callaway H (Eds.), *Anthropology and autobiography*. London, Routledge.

Crouch, C. (2010). Geographies of tourism: (un) ethical encounters. *Progress in Human Geography*, *34*(4), 521–527

Cuthill, V. (2007). Consuming Harrogate: Performing Betty's cafe and revolution Vodka bar. *Space and Culture*, *10*(1), 64–76

Delamont, S. (2007). Arguments against Auto-Ethnography. *Qualitative Researcher*. 4. Retrieved 3 March 2009 from http://www.cardiff.ac.uk/socsi/qualiti/QualitativeResearcher/QR_Issue4_Feb07.pdf

Douglas, M., & Isherwood, B. (1979). *The world of goods: Towards anthropology of Consumption*. New York: Routledge.

Edensor, T. (2002). *National Identity: Popular culture and everyday life*. New York: Berg Publishers.

Ellis, C. (2004). *The ethnographic I: A methodological novel about Autoethnography*. Walnut Creek: AltaMira Press.

Ellis, C., & Bochner, A. (2000). Autoethnography, personal narrative, reflexivity. Research as subject. In N. Denzin & Y. Lincoln (Eds.), *Handbook of qualitative research*. Thousand Oaks: Sage Publications.

Frank, A. (2010). *Letting stories breathe: A socio-narratology*. Chicago. The University of Chicago Press.

Foucault, M. (1975). *Birth of the clinic: Archaeology of medical perception*. New York; Vintage Books.

Geertz, C. (1988). *Works and lives: The anthropologist as author*. Stanford, California: Stanford University Press.

Gergen, K. (1991). *The saturated self*. New York; Basic Books.

Gibson, H., & Yiannakis, A. (2002). Tourist roles: Needs and the lifecourse. *Annals of Tourism Research*, *29*(2), 353–383.

Giddens, A. (1990). *The consequences of modernity*. Cambridge, UK: Polity

Goffman, I. (1983). The interaction order. *American Sociological Review*, *48*, 1–17

Grant, A., Biley, F., & Walker, H. (Eds.) (2011*)*. *Our encounters with madness*. Ross on Wye: PCCS Books.

Haldrup, M., & Larsen, J. (2003). The family Gaze, *Tourist Studies*, *3*(1), 23–45

Hall, D. (2000). Tourism as sustainable development? The Albanian experience of 'transition' *International. Journal of Tourism Research*, *2*, 31–46

Hardcastle, M., Kennard, D., Grandison, S., & Fagin, L. (Eds.) (2007). *Experiences of mental health in-patient care: Narratives from service users, carers and professionals*. London; Routledge.

Harrison, P. (2000). 'Making sense': Embodiment and the sensibilities of the everyday *Environment and Planning D: Society and Space*, *18*, 497–517.

Harrison, J. (2003). *Being a tourist: Finding meaning in pleasure travel*. Vancouver: University of British Columbia Press.

Hinchman, L., & Hinchman, S. (2001). Introduction. In L. Hinchman & S. Hinchman (Eds.), *Memory, identity, community: The idea of narrative in the human sciences*. Albany: State University of New York Press.

Kafka, F. (2000). *The trial*. London: Penguin Books.

Kahn, B. (1987). *Cosmopolitan culture: The gilt edged dream of a tolerant city*. New York: Atheneum.

Kemp, S., Burt, B., & Furneaux, L. (2008). Test of the peak-end rule with extended autobiographical Events. *Memory & Cognition*, *36*(1), 132–38.

Kobayashi, A. (2003). GPC ten years on: Is self-reflexivity enough? *Gender, Place and Culture*, *10*(4), 345–349.

Lefebure, H. (2002). *Critique of everyday Life*. London: Verso.

Lowry, L. (2012). Lowry quote seen in *The lowry art gallery*, Salford Quays, 19th January 2012.

MacCannell, D. (2001). Tourist agency. *Tourist Studies*, *1*, 23–37

Moore, K. (2002). The discursive tourist. In G. Dann (Ed.), *The tourist as a metaphor for the social world*. Wallingford England: CABI International.

Nawijn, J. (2011). Determinants of daily happiness on vacation. *Journal of Travel Research*, *50*(5), 559–566

Noble, G. (2005). The discomfort of strangers: Racism, inactivity and ontological security in a relaxed and comfortable nation. *Journal of International Studies*, *26*, 107–120.

Rapport, N. (2003). *I am Dynamite: An alternative Anthropology of Power*. London: Routledge.

Richardson, L. (2000). Writing. In N. Denzin & Y. Lincoln (Eds.), *Handbook of qualitative research*. London: Sage Publications Ltd.

Rojek, C. (1993). *Ways of escape: Modern transformations in leisure and travel*. London: Macmillan.

Saunders, P. (1990). *A nation of homeowners*. London: Unwin Hyman.

Short, N. (2005). Vocal Heroes: The views of two people who experienced a cognitive behavioural approach for their difficulties. Their narratives are accompanied by a commentary from the therapist. *Journal of Psychiatric and Mental Health Nursing*, *12*, 574–581

Short, N. P. (2010). *An evocative autoethnography: A mental health professional's development.* Unpublished Professional Doctorate.

Sibley, D. (1988). Survey 13: Purification of space. *Environment and planning D: Society and space, 6,* 409–421.

Valentine, G. (2008). Living with difference: Reflections on geographies of encounter. *Progress in Human Geography, 32*(3), 323–337.

Van Maanen, J. (1988). *Tales of the field: On writing ethnography.* Chicago: The University of Chicago Press.

White, N., & White, P. (2008). Travel as interaction: Encountering place and others. *Journal of Hospitality and Tourism Management Annual*

JONATHAN WYATT

ASH WEDNESDAYS: AN AUTOETHNOGRAPHY OF (NOT) COUNSELLING

ONE WEDNESDAY, NOW: APPROACHING THE COUNSELLING ROOM

You walk off the suburban street, its tarmac ravaged by potholes, come to the front door and ring the bell. Hear its echo. Without waiting you walk left, to the path down the side of the house, through the gate propped open by a white stone, and between the red brick walls of his house and the neighbours.

It's a summer evening so you can see along the path to where it dog-legs right. In winter, you would feel your way in the dark along this dank passageway until a sensor noticed you and a light flicked on; and you would wonder if he might be thoughtful enough to put up another light nearer the gate. At the end as you turn he's standing waiting for you between the main house and the outside counselling room. He heard the bell ring and meets you here, as he always does, wearing a button-down shirt outside blue jeans. Today's shirt is freshly ironed cerulean. He smiles, makes that gentle gesture with his right hand, and you follow his lean frame inside.

Gentle. That's how you find him. Measured, calm. You like that about him; and find it irritating.

You go to the blue sofa, walking past the chair on which he likes to swing back as he listens. Before you settle, you take in the vista of garden, mown grass and fruit trees that unfolds behind the room. You sit. You place your stuff on the floor. The storage heater makes the room too warm this evening and he has opened the window. On other days it's too cold. He struggles to regulate the temperature. A red Persian rug lies between you and him. Valuable, you think. He's still, as if waiting for you to begin.

"Why did you want to see me?" you ask.
You see him pause.
"Because I don't. Anymore. At the moment. See you."

He pauses again. You do that trick he does: you wait. You don't want to rush him, don't want to push him too hard. Not yet. You trust him to find the words.

ONE WEDNESDAY, NOW: WRITING AT MY DESK

My last counselling client finished four months ago, as our winter drought turned to sodden Spring: a young woman of nineteen who stopped coming. I'd misread her,

N. P. Short et al. (Eds.), Contemporary British Autoethnography, 127–137.

I think; hadn't picked up the clues she gave me, hadn't been sharp enough to let myself notice – and to tell her that I noticed – what she was finding so difficult to tell me. Those secrets she was keeping from both herself and her family.

She was my second client since I left the UK's National Health Service (the 'NHS'). My first came via a colleague at the practice. He came three times, then phoned to say that he was feeling better, thank you, and would like to stop. He never paid me. I wrote to him twice.

I have had clients for nearly twenty years. I can remember my first, at a counselling service for young people in Oxfordshire. Pam? No. Yes. Maybe. I remember what she looked like, some of what she talked about. School. Home. Friends. I saw her once a week, then once a fortnight. At the start, I remember my anxiety, waiting to hear her footsteps on the stairs, attempting to ease my breath and slow my heart rate.

I left the NHS after ten years of Wednesdays, just over a year ago. I told my colleagues, my family and myself that I would establish a small private practice, but now I am not counselling. In this lull or cessation – this space – I am pressing out the meanings I make of both being and not being a counsellor; tracing letters in the ashes of the day which was for so long set aside for clients, the day on which I now write. What sense(s) can be made of not carrying my body through the door of my consulting room once a week, as planned; not being a therapist in private practice? What do I make now of the people I saw during ten years at the health centre? Do my "enchanted encounter(s)" (Gordon, 2008, p.55) with them stay with me, affect me, haunt me? This chapter writes into these transitions, into these presences and absences, pursuing an inquiry into what it means (after Deleuze & Guattari, 2004) to be a becoming-(non-)counsellor.

I worked my NHS Wednesdays as a paid counsellor in a medium sized medical centre in a medium sized market town. Two years before I left, this medical centre became a pilot site for the much-trumpeted, incipient national government initiative, 'Improving Access to Psychological Therapies' (IAPT). I received a letter one Wednesday morning from the manager of our freshly re-branded 'Talking Space.' It had a five page questionnaire attached, which he asked me to complete with each patient every time I saw them, in order to provide 'evidence' as to whether or not this redesigned service for patients was working. These forms and my clinical notes were the equivalent of the medic's hospital charts; the official records of my work and its outcomes. The forms described the week-by-week improvements (or not) that the patient was making, monitoring how they were faring against the 'PHQ-9' depression, the 'GAD-7'[1] anxiety, and the phobia scales, even if they did not present with depression, anxiety, or phobias.

This 'Talking Space' was the context in which I now met patients. But there was always another context, a parallel talking – and listening – space, where what was at stake was a complex encounter between two people, not forms that I refused to fill. If, like Phillip Pullman's (1997) Will, you could have sliced the air with a 'subtle knife' and slipped through the gap, you would have found a different counselling world, where two people face each other telling and re-telling stories in unspoken faith that through shared and indeterminate brokenness, there is the capacity to heal, if healing is to be done. As Nancy writes:

> To listen is to enter that spatiality by which, *at the same time*, I am penetrated, for it opens up in me as well as around me, and from me as well as toward me: it opens me inside me as well as outside, and it is through such a double, quadruple, or sextuple opening that a 'self' can take place. To be listening is to be *at the same time* outside and inside, to be open *from* without and *from* within, hence from one to the other and from one in the other. (Nancy, 2007, p. 14, italics in the original)

This intricate, intimate – and everyday – process, this sense of 'assemblage' (Deleuze & Guattari, 2004), of 'intra-action' (Barad, 2003), and its memories and encounters in my material and imaginary counselling spaces, is the space that I am waiting at my desk to write into meaning.

ONE WEDNESDAY, THEN: MY COUNSELLING ROOM AT THE MEDICAL CENTRE

I head into the admin office to collect from the front desk the list of people I'm seeing today, bidding good morning to colleagues as I pass. The doctors meet in the staff room, and I join them, smiling at their banter and their warmth and sensitivity towards patients. Sometimes they let slip their despair at the most recent unreasonable bureaucratic burden placed upon them or the outrageous behaviour of a patient. At 8.40 a.m., they scatter to their rooms, weary but purposeful. "Time to save more lives, then," one says as they rise from their seats. I wait a few moments, taking stock, and then head to my room.

Tanya is my 9.00 a.m. client and the medical centre is at its busiest: I can hear the bustle of the waiting room beyond one wall. Today this doesn't distract me; she has my attention, which, over the three weeks we have been meeting, I have found easy to give. With her, my mind rarely wanders.

Her cough is bad, emanating from deep in her chest. It interrupts our discussion about 'Angie', as she has called her, this part of herself that berates and persecutes her. I look at Tanya as she turns away from me, hand over mouth, thin blonde hair now covering one sallow cheek. In a moment's quiet she turns to apologise, then the cough begins again, more insistent. Attacking.

I tell her that it's fine, not to worry.

This has been the pattern today, even before the cough began ten minutes into the session: "I'm sorry. I'm sorry. I'm sorry."

She is not apologising for the cough, I realise, but for Sunday. I reply that it is fine, really fine, though I know that reassurance is no match for Angie, her familiar, internal bully.

On Sunday afternoon, unshaven, I had been standing in Oxford's city centre in the rare summer sunshine stroking my alarmingly grey stubble. I saw my semi-bearded self as being slightly dangerous; and was enjoying it. A kind of middle-aged

English Clint Eastwood ready to take on some punks. The family was due to arrive as arranged in a short while. Starbucks beckoned.

She was suddenly standing there. "Hello," she smiled. "I saw you and thought it would be rude to walk past without coming up."

I was shocked. "Well…Yes... Of course. Hello."

Clint fled.

"Hello!" I announced again, laughing, stuck. But she seemed different, younger, the young woman she is; bright, buoyant almost.

The silence went on for too long. Beyond her I caught sight of Holly, who was running towards me.

I said to Tanya, "It's good to see you but… I'm sorry, I have to go. I'm meeting my family."

"Yes, of course." Hesitancy in her eyes. Embarrassed. Deflated.

Holly was with us, grabbing my hand. They looked at each other. We turned and left.

Now she coughs.

Angie has given her no respite since Sunday. She tells her that it was unfair to approach me, in my time, when I want to be with my family. But then Angie tells her relentlessly that she is a disappointment, that she has made nothing of her life, that she is useless.

Her plea back to Angie is that, for a moment, on Sunday, she wanted not to be a "client". She wanted to be normal.

The coughing seems to take her over. She clutches her stomach, stands up, moves to the sink and vomits.

I remain seated.

Angie is a looming, terrifying presence.

ONE WEDNESDAY, NOW: THE LIVING ROOM AT MY HOUSE

On Wednesdays at the practice, in the times between clients and during my two-hour afternoon break, and in the weeks and months since I left, I would sometimes write about being and working with clients.

Therapists writing tales of their encounters with patients has a long history. Freud told a good story – Dora, Little Hans (Freud, 1990) and the rest – and there are the endless 'case studies' and 'case examples' in the traditional psychoanalytic literature. Irvin Yalom, arguably the most compelling current therapist-writer, describes himself as both storyteller and teacher (see Yalom, 2006, p.247). Where these roles sometimes conflict, he states that he puts the story first and finds a way to make the pedagogical point elsewhere. I think of such writing as being like 'parallel charts', the reflective writing process developed by Rita Charon in her work developing medical clinicians (Charon, 2006). Unlike the medic's hospital charts or my notes and questionnaires, parallel charts try to shed light on the counselling experience; they are an acknowledgement of the complex human encounter; and are, perhaps, a counter-narrative to IAPT. The writing about my clients mattered because they mattered. The writing enabled me, as Charon puts it, to "[take] the measure of [my] own awe" (Charon, 2004, p.34). The writing was about the emotional connection that lies at the heart of therapeutic work (Wright, 2009).

My clients (and my writing about them) matter still: because their 'ghosts' speak of how to live, and how to live more justly (Derrida, 1994). Perhaps this is just po-faced *post hoc* rationalisation. Maybe writing about clients was just – or was as well – vicarious and parasitic.)

In my last two years at the practice, drawing on narrative therapy practices[2], on occasions I wrote *for* clients. I would write between sessions, then read my writing to a client and/or give it to them. Towards the end I stopped writing for clients; a colleague warned that it could be awkward, like getting poetry from an ex-boyfriend (Tamas & Wyatt, in press). I stopped writing about clients too; I no longer could, no longer wanted to. This is part of what happened: I lost needing clients to write. I became able to write without them. Except now.

This writing has been vexing me for days, weeks, months. I have not been able to find a hook, a thread, a metaphor to write with, to live by, one that calls me to follow. It has been – and remains – a struggle to work with and through. I have tried moving myself into different spaces to find what I – a plural 'I' – am looking for. Cafés, my usual writing haunt, have been too distracting; in my cramped cube of an office at home, I feel crowded and glum. A couple of nights ago, on Monday evening, I experimented with sitting here in the living room with the television on and the lights up, typing. One key after the other, one word then another. Writing's slow, painful accrual. I tried to hoodwink myself into believing that I was not writing these impossible stories but watching Rookie Blue.

Last Saturday I tried the train, on my usually productive monthly journey to my mother. It seemed an ideal opportunity to write my way into this. I planned to jump on board, open the laptop and write from Radley to Didcot (ten minutes), Didcot to Reading (twenty), Reading to Guildford (fifty), and Guildford to Godalming (ten). And back, at the end of the day. Sit, open, write; repeat.

It worked in a way. I was focused and disciplined, apart from checking the football scores every twenty minutes all the way home. But letters stumbled out doubtfully, producing a little aimless crowd of 500 words. I couldn't *feel* the writing; I hadn't reached that point – which I long for – where writing finds momentum and direction, becomes a fluid gesture that moves with a kind of inevitable grace until it rests, and I pause, read, return and write again.

Yesterday, Tuesday, my self-exhortation was to travel to my office in Oxford, catch up on my correspondence, then turn to this. I didn't. Other, more pressing tasks came into view. The late novelist, David Foster Wallace, described the combination of disgust and love the fiction writer feels for a text s/he's working at. For me, it's more like greeting a stranger I feel wary of; and it's not yet love, though there is desire. The way through it for Wallace is to hold onto the 'fun', by "[going] deep inside yourself and [illuminating] precisely the stuff you don't want to see or let anyone else see, and this stuff turns out (paradoxically) to be precisely the stuff all writers and readers share and respond to, feel." (Wallace, in The Guardian, 2012, para. 9). *Pace* David, but this emotional pot-holing is anything but fun.

I am not sure if this points to a crisis in and of autoethnography, or a crisis in me. As Gale and I wrestle with elsewhere in this collection, the 'I' – the plural 'I', as multiple as the 'we' of co-authorship – has choked. The delightful, liberating poststructural view of the fragmented, de-centred subject has stuck like a boiled sweet in the throat of the reflexive writer and therapist. I sign up to Deleuzian conceptualisations of subjectivity whilst I continue to write, both alone and with others, in the first person. I write about 'my' experience while I purport to disrupt the unified subject. How can a poststructuralist writing about personal experience be anything but ironic, and how can a therapist write about their clients ironically? It is 'my' body that sits – that sat – with clients and registered their rage and pain; 'my' stomach that growled indelicately. The 'I' that will die and be mourned and missed (or not) is not just some postmodern blob of subjectivity; it has palpable edges, a perimeter of permeable skin within which this writing happens.

But I am tired of this body's voice, like the voice of the client whose earnest complaints once lulled me, jet-lagged, to sleep. I cannot find my way into this writing because I am trying not to write from this familiar smooth and seamless place. The subject position from which I want to speak looks beyond itself towards the other; it loses itself in and with the reader and the subject, allowing us to connect with each other and with others, offering a small and vibrant gift; a very local act that moves with care and humility toward the global (Braidotti, 2011).

In their challenge to the 'I' of autoethnography, Jackson and Mazzei (2008) invite us to disturb the easy, glib comfort of writing about personal experience. Autoethnography, they argue, assumes "a coherent, explanatory subject who gathers up meaning and reflexively lays bare the process of knowledge-production" (p.303), as if this process is straightforward and innocent. Instead, they argue for a "performative 'I'", one that:

> ... has the potential to produce evocative, ethical, and failed practices that result in a telling with the potential to open the gaps and produce different knowings. The desire is not for a truthful story, but a story that confronts the truths and traces that are both possible and impossible. (p. 314)

I am with them in their call for suspicion, uncertainty, and deconstruction, and their mistrust of the innocence of "experience," but cannot make this fit into my room at the medical centre with Tanya and Angie, and the knowing that is necessary there. When Derrida writes that "we are only ever *ourselves* from that place within us where the other, the mortal other, resonates" (Derrida, 2003, p. 117, italics in the original), he both affirms the possibility that there is something we can call, at least provisionally, a 'self' and makes a claim for contact. The imperative and the impossibility of starting from "the micro-instances of the embodied and embedded self" (Braidotti, 2011, p.76) encounters the desire to lose that self in connection with others, human and non-human. They cancel each other like opposite sound waves; my pen hovers in the silence, in the café, on the train, waiting for words that have no place to come from.

This "sole-authored" chapter is as "solo" as Davies' flooding Brisbane River, which "we think of it as an entity, but it is certainly not fixed." (Davies, in press). Its voice(s) attempt not to fix, but to free; to be one thing folding into another, then another and another (Deleuze, 1995).

Slumped in the living room, I drop my hands and sigh; another false start, looping aimlessly through an obvious theoretical conundrum. It is Wednesday lunchtime. If I lean forward, twist to my left and look through the window's open green curtains, I can see the outside room, my counselling room. It is empty. Between 9.00 a.m. and 9.45 a.m. I saw the talented and experienced counsellor whom I supervise. She is the only person I see. When she left, I turned down the storage heater because the room will not be used for another fortnight, shut the window, turned off the light, shut the door, walked down the path, closed and bolted the gate, opened the back door into the utility room, and walked through the kitchen. I sat down, put my feet up, switched on the laptop and started to write. Today's regime is that I shall write for 50 minutes, take a ten minute break, write for another 50, and so on. The rhythm of counselling.

ONE WEDNESDAY, THEN: MY COUNSELLING ROOM AT THE MEDICAL CENTRE

It's 5.15 p.m. Rosa is my final client of the day. It's our third session. She folds her hands on her lap. I wait.

I say, "I've written something. It's about how I've understood what you've been describing; I've tried to capture the story. The stories."

"Yes. And…" She trails off.

"I wonder if it might be ok for me to read it to you. I might not have it right. It might not be how you see it, but…Or I could just give it to you. Or not." And I laugh.

"Yes. Please. I'd like you to read it."

"Ok."

I take the paper that I have placed on the low cabinet beside me and look at the one page of typescript. I can feel my heart. I clear my throat. I shall take my time.

"Ok. Here it is:

'I carry my story with me through each day, each night. It is in my body: in the angle of my hands as I reach for the telephone, or how I raise my head from my pillow. My mouth shapes into a smile that it doesn't feel and it is this story that it tells. If the curl of lip, the arc of neck and the angle of wrist could talk. But they do not speak. I do not let them give it away, though, if you pay close attention, look at the fine detail, you might ask questions.

I am practised at this. At keeping it in. So no one will know. Ever. I have held onto it for years. Thirty, forty. Forcing it down each time, putting it back inside, pretending, wearing my brightness and energy, my warmth and care, as a mask. Each day.

Till now. Now, I can't. It has become too heavy to carry, this story. But still I can't tell. Only she knows, and this is her story too so she has her own heavy burden to carry; and talking about it with her serves, often, only to add new weight to each of us as we are faced with our responsibility to not tell.

Telling or not telling. Telling sounds like betrayal. 'Don't tell', 'if you tell', children say. So 'telling' would bring guilt, guilt about all those who would be drawn in, all those ideals destroyed, relationships irreparably damaged, long-held faith undermined, lives disrupted, lives conceivably lost. Telling would mean living with the consequences.

Not telling, I preserve others. I keep them safe in their perceptions of how things are. I protect.

Telling would mean living with fewer secrets. Would mean learning to live with others knowing a 'me' they might prefer not to know. A 'me' I might prefer not to know.

Not telling I have to live with how this story gnaws me; it devours me, restless, insatiable, risen from its dormant state, demanding reparation, desperate to be fed by the air of being known, by the nourishment of justice and fairness, to be appeased and, maybe, allowed to rest.

And still, each week, I must tend to the needs of he whose story this also is, must show him care and love now he is near the end, saying nothing, giving him no indication that I know, that I remember. I lift, I tidy, I clean, biting back the anger I am at times aware of. 'Do you know what you did? Do you remember? Do you? Do you know what you have caused?' But I smile. I don't tell.'

My eyes are full, my voice thin.

I look at her and she says, yes, that's it. That's what it's like. That's how I feel.

At the end of our time she takes the page with her, folding it into her bag as she stands.

ONE WEDNESDAY, NOW: THE COUNSELLING ROOM AT MY HOUSE

It's getting dark. He has a red notebook by the side of his chair. He reaches down, picks it up, takes out a sheet. One page of text. Holds it. Offers it to you. You look at the page. You feel awkward, like he's given you poetry.

"It feels different this time," you read to yourself. *"Before, although I was in pain – such pain – I knew what I had to do. I knew where I had to go, how I had to be. This time...oh, I am nowhere. Lost...."*

He interrupts you as you read and you lose your place.

"This is someone I worked with before. Petra[3]. She'd lost a pregnancy – lost her baby – and I'd written about working with her, and how she'd travelled to her favourite beach to grieve him. Three years later, she came back to see me at the medical centre. May I?"

You're surprised but you're pleased and pass it to him. He starts reading aloud. You sit back and listen.

It's as if you aren't in the room. When he reads, he wears glasses, and you think he seems uncomfortable, as if he feels he shouldn't be wearing them. When he pauses, which he often does, he looks over them beyond you through the window onto the garden, his voice projected to some other listener.

"It feels different this time. Before, although I was in pain – such pain – I knew what I had to do. I knew where I had to go, how I had to be. This time...oh, I am nowhere. Lost. Lost amongst the long list of tasks to be done, details to pursue, obligations to meet. I wake early to make the necessary calls. I read the reports, the endless reports, so that I can interpret them for my family, whom I painstakingly consult, each in turn, so that all feel that they have had their say. I am PA, manager, communications officer, translator, teacher.

I am all of these. And somewhere, somewhere in a part of me that I have lost touch with these past months, I am sister. I am a bereaved sister looking for my sense of loss, trying to connect with the sadness, the regret, the longing, the anger perhaps, the love; attempting to recognise, as before, what it is that my soul needs, what I must do, however long it takes, however difficult I may find it.

Meanwhile, my workplace, which used to sustain me, has shut itself down, unable any longer to be at ease with its humanity. Fearful of what it imagines will ensue if it permits itself to risk embracing the wholeness of the people who make it what it is, it denies my pain, is intolerant of how I am affected and seeks only to ensure that it gets the required 'outputs'.

I will go back to myself. I will find the stories I need to tell – her stories, our stories. I will find a way to pay attention to my newly developing relationship with her, with Niamh. It is not how I wanted it; it is not how we imagined; but it is where I am and I will find a way to go where it leads me."

He removes his glasses and looks to you, intent, as if he has shown you something.

"I read it to her at the time, like that," he says. "I'm not sure what work it did, but she heard it and stayed quiet. She said it was good to hear herself being offered back to her. At the end of the session she asked to keep the text. She folded it and left."

He is waiting for you to respond. You are thinking of Rosa's hand folding the paper into her own purse, of Tanya's thin blonde hair, of Angie's wrath. You hear Agamben (2008) saying that testimony's value lies in what is absent, that which is impossible to bear witness to.

You sit, more or less present with the 'him' that he is showing you, the hints of the stories he doesn't. The counsellor has folded himself, been put away thoughtfully, and left; a piece of paper to be pulled out of a purse or pocket now and then, to see what sense it makes.

You are reader, viewer, writer; you are witness, critic, friend. A charitable fiction. You are client: the ones he's encountered and helped; those who have left his room at the practice confused, or warmed, or less alone; and those he will not see. You are those parts of him that no longer need his attention in that way, or those he has given up on, or can no longer help.

He seems tired of helping; and relieved he doesn't have to anymore. You smile, a little; though it has cost him, he has written you into this room in order to tell you how much he does not need you.

He says, gently, that he does not need you now. That you, perhaps, never really needed him, and certainly don't anymore, not as he is now. You feel proud of him and relieved and a little dejected. You suspect that he has missed some crucial point. It is not the need that has shifted; but perhaps it has come unmoored from its agents and propulsion, exceeded its terms. The thin skin around his eyes looks worn, almost translucent. You offer an encouraging smile. In Shakespeare's tragedies, "when remedy is exhausted, so is grief" (Mamet, 2000, p. 21).

You pick up your stuff from beside you, stand, take one more look around this room. "I don't suppose there's a fee, for today, is there?" you ask. He is not sure if you're being funny. You continue, "Don't get up. I can see myself out." He smiles, looking up at you, and reaches a hand to touch yours. "Yes," he replies, "I know."

You open the door, linger too long outside, see the drawn green living room curtains – what kind of household is this? Who lives here? Is he happy? – and return down the path, out onto the gravel and the pock-marked road, leaving him to his Wednesdays.

NOTES

[1] These are each well-established screening tests. They involve patients completing short questionnaires, the outcomes of which carry scores that measure, respectively, depression and anxiety.

[2] e.g. using writing – by/with therapist and/or client – to 're-story' a person's familiar, well-established narratives. (See Payne, 2000.)

[3] See Gale et al., 2012.

REFERENCES

Agamben, G. (2008). *Remnants of Auschwitz: The witness and the archive*. New York, Zone Books.
Barad, K. (2003). Posthumanist performativity: Toward an understanding of how matter comes to matter. *Signs, 28*(3), 801–831.
Braidotti, R. (2011). *Nomadic subjects*. New York: Columbia University Press.
Charon, R. (2004). *The ethicality of narrative medicine*. In B. Hurwitz & T. Greenhalgh & V.
Charon, R. (2006). *Narrative medicine: Honoring the stories of illness*. Oxford: Oxford University Press.
Davies, B. (in press). Reading anger in early childhood intra-actions: A diffractive analysis. *Qualitative Inquiry.*
Deleuze, G. (1995). *Negotiations (1972–1990)*, (M. Joughin, Trans.). New York: Columbia University Press.

Deleuze, G., & Guattari, F. (2004). *A thousand plateaus*. (B. Massumi, Trans.). London: Continuum.

Derrida, J. (1994). *Spectres of Marx: The state of debt, the work of mourning, and the new international*. (P. Kamuf, Trans.). New York: Routledge.

Derrida, J. (2003). *The work of mourning*. Chicago and London: The University of Chicago Press.

Gale, K, Pelias, R, Russell, L, Spry, T., & Wyatt, J (2012). *How writing touches: An intimate scholarly collaboration*. Newcastle-upon-Tyne: Cambridge Scholars Publishing.

Gordon, A. (2008). *Ghostly matters: Haunting and the social imagination*. Minneapolis: University of Minnesota Press.

Guardian Online (2012). *David foster Wallace on the nature of fun*. Retrieved from http://www.guardian.co.uk/books/2012/nov/16/david-foster-wallace-nature-of-fun. 29 November 2012.

Jackson, A. Y., & Mazzei, L. A. (2008). Experience and "I" in autoethnography: A deconstruction. *International Review of Qualitative Research, 1*(3), 299–318.

Nancy, J.-L. (2007). *Listening* (C. Mandell, Trans). New York: Fordham University Press.

Payne, M. (2000). *Narrative therapy: An introduction*. London: Sage.

Skultans (Eds.), *Narrative research in health and illness*. Oxford: Blackwell.

Tamas, S., & Wyatt, J. (in press). Telling. *Qualitative Inquiry*.

Wright, J. (2009). Autoethnography and therapy: Writing on the move. *Qualitative Inquiry, 15*(4), 623–640.

Yalom, I. D. (2006). *Momma and the meaning of life: Tales of psychotherapy*. (Originally published in 1999). London: Piatkus.

KEN GALE & JONATHAN WYATT

ASSEMBLAGE/ETHNOGRAPHY: TROUBLING CONSTRUCTIONS OF SELF IN THE PLAY OF MATERIALITY AND REPRESENTATION

INTRODUCTION

We have been writing together, and together with others, about and through collaborative writing for many years (e.g. Gale & Wyatt, 2009; Wyatt, Gale, Gannon & Davies, 2011; Gale, Pelias, Russell &Wyatt, 2012). In this chapter we make a claim for a new ethnography that both builds upon and challenges earlier influential models and practices that can be seen to have constructed autoethnography in particular and actively differentiating ways. We work to propose collaborative, spatially and temporally distributed ethnographic practices that destabilise, reconstruct and deterritorialise the existing theory and practice of the signified generalisation 'autoethnography'.

In offering this we develop the theory and practice of *assemblage/ethnography* (Wyatt & Gale, 2013) that works to elude and trouble the potential discursive construction that the naming of a category of difference can create and, at the same time, offer a mode of practice that always brings the materiality of relational space into play as a method of inquiry. We take a lead from Haraway (2000) in seeing this as a space of 'diffraction' and 'interference', rather than one of reflection or reflexivity, from Barad (2007) in attempting to work with the 'entanglements' that inhere within, through and around the 'intra-actions' of material and discursive exchange, from Thrift in working with a 'processual sensualism that a material schematism provides' (2006, p. 139) and from Deleuze and Guattari in living with the creative challenges and anticipations that a world with no heaven for concepts can be seen to offer (1994).

In attempting to achieve this we display in the following pages a collaborative and collaborating modality of ethnographic practice that places the category of difference of individualised subjectivity and the differentiating practice of the individualising subject, of what has been referred to as the 'autoethnographic I' (Ellis, 2004), under erasure. In this we value the methodological leads offered by Foucault of 'getting free of one self' (2000) and of Lather of 'getting lost' (2007) and in so doing rhetorically engage with the fluid and transmutational qualities proffered by the Deleuzo-Guattarian figures and conceptualisations of 'multiplicity', 'becoming' and the 'assemblage' (Deleuze & Guattari, 1988). To do this the chapter offers a

N. P. Short et al. (Eds.), Contemporary British Autoethnography, 139–155.

schematised series of exchanges, via emails and their attachments, that took place over a period of a few months.

In producing this account our 'ethnographic imaginations' work at the interstices at play between the flurried narrative accounts of our original 'writing down' and what presents itself on these pages as our 'writing up' (Atkinson, 1991) and in so doing works to both examine and trouble the material and textual constructions of the reality of our collaborative engagements into the not yet known.

Although we trouble claims to individualism and individual author/ity, a provisional hypothesis might be that in what follows Jonathan's writing is in italics, Ken's in plain text.

THINKING (NOT) OF SELF

I am thinking (not) of self and how indeterminate that is and yet how determining it also is. How that sense of self that emerges out of habit, out of discourse, out of not allowing diffractions to play a part: a part to alter 'concept, percept, affect' (Deleuze & Guattari, 1994, p. 163).

I find you writing recently:

I sign up to Deleuzian conceptualisations of subjectivity whilst I continue to write, both alone and with others, in the first person. I write about 'my' experience while I purport to disrupt the unified subject. How can a poststructuralist writing about personal experience be anything but ironic, and how can a therapist write about their clients ironically? It is 'my' body that sits – that sat – with clients and registered their rage and pain; 'my' stomach that growled indelicately. The 'I' that will die and be mourned and missed (or not) is not just some postmodern blob of subjectivity; it has palpable edges, a perimeter of permeable skin within which this writing happens. (Wyatt, 2013)

This incessant *nouning* is so disabling because it is not really what we mean, or what we feel, or who we are or how we are.

I am arrested. Checked. Isn't it what we mean? Or what we feel? Not who or how we are? Maybe it's that they are so very difficult to let go of, to mourn. When I call you, write to you, think of you, tell Tess that I'm writing this with 'you', there is at least a moment of capture: a press of the button that holds a you, today's you, this moment's you, the singularity of Ken, the you that is full of the recent Cadiz trip – effervescent, restless, excitable, passionate – in frame. I treasure that capacity: there is a Ken whom I am coming to know, the knowing of whom is always in flux – temporary, provisional, partial; a Ken(ning) who is different and distinct from all others, all other Kens, all other friends, all other people I have met, a sense of whom I feel that I have, 'trembling at the horizon of all that 'I' don't know about 'you'' (Pollock, 2006, p.93).

It is, I think and feel, naming that I wish to hold onto in our assemblage/ ethnography. The possibility of stories. I am with you about saying no to 'nouning' and fixity and yes to fluidity, verbs, dispersal of the self, uncertainty – yes, all of these.

Let's tell stories. Tell me a story, Ken. Let's "go visiting" through stories, as Hannah Arendt (1982) encourages. Like the ones of you travelling across the USA in 1989[1]. The you in all your becoming then. The events in all their becoming then. Tell those. With their senses of place and space; the friend you were with, the cities you drove through, the escapades. Do these 'noun' you? Not for me. Not in my imagination and memory of your telling of them. I celebrate the sense they give me of a Ken, or, more accurately, the Ken-ing haecceity as "unique existent" (Cavarero, 2000).

We have been working toward these human and post human senses of becoming and assemblage/ethnography and yet we seem tied to those very nouns that identify us within humanist and phenomenological individualism. As I open this up I am drawn back to thinking about identifications, representations and the discourses that work to bring these constructions into place. I started to write the other evening:

Slowly over these last few days I have sensed my self breaking away from another self that was constraining and forming me at the same time: a self that was becoming me and yet, in terms of living in relation to a me that I might live on some kind of plane of immanence, taking me away from that living, limiting, moulding, denigrating and disallowing a massive pregnant well spring that has been wanting to burst forth and flow out of me and into me for ages now.

I struggle with intensities that seem to emanate from the objective conditions that attempt to regulate me with their administrations, their legalities and their structures. I am on the cusp of divorce, of retirement and death and I swim in the whirlpools and currents that these conditions prevail upon me.

I know that the only way that I can live with and against these conditions is with a my self that is driven, that is focused, that needs to do, to act, to energise, to live. Without this I know that I am dead.

I am here with you as you write, knowing something further, something now, of the 'singularity' of Ken? A sense of you, not one that pins you, fixes you, but one that suggests you are knowable, that prompts me from reading this to root for you, to wish for your happiness, to be beside you in the struggle you describe.

As these concerns try to make themselves felt and heard, as passion and affect work to infuse and bring to life these writings, it is like a young body trying to live healthily, through the use of exercise and eating good food and still being covered in the disabling and scabrous effects of eczema or acne. The writing above is full of scabs; there is a profusion of 'I's', 'we's', 'me's' and so on. This writing is about infection: it is infected. Its sores are virulent; they seep all over the page, messing with its honest intent, staining its integrity with the irrevocability of their creeping presence.

No, no, no, I cry: they are not scabs or sores; they are not virulent. The I's, we's and me's convey the vibrancy and struggle of Ken. Ken-ing. I don't want to lose that, don't wish that sense of you to be erased. Show me how we can.

Paragraphs of writing work like teenagers squeezing unwanted spots. As one spot is destroyed by the pressures of frustrated fingers another shows its presence in a hitherto hidden manner. It seems to be impossible to exorcise 'I', 'we', 'you', 'our', 'us' and 'them'. If they are our spirits; if they matter, if our materiality of self is to live with representations and the pervasive discursive constructions that pollute lives like these, how are we to talk and write about them? In our *becoming-Ken-Jonathan* (Gale & Wyatt, 2009) we have reached this point of assemblage/ethnography. In our mappings and our 'between-the-two's' this seems to be significant. It seems that we have struggled to bring this to life and it seems in our becomings we are giving birth to something that wants to grow, wants to live and wants to disturb the comfortable habits, customs and traditions of those who live without reflexivity in worlds of identification, representation and wanton repetition.

And so, as time has elapsed, there has been space to think and feel and sense and perhaps value a writing that does not talk of 'I', 'you', 'we' and 'us' …

I am left, just now, finding that difficult. Writing this to 'you', from 'me', still has meaning. You say 'we' ('we have reached this point…we are giving birth'): it is not all of what I notice of/in me.

I hold onto the hope and the possibility of stories. Stories embroiled and imbricated within matter, flux, and provisionality.

Beginning again through a fleeting remembering of Borges' essay/short story Tlon, Uqbar, Orbis Tertius in Labyrinths and in it the phrase which has always resided and never completely disappeared and so that when re/collection is sparked it appears in re/citation.

'upward behind the onstreaming it mooned' (1971, p. 33)

Starting to inquire into the nounless world that is Tlon, the feeling of pointlessness is ever present, lurking around corners, pregnant with anticipation, desirous to trip up the unsuspecting novitiate writing self into the world. When he speaks of those who inhabit Tlon Borges says, 'the world for them is not a concourse of objects in space; it is a heterogeneous series of independent acts' (p. 32).

The swirling dementia induced by fleeting words and cries. The brief fragment of a scream carried across the crowdedness of a room. Sensing sighs in the silence of a brief moment. The tantalising encounters with momentary body smells in movements of passing on the street. It is 'body-without-organs' (Deleuze and Guattari, 1988); always disembodied. The organisation of the body is at best a sham and at worst an artefact that disciplines and controls. Body is never fixed: it is its appearance; it is its representation, its identification that is fixed by name, classified through order and frozen by type. Therefore its fixity creates an illusion whose ephemeral qualities gives perpetuity to myths and beliefs that rinse all magic from its reality and fixes the image in the repetition of the process, the different trays of chemicals, the certainty of different reactions. These replications are only the stuff of life that are wrapped up in the severity and machinic force of systems of power. The simple beauty of a Warhol silk screen that screams over and over again 'I am not the only one', 'I am not the only one'. Elvis says, 'I am not the only one', Mao says, 'I am not the only one', Marilyn says, 'I am not the only one'. The simple beauty that comes from the knowing that the process of silk screening can never produce the same image. The repetition of the process creates its own differentiation: each one is different.

Really, each one is different: though they appear to be the same. *Yes, yet they have names; they are/have stories that we tell of them.*

And so with everything?
Really, each one is different: though they appear to be the same.
And so with collaborative writing?
Collaborative writing as a method of inquiry?
Collaborating with whom?
Inquiring into what?
Into whom?

Collaborating with a person, someone with a name, someone someone knows, invariably involves collaborating with a cipher, a representation of a reality that always has to be displaced by the representations that bring it to life, that locates it within time and space. It makes sense to talk about *becoming-Ken-Jonathan* only because this hyphenated, Deleuze inspired trope carries with it certain associations, associations of plurality, of differentiation, of emergence, of liminality, of always becoming other. In these dust storms, these ever shifting sands, 'I' is always indeterminate, always unsure, never safe, its threats of fixed embodiment are always challenged by lost histories, by secrets that live unhaunted lives, by stories that never can be, never will be told. These collaborators are named: Davies & Gannon, Denzin & Lincoln, Wyatt & Gale and so on and what do these collective signifiers mean? Associated with each of these pairs are bodies of work, within these bodies, whilst protests might be made, are organised conceptual arrangements, there is rhetoric, critique and the humblest of invitations to question the artifice which makes each pair, with their associated bodies, recognisable, understandable and, dare it be said, citable. In this has the beautifully candid exhortation of Deleuze when he says of working with Guattari been lost?

Félix and I, and many others like us, don't feel we're persons exactly. Our individuality is rather that of events, which isn't making any grand claim, given that haecceities can be modest and microscopic. I've tried in all my books to discover the nature of events; it's a philosophical concept, the only one capable of ousting the verb "to be" and attributes. From this viewpoint, writing with someone else becomes completely natural. It's just a question of something passing through you, a current, which alone has a proper name.

Even when you think you're writing on your own, you're always doing it with someone else you can't always name. (Deleuze, 1995, p. 141)

So let us use these names; or let us use names in this way – Ken as a 'current passing through you'. When we talk about 'you' let us tell the stories of this force that is you at that moment.

Bronwyn Davies says in her recent use of this powerful and potent quotation, 'By putting oneself out where thought is happening, one cannot always name whoever it is one is writing with' (Davies, personal communication). This carries great force. Though in the preceding sentence there are names that inevitably have substance and substantial tangible life within and through their representational and identifiable histories, this sentence of Davies' bares a pulsing naked and intelligible heart when it gives the words 'where thought is happening, one cannot always name whoever it is one is writing with'. There is a worry about the elision of 'oneself' and writing life might be more comfortable if the potentialities and transitions that are incumbent in the pregnant space that lives between 'one' and 'self', qua 'one self' were made more evident. And of course it is not simply the world of thought that is always becoming; it is the differentiations that are always emergent as the world of thought lives in and with the constant repetitions of those multiplicitous encounters with sense and affect, intuition and value. Nothing is fixed, there is always change. With assemblage/ethnography it seems so important that there is a living, not simply with a sense that 'one cannot always name whoever it is one is writing with', but also that there is a living with the intensities and senses of selves and others that in multiple and diverse settings of time and place coalesce and conflict, confer and differ, and sometimes reflex and also, inevitably, diffract. In the not yet known of these always collaborating diffractive possibilities there will be a subsequent and creative interplay of matter and discourse, body and words. And so it seems that this assemblage/ethnography cannot only be about the 'whoevers', it will also have to involve the withevers and in each of these both gain and attempt to convey a sense of what Kemmis has called 'happeningness' (2010, p. 417), of living in and perpetuating 'moments of being' (Woolf, 1985), and always in becoming alert to and present with the creativities, pluralities and endless possibilities of worlds of haecceity.

Ah yes, I am with you here.

How about a brief return to Borges and the world of Tlon for a moment of curiosity and temporary respite?

...the colour of the rising sun and the far-away cry of a bird ... the sun and the water on a swimmer's chest, the vague tremulous rose colour we see with our eyes closed, the sensation of being carried along by a river and also by sleep ...these ... can be combined with others ... the process is practically infinite. There are famous poems made up of one enormous word ... the fact that no one believes in the reality of nouns paradoxically causes their number to be unending. (p. 33)

Even Borges could not write against nouns in his imaginary noun-less world without using them.

It is 4.22 p.m. In 10 minutes we will leave for the cinema, but I want to write here, to type into this shared electronic space, neither yours nor mine. Ours. Although it may seem disconnected to your writing here, the prompt is in the just-this-ness, the haecceity, of the clearing of our attic today, the handling, sifting, keeping and binning of assorted items accumulated over the past twenty three years in this house. Thirty bags of clothes, stored for winter or summer or for when they came back into fashion or for when weight is lost or gained; some twenty cardboard boxes, all empty save for blocks of polystyrene and clear plastic bags; five years' worth of my back issues of the football magazine '442'; my stamp collection from when I was a child; miscellaneous toys, cards, fairy lights and books, all belonging to the Joe and Holly, that they have stored as each stage of growing up has left others behind; and cases, sports equipment, curtains, cots, Christmas decorations and sheet music.

There have been five trips to the tip over the weekend and there will be more; we have two bedrooms filled with bags and cases to sort, items in piles, many – of mine, at least – kept for sentimental reasons when, two decades ago, I was unable to let them go. I have already begun to find it easier this time. There seems to be no point holding onto objects that had meaning, that I was attached to, that attached those selves to me, then. Letters from old friends, cards from my first classes as a teacher. Those students will be in their forties now. I have not looked at those things since I lifted the boxes up the unstable step ladders (which I still use) and placed them in the corner of the attic. I will not look at them again if I place them back there. Why not just wedge them into the back of the car and be done with them?

That is easy to write. I am not sure, when I climb the stairs later, that I shall be able to see it through.

'Ah yes, I am with you here'
And yes it feels that treading carefully is what this nomadism is all about. It is the use of these 'me's' and 'you's', 'we's' and 'them's' that are potentially so disabling. The problem seems to be intractable, so for the moment I, yes I, am going to continue using them. There seems to be no choice.

We walked, you and me, last Saturday afternoon, in the brightness of a warm October afternoon, in all the particularity of that day, above Ammerdown², talking as we dodged the mud, climbing steadily until we reached the monument, the folly whose history I must have known at some point. We caught up, talked about writing, and paused to hail our fellow writing weekenders.

'You' and 'me'. 'We' did that. I use those terms with caution, aware of their provisionality, their contingency. I do not seek to fix - not you nor me nor them nor 'it': those moments, those haecceities.

Is writing like this 'disabling'? A 'problem'? 'Intractable'? Not for me.

145

I am so aware of the way in which, in our nomadic inquiries, the smoothing and the striating still goes on: space is never still, never fixed because of this. As I smooth out the network of striations that might pre-exist I replace them with new ones and the realism of my ontology is happy that these are then further smoothed by new forces, by fresh winds that blow across and unsettle and disturb, as the desert becomes more populous. I am happy with this. I have an understanding. I am happy that this understanding is shifting, in flux, always open to change. I like it that this has the power to say that, that there is always an endless process of differentiation and that, therefore, my subjectivity is always in play.

I cannot help but believe in the post human possibilities that lie within the scope of bodies not ending with skin, of somehow living in these very real moments of knowing the heterogeneity, the contingency of self as subject, of knowing that my boundaries, my very edges are always shifting and breaking down, that there are these forces at play in and about me, that this very molecularity has the potential, through particularity, to be energising, creative and always renewing. And then I hear you cry in the near distance of my dreams and my unstable worlds of affect,

> *A sense of you, not one that pins you, fixes you, but one that suggests you are knowable, that prompts me from reading this to root for you, to wish for your happiness, to be beside you in the struggle you describe.*

And I wonder about this sense you have of me and of course anyone, anything, being 'knowable'. I have shared with you and others my sense of trouble about this: I express concerns about representation, I search out the patterns of interference, the 'diffractions' that Haraway talks about and my body lurches and reacts to what this being 'knowable' says. I sense that the 'knowable' somehow relies upon representation and I sense that these representations have to be elusive and mercurial, always shifting: this is the nature of our becoming.

> *Yes. 'A sense of you...one that suggests that you are knowable' – you, me, your children, mine – has the emphasis on 'sense' and 'suggest'. It is the sense of Ken, like the way I can picture you throwing back your head when you lose yourself in laughter, which hints at the possibility of 'knowing', at a something or somethings – flows, intensities – that mark(s) you as 'unique existent', which leads me as your friend to stay being curious, intrigued, involved, wishing to see what further intensities emerge and assemble. Maybe 'knowable' is not what I mean: maybe, in this sense, I mean 'narratable' (Cavarero, 2000).*

Without this we have what Foucault has called 'fixity' and with this comes the etching, the somehow forceful, deep cutting kind of fixing of the striation in a more permanent form; it forces through materialities, it incises and cuts deep and in this doing resists the reflexive and indeed diffractive energies that would smooth its fierce indentation.

I am wondering how we can move our between-the-two's toward the kinds of processes of subjectification that Deleuze (2004) talks about in *Difference and*

Repetition. I love the way in which the writing in that book shifts the attention away from the kinds of knowing that we have grown up in within post-Enlightenment thinking, a form of thinking that we have become so ingrained in that we can't think without 'I', 'me', 'you' and so on. In a way he starts with intensities and works from there. In doing this it seems to me that he is re/cognising the troubled, unstable nature of existent selves not as fixed beings but as contingent and heterogeneous elements in always becoming force fields of flow and exchange. He says that with intensity there is always difference, or intensities are always different and that through and with these multiple irruptions and eruptions of intensity differentiations are always produced that invariably create our sense of selves, of other selves, of matter and so on. The crucial element in this is that differentiations produce the 'I's', the 'me's', the 'you's' and so on, not the other way around. If we express it the other way around it seems that there must be at the very least the implication of or the inference toward essence. This is the logic of Plato's argument about forms which positions being as prior to becoming. Within this usage Deleuze also sets up a fascinating argument to support a reconceptualisation of empiricism in which the conceptualisation, say of self, of Ken, of Jonathan and so on is an 'object of encounter, as a here-and-now, or rather as an Erewhon from which emerge inexhaustibly ever new, differently distributed "heres" and "nows" (2004a, p. xix).

I am left, just now, finding that difficult. Writing this to 'you', from 'me', still has meaning. You say 'we'…: it is not all of what I notice of/in me.

Yes, I feel that I want to agree with you and in so doing I want these 'I's', 'me's' and 'you's' to be a part of the kind of empiricism that Deleuze describes, something that is beyond the kinds of 'anthropological predicates' (op. cit) that have the insidiously discursive tendencies to fix us in ways that are more suffused with the toxic addictions to representation than the healing antidotes to be found in the diffracting materialities of contingency, heterogeneity and flux. I sense that in the repetitions of our discussions, discussions that have been reverberating and enthusing our between-the-two's for many years now we have multiplicity and difference. Working with Difference and Repetition again I feel that these are our intensities, they are the intensities of an assemblage we have called elsewhere Becoming-Ken-Jonathan and I like that because it seems to have a freshness and a vibrancy of life that will never harness us to coded signifiers and representations of self that obscure and deflect by the stoutness of their rigidities. And so with Deleuze I want to 'make, remake and unmake my concepts along a moving horizon, from an always de-centred centre, from an always displaced periphery which repeats and differentiates them' (op. cit).

The I's, we's and me's convey the vibrancy and struggle of Ken. Ken-ing. I don't want to lose that, don't wish that sense of you to be erased. Show me how we can.

Well we start with Erewhon! And perhaps in so doing, we do not do away with the I's, the 'me's' and the 'you's', partly because we can't! Instead we displace them,

147

we don't divorce them and we will not lose them. We will repeat them and as we do this we will do this always with the presence and action of diffractive possibilities, always in acknowledgement of and always in play with the exponentially existent possibilities of contingency and flux. We will be using this in intensity to activate and create further intensities.

Perhaps it is, as you suggest, in and through our stories that this will emerge.

It is, I think and feel, naming that I wish to hold onto in our assemblage/ ethnography. The possibility of stories. I am with you about saying no to 'nouning' and fixity and yes to fluidity, verbs, dispersal of the self, uncertainty – yes, all of these.

I hold onto the **hope and the possibility of stories**. *Stories embroiled and imbricated within matter, flux, and provisionality.*

So let us use these names; or let us use names in this way – Ken as a 'current passing through you'. When we talk about 'you' let us tell the stories of this force that is you at that moment.

I sense intensity in your words. I know what those stories can do. I sense how they bring together worlds of concept, affect and percept and I have a knowing of how their very presence substantiates the materiality of the relational ontology of our Becoming-Ken-Jonathan assemblage. So perhaps it is not so much the pleasure of the stories in their writing, telling, reading and listening it is more about what we do with them, how we use them how we instantiate them in our becoming.

Tell me the stories, then, of the Cornish flag. Of your Cornish becomings[3]. I have often wished that I was 'from' somewhere, that I belonged to a place. I think that is why I spent much of my twenties in places – Liverpool, Newcastle – where people seemed so sure of who there were, not that this was unproblematic. I think it is why I have no loyalty to a football team. Manchester City? Only when they are doing well. I have been to Manchester less than half-a-dozen times; and to watch City there just once.

Tell me about your Reuben and Phoebe and Katy; and Rohan[4]. About America. Write about the struggles and joys of these current days. What I mean to say is:: There is such a richness to Ken-ing. I am glad to name you. .

Sleep-writing

I have been writing this in my sleep these last two nights; when its intensities have become too much, the writing has been waking me. I turn and turn, and it will not let me go. I am beginning this at work in my office, with an indecisive low sun of late autumn mid-afternoon causing me to raise and lower my blinds every few minutes, and I both welcome and am irritated by it.

A question has come into view, one that seems to be (at) the heart of this chapter, this assemblage/ethnography; even, perhaps, at the heart of autoethnography in general. I shall try to frame it:

To what extent can writers – people? – we? – lay claim to singularity? In our writing, in our lives.

No, that's not right. Well, yes, maybe, but perhaps this is better:

To what extent can we – do we, inevitably – create such singularity through writing; in writing between us; in this assemblage of (the verbs) Ken and Jonathan.

No, that's still not right. Yes, maybe it is; but there's more:

To what extent is it our political, ethical charge that we do so? That we must, because there is so much at stake.

You see, what, I think, is keeping me awake is how much these questions matter (in that word's various meanings) to me, to us, to the work. Here are today's answers to them:

However inadequate, however provisional, however misleading, we can and we must claim the possibility of singularity; we can and must aspire to, work at, creating such singularity through writing. It is indeed our political and ethical charge. We have to. When I talk about singularity I am talking here of the 'singular existant' of Nancy (Nancy, 2000), *which "may be singular plural or something else entirely, outside of the order of the calculable" (Callus and Herbrechter, 2012, p. 246); a "haunted subject, haunted by what comes after it just as much as by what comes 'before', it can never be fully present to itself".*

I am with Rosi Braidotti in viewing the subject as:

an entity fully immersed in the process of becoming, in productive relations of power, knowledge, and desire. This implies a positive vision of the subject as an affective, productive and dynamic structure. (Braidotti, 2011, p. 17)

You see, I am with her in seeing the subject as a – fluid, open, permeable – 'structure', an 'entity' (see also Brians, 2011) and, the term she invokes later, 'a figuration'. I am with her in a call to the notion of 'bodily materialism', the 'embodied or enfleshed subject' (Braidotti, 2011, p. 15), one that is always 'emerging out of a process of becoming'(Brians, 2011). With her in seeing nomadism as about 'becoming situated, speaking from somewhere specific and hence well aware of and accountable for particular locations.' (Braidotti, 2011, p. 15)

I am with Kottman, talking of Cavarero, when he describes how she:

insists that the self is narratable and not narrated. It is an existence that has not been reduced to an essence, a 'who' that has not been distilled into the 'what'. In short, for Cavarero, it is the unique, individual existent – who is in constitutive relation with other existents, and who is not yet, or no longer, a subject – who takes 'priority', so to speak. (Kottman, in Cavarero, 2000, p. xii)

This is why I am calling you, calling us, to stories in (this) assemblage/ethnography. Cavarero, like you, like me, is against categorisation, simplistic representation, fixity, all of these, but argues that "narration reveals the finite in its fragile uniqueness, and sings its glory" (ibid.: 3). This is why I keep coming back to you to tell stories

149

– not ones that are simplistic and unitary but ones that provide, create, something of the embodied, the embedded, the particular. You. Us. Me: writing this here, troubled, disturbed, angry, passionate, joyful.

You see, in part I am fuelled by how I experience you. The theory you espouse is not how I find you (the verb), today, in this moment. I don't believe you want to live without calling on 'Reuben', 'Phoebe', 'Katie' and those intimate others in your life; I don't believe that you want to live without telling me – you, others – how intense was yesterday's swim, say, your body's immersion in the waves, its pull against the currents, the thrill; ;you will always call on your trip to the US in 1989. You talk about yourself and your life, your histories and your futures, your longings and desires, your fears and anxieties – and so you should. You must. Dosse (2010) talks of Deleuze and Guattari's 'intersecting lives', and tells their complex, nuanced, incomplete stories. You and I joke about Deleuze's dodgy hair; we speak of their differences, and of Guattari's work at La Borde and of his influence of upon their collaborative work.

Intensities, haecceities, flows, assemblages, all. I can't quite believe you would want to live in Borges' world, though I know it only from what you have told me. I wouldn't want to.

I am writing in a different but connecting space, in a file with a different name about no longer counselling; and I am with the stories of those I saw in my consulting room over ten years; I am writing into their haunting. There, as here, I am with Gannon in arguing for 'a relational autoethnographic [or, rather, assemblage/ethnographic] subjectivity, a self that is contingent on the recognition of others, and a self who finds voice through that relation.' (Gannon, 2012, p. 1). By 'self', I mean that which is – echoing you above – a "contingent result of an ongoing process" (Brians, 2011, p. 132).

We must hold onto the possibility of the personal, the personal pronoun, the person, the relational. There are politics at stake here. For Braidotti, memory and narrative are crucially linked to 'practices of accountability (for one's embodied and embedded locations) as a relational, collective activity of undoing power differentials'. To not do so is disabling and nihilistic: 'The world without me, the-world-without-us...(is) the folk tale of the end' (Callus and Herbrechter, 2012); and it is to abdicate responsibility; to fall, ironically, into self-referential indulgence.

This is where I will end today. I will not place the personal pronoun in inverted commas.

It's now Saturday morning. I'm at home. Tessa[5] has gone out for a day with her fellow students and tutors on the Masters programme she is so much in love with. You have sent me more writing that I have glanced at but now want to engage with fully. You have sent me an email about your antics last night, and about how much you enjoy Friday nights, which I do too – better than Saturdays by far, I agree. Now I must wrest myself from this writing and take in some air. And get coffee.

150

WONDERING ABOUT OTHERS

... effervescent, restless, excitable, passionate – in frame. I treasure that capacity: there is a Ken whom I am coming to know, the knowing of whom is always in flux – temporary, provisional, partial; a Ken(ning) who is different and distinct from all others, all other Kens, all other friends, all other people I have met, a sense of whom I feel that I have, 'trembling at the horizon of all that 'I' don't know about 'you'"

I am coming to something here.

We talked on the phone recently about other matters that have troubled us, that have lurked within our assemblage for years now and have configured it in uneasy, wriggling and tenacious ways. That sense of forces that are there, that sense of sensing that sometimes is so highly pressured and that at others is so slight that we blithely drift through our everyday, oblivious to the play that is upon our bodies, in ways that in our bareness we hardly notice: the sun in its grace pours on our bodies, giving us energy and we offer nothing in return. That's how it feels sometimes.

I am coming to something here.

I wonder how we are conditioned by these binaries. Are we too polarising in the play that we are acting out here? May be it is not about whether or not we expunge the personal pronouns from the writing that infects our 'we's' and our 'us's' and our 'our's' maybe it is about accommodating them within and by the use of our 'ands'. As I have been feeling my way in to your most recent writing and as I have also gone back over the to-ings and fro-ings of our recent correspondence, a powerful sense of feeling fine about you using these personal pronouns in relation to me, you and us is beginning to emerge. When you talk of having a 'knowing' I get that, I get that in relation to what seems to happen in our assemblage/ethnography. This feels real and whilst the signifiers have to represent, that is what they do, the representations seem less likely to carry out the kinds of tasks that I have been railing against in my recent writing. I gain a sense that in this assemblage/ethnography we have a collective ontology that is realist and that wouldn't allow for representations to dis-able, control and mis-represent how we go about things. I might be (mis) representing us in ways that others might consider to be fallacious, incorrect and even naïve and if so I am always open to the diffracting possibilities that this might offer but for the moment this feels better.

> Clichés, stock phrases, adherence to conventional, standardised codes of expression and conduct have the socially recognised function of protecting us against reality, that is, against the claim on our thinking attention that all events and facts make by virtue of their existence. (Arendt, 1978, p. 4)

It feels to me that you and I write in ways that are not designed to protect us 'against reality'. It feels to me that we immerse our selves in reality as a way creatively enriching and bringing reality to life I am excited by the movement of the writing

151

of Barad, Haraway and others into the here and now of our own and by the way in which the materialist complexities of this writing works to intensify our own. I am drawn back to earlier struggles in our work when we considered Maggie MacLure's observation that 'the space opened up by language is an ambivalent one. It is both productive and disabling.' (2003, p.3) The quotation that she includes from the writing of Derrida is both illuminating and infuriating in the way in which it also adds complex energy to these considerations:

> Without the possibility of différance, the desire of presence as such would not find its breathing-space. That means by the same token that this desire carries in itself the destiny of its nonsatisfaction. Différance produces what it forbids, making possible the very thing that it makes impossible. (Derrida, 1976, p. 176)

We search for each other's presence in our writings: it seems as if we always have done. As we engage in this there always seems to be something alluring, always enticing, and invariably incomplete and ambiguous that drives our collaborative writing as a method of inquiry forward. We can no longer avoid talking about our work with each other and with other others in the aeons and multiplicities of relational space as *assemblage/ethnography*: how could it be anything else!?

> *There seems to be no point holding onto objects that had meaning, that I was attached to, that attached those selves to me ... I will not look at them again if I place them back there. Why not just ... be done with them ...That is easy to write. I am not sure, when I climb the stairs later, that I shall be able to see it through.*

I too am sensing the power of memory working on me this morning as the bright autumn sun illuminates my home and works to pull my body out into its glow and its freshening radiation. I love the lack of cliché that living with the convolution of memory activates. It is like re-kindling an affair to bring Maggie's thoughts back into play here. This repetition is of course difference: without this the affect of respect and the concentration of animate lucidity would be dead. And so with this licence I also remember Irigaray and want to use and adapt a quotation of hers that we have considered before in relation to her argument for *parler femme*:

> (They) are contradictory words, somewhat mad from the standpoint of reason, inaudible, for whoever listens with ready-made grids, with a fully elaborated code in hand. For in what she says too, at least when she dares, woman is constantly touching herself. She steps ever so slightly aside from herself with a murmur, an exclamation, a whisper, a sentence left unfinished...When she returns it is to set off again from elsewhere...One would have to listen with another ear, as if hearing an "other meaning" always in the process of weaving itself, of embracing itself with words; but also of getting rid of words in order not to become fixed, congealed in them. (Irigaray 1974, p. 29)

I now want to adapt this important and well known passage and use it in relation to the multiplicity and intensity of assemblage/ethnography. I want the passage above to be read using 'we' instead of 'she'. I don't want to hi-jack or contradict the intensity or rhetorical force of her words, I want to repeat them in application and in so doing show respect for them and argue for the difference of the 'and' that allows for them to be used with energy and force within our collaborative space and, I would argue, with that of others. It also feels to me that in this re-cognition and application of difference we are also moving away from the influence and the locus of reflection and reflexivity. So often in the past we have put the mirror up to our relational selves, we try to gain a sense of our becomings, we try to make sense of our selves and a sense of our selves in relation to one then the other. And, of course, all that is great and at the same time it is not enough. We also live looking out and in at those *'temporary, provisional, partial'* selves we talk about above and in so doing sense a *'trembling at the horizon of all that (we) don't know about (us)'* (Pollock, *2006, p. 93).*

It seems that trembling at these horizons is like swimming in the rising and falling of the surf, always anticipating the next big wave, treading water, looking out over the swells, waiting with an energising nervousness for its slowly rising arrival, being ready for it and then quickly turning, body moving to be in an instant at one with its tumbling flow. And in the intensity of these moments there is always interference, always the thrilling uncertainty of not knowing where the ride with the wave will take you.

Haraway (2000, p. 103–4), in troubling the somewhat dominating influence of reflection as a trope for self-knowing and whilst not against self-reflection, argues for the use of the optical metaphor of diffraction:

> So what you get is not a reflection, it's the record of a passage ... (a)s a metaphor it drops the metaphysics of identity and the metaphysics of representation and says optics is full of a whole other potent way of thinking about light, which is about history. It's not about identity as taxonomy, but it's about registering process on the recording screen.

This has great force for me. I sense the powerful liminality of self that both literally and figuratively trembles at the horizon, feeling myself into the differences that are always in between and endlessly becoming. I am learning as I write to trust you in your use of 'me', 'you, 'us', 'them', 'Ken', 'Jonathan' and so on. I am slowly getting this in relation to the differentiating repetitions that energise the diffractive possibilities of our 'touchings' and settings off in other directions. However, I remain uncertain and concerned about this usage as I activate my senses on the edges of this assemblage, feeling hesitant and nervous as others name me and exercise their reality through representations that I find opaque and often oblique. In the becoming of our relational space, where affect and percept seem ascendant, I sense also the powerful growth of concept, where knowing through naming exercises a forceful particularity and possesses a realist ontological force that is illuminating, vibrational and creative in the ceaseless haecceity of (our) assemblage. So living trustfully in the critically affective concern of this tentative usage, writing here, with you, in these moments, I am feeling better.

NOTES

[1]   Jonathan teases Ken about his regular allusions to this epic trip.
[2]   In October, 2012, we participated in a collaborative writing weekend in Ammerdown, a village outside Bath, UK.
[3]   Ken was born and brought up in Cornwall and continues to live there.
[4]   Ken's children and grandson.
[5]   Jonathan's partner.

REFERENCES

Arendt, H. (1982). *Lectures on Kant's political philosophy*. In R. Beiner (Ed.). Chicago: University of Chicago Press.

Arendt, H. (1978). *On thinking*. New York: Harcourt, Brace Jovanovich.

Atkinson, P. (1991). *The ethnographic imagination: Textual constructions of reality*. London: Routledge.

Barad, K. (2007). *Meeting the universe halfway*. London: Duke University Press.

Borges, J. L. (1971). *Labyrinths*. Harmondsworth: Penguin.

Braidotti, R. (2011). *Nomadic subjects*. Originally published in 1996. New York: Columbia University Press.

Callus, I., & Herbrechter, S. (2012). Introduction: Posthumanist subjectivities, or, coming after the subject...*Subjectivity, 5*(3), 241–264.

Cavarero, A. (2000). *Relating narratives: Storytelling and selfhood* (P. A. Kottman, Trans.). Abingdon: Routledge.

Davies, B. *Personal communication*.

Davies, B., & Gannon, S. (2006). *Doing collective biography*. Maidenhead: Open University Press.

Deleuze, G. (1995). *Negotiations: 1972–1990* translated by Martin Joughin. New York: Columbia University Press

Deleuze, G. (2004). *Difference and repetition* (translated by Paul Patton). London: Continuum.

Deleuze, G., & Guattari, F. (1988). *A thousand plateaus: Capitalism and schizophrenia* London: Athlone.

Deleuze, G., & Guattari, F. (1994). *What is philosophy?* (Translated by Hugo Tomlinson and Graham Burchill). London: Verso.

Derrida, J. (1976). *Of grammatology* (Transl. G. C. Spivak). Baltimore, MD: Johns Hopkins University Press.

Dosse, F. (2010). *Gilles Deleuze & Felix Guattari: Intersecting lives*. Chichester: Columbia University Press.

Ellis, C. (2004). *The ethnographic I: A methodical novel about autoethnography*. Walnut Creek: Altamira Press

Foucault, M. (2000). *Ethics: Subjectivity and truth*, edited by Paul Rabinow, translated by Robert Hurley. London: Penguin.

Gale, K., & Wyatt, J (2009). *Between the two: A nomadic inquiry into the collaborative writing and subjectivity*. Newcastle-upon-Tyne: Cambridge Scholars Publishing.

Gale, K., Pelias, R., Russell, L., & Wyatt, J. (2012 forthcoming) *How writing touches: An intimate scholarly collaboration*. Newcastle-upon-Tyne: Cambridge Scholars Publishing.

Gannon, S. (2012, forthcoming). Sketching subjectivities. *International Review of Qualitative Research*.

Haraway, D. (2000). *How like a leaf: An interview with Thyrza Nichols Goodeve*. London: Routledge.

Irigaray, L. (1974). *Speculum of the other woman*. New York: Cornell University Press.

Kemmis, S. (2010). What is to be done? The place of action research. *Educational Action Research, 18*(4), 417–427.

Lather, P. (2007). *Getting lost: Feminist effort toward a double(d) science*. New York: SUNY.

MacLure, M. (2003). *Discourse in educational and social research*. Buckingham: Open University Press.
Nancy, J-L. (2000). *Being singular plural* (Transl. R. D. Richardson & A. E. O'Bryne). Stanford: Stanford University Press.
Pollock, D. (2006). Memory, remembering and histories of change. In D. S. Madison & J. Hamera (Eds.), *Handbook of performance studies* (pp. 87–105). Thousand Oaks: Sage.
Thrift, N. (2006). Space. *Theory, Culture and Society, 23*(2–3), 139–155.
Woolf, V. (1985). *Moments of being*. In Jeanne Schulkind (Ed.), (2nd ed.). London: Harcourt Brace.
Wyatt, J. (2013). Ash Wednesdays: An autoethnography of (Not) Counselling. In N. P. Short, L. Turner & A. Grant (Eds.), *Contemporary British autoethnography*. Rotterdam: Sense Publishers.
Wyatt, J., & Gale, K. (2013, forthcoming). Getting out of selves: An assemblage/ethnography? In T. Adams, C. Ellis & S. Holman-Jones (Eds.), *The autoethnography handbook*. Thousand Oaks, CA: Sage.
Wyatt J., Gale K., Gannon S., & Davies B. (2011). *Deleuze and collaborative writing: Writing on an immanent plane of composition*. New York: Peter Lang.

DAVID GILBOURNE & PHILLIP MARSHALL

WRITING FORMS OF FICTION: GLIMPSES ON THE ESSENCE OF SELF

INTRODUCTION

The chapter to follow is structured around three story-lines. Two of these (the first and second) offer reflections from different elements of the first author's sporting life, the third and final story draws from the sports coaching and research experiences of the second author. The opening storyline, '*Landscapes and Lives*' is a short extract taken from the opening sections of a longer story that exists in narrative and drama script format. Part auto-ethnographic part fiction , the full story examines a young player's life in professional football and highlights the different roles that family and friends might play any player's life. The second, '*Two banks of four and spot-faced rock drummer*', is a fiction based around the auto-ethnographic theme of applied sport psychology practice. The third story, '*Little things*', is a further auto-ethnographic fiction based around the dilemmas of a coach/educator; the focal point of this final story 'Steve' is deployed in a creative non-fiction style to convey the frustrations and ethical challenges associated with coaching practice. Three stories, all with differential auto-ethnographic content and with different degrees of fictional content in terms of style and or people or context, yet, these stories help to reflect the authors own psyche, aspects of their own essence, in that regard they all offer a glimpse of the auto-ethnographic self.

As the text and three stories unfold I (David) have opted to maintain an opaque approach to the way I frame and introduce them and I also introduce the final story on Phil's behalf. The stories are deliberately left in 'mid-telling', allowing readers to ponder on the way each story might continue and conclude. The stories have all been written at different times in different spaces and with different purposes in mind. To explain a little further, '*Landscapes and Lives*' is taken from the opening lines of another story '*Family, Fate, Mates and Moments*' a project that is, in writing terms, in-progress; the selection of text presented here introduces the stories main character 'Ade'.

In contrast '*Two Banks of Four and Spot Faced Rock Drummer*' emerged out of the strain of a dull night at a hotel in the East Riding of Yorkshire. On my own, with nothing to do, and being the only resident sat in a deserted hotel bar, I sat down to write in order to keep myself entertained. Though this might seem a harmless even trivial way to spend a few hours, yet as the story emerged I learned a little more about myself.

N. P. Short et al. (Eds.), Contemporary British Autoethnography, 157–167.

Finally, *'Little Things'* was initially written for a peer review manuscript on the topic of evidence-based practice, but as myself and Phil shared in the re-writing and drafting of his own story the tale progressed into a wider-ranging fiction. As the direction of the peer review paper also changed we (that is the author team) decided not to use Phil's story, so we filed it away for another day. The efforts taken in talking about and writing the story did seem to consolidate Phil's own commitment to his own auto-ethnographic journey and so it seemed like time well spent.

In these examples it seems to matter very little 'how' or 'why' or 'when' or 'for what purpose' stories might get written, for they all, in some way or other, reflect a little bit of the self in a particular moment in life, they reflect the self in a specific space-in-time and that might be revisited later through what the lines say and in how they say it. I hope you enjoy the stories, I hope they make you smile at times, and I hope they make you reflect a little on your own life and on the things that meander around in your own thinking and, possibly, in your own writing.

LANDSCAPES AND LIVES

I grew-up in Nottinghamshire and enjoy travelling back and looking at the landscape and year-on-year I find that it absorbs more and more of its industrial past. Going home is always special to me, hearing the accent makes me feel warm inside, the people have warmth about them too, they have a dry humour, going home makes me smile and it seems important, through it all, that we smile...

****

A Sheffield to Nottingham train winds its way steadily across the post-industrial wastelands of Yorkshire, traverses more open greenery on the edges of Derbyshire, before, finally, travelling through flatlands that signal the Nottinghamshire border. All these counties house remnants from the days of heavy industry and coal. Old pit spoil heaps litter the landscape; many are masked now, re-seeded with rye-grass and the formulaic planting of ash and silver birch, a poor disguise to the chaotic structure of nature. Ade, one shoulder scrunched up against the carriage window, blankly surveys the late autumn landscape. Something catches his eye, a man, out walking with his dog. He strains to follow them before they disappear from view. Shuffling back into his seat he reflects on the scene, the man had looked old and limped as if his hip was sore. Ade's fingers draw circles on the window he ponders serious things, age, life-span and death. He takes a deep breath and turns his thoughts to the man's dog, a young energetic beast it was, he re-runs images of it bounding and sprinting and smiles, briefly. As the afternoon light fades away Ade's mood deepens, today, on this day, his world seems cold and brutal. Another train going into Sheffield flashes past. In the seats opposite, an old couple glance in his direction and whisper. Further down the carriage two girls noisily exchange a series of unconnected stories, inane chatter that occasionally brakes into Ade's consciousness:

"He slapped me across me face...showing off in front of his mates."

"Hit ya?"

"Yeah...and I said like...'don't do that like ya just showin off in front of your mates'...then he punched me."

"Don't get pregnant with him."

"I'm not pregnant..."

"He's like his Dad he is."

The train stopped at Langley Mill, a litter strewn, desolate station populated on this day by three teenage girls. They sit huddled from the wind in an ugly plastic and metal shelter. Two of them smoke and laugh. The other, part-turned away, types a text-message into her mobile. The girl with the phone looks up and takes a step forward, a bold step, and as she looks into the carriage the old woman returns her gaze. The girl, tall and thin, draws unconvincingly on her cigarette turns her head to one side spits out the smoke and returns her eyes to the carriage; her gaze, now a glare, pierces the glass. As the train pulls away Ade looks back as if mesmerised, the girl watches him, shoves one finger into the air and scowls a smile.

"See that girl?"

"Loser"

"Yeah"

Ade slumps back onto his seat, takes a deep breath and searches for sleep; the old lady looks across at his pale face and wonders. Behind closed eyes his mind wanders back to the River Trent, he remembers a warm day, he's sat on dry grass looking across the water, families walk past on the other side, laughing and running, then, he sees old knarred hands gripped together shaking. Another bout of emotion wells up. His eyes open briefly then close again as another memory overwhelms him:

"Ade come on...race ya."

"Dad wait..."

"Go on...I'll give ya a start."

Ade is running and running, arms driving, legs reaching, bare feet sink into soft warm sand then into cooler harder sand left in deep grooves by the tide, then wet heavy sand, he can hear the sea now...

The old lady watches his daydream unfold and, as a smile meanders across Ade's face, she sighs and reaches for her husband's hand.

Ade's nearly there, Dad's closing in. Two bodies side-by-side, alongside. Dad is first into the sea:

"You cheated Dad....Dad you cheated"

Sometime later as the train jostles its way into Nottingham station Ade shuffles in his seat and re-engaged with reality...the girls just can't seem to stop talking...

"I like the new manager."

"Yeah he's nice."

D. GILBOURNE & P. MARSHALL

"He came in the toilets today I'm havin a wee and he ses 'is that you in there?'...I said no it's not and don't come in I'm havin a wee."

"Aaar"

"We just laughed."

"He's nice though."

"Yeah"

The old man smiles, shakes his head and reaches to collect his bags off the rack. Ade, as if unfairly forced to wake from a deep sleep, looks bemused. He lost his Dad today, he lost his Dad, he lost his Dad...today. He grasps at a seconds hope...did it really happen? He feels empty, washed-up. The train lurches forcing the old couple to wobble and reach towards each other as they struggle to put coats on. Twice the old woman turns towards Ade each time his eyes are downwards checking his mobile. The opportunity to speak passes. As she walks along the platform arm linked with her husband, she watches Ade disappear over the railway bridge. Later that evening, and with her husband snoring gently on the sofa, she thinks about the boy on the train and wonders if he might have wanted to talk. She considers why she had said nothing, concludes that her confidence is on the wane, ten years ago, a stronger and more assured woman then, she would have spoken, she would have asked if he was alright. Her husband wakes and stretches:

"I wish I'd asked that boy what the trouble was..."

****

TWO BANKS OF FOUR AND A SPOT-FACED ROCK DRUMMER

As the years of University life have come and gone and PhD's have come and gone I have arrived at a view that we should appreciate the complexity of lives a little more. We seem, at least I sense that 'we seem' to be content with data that might be described as shallow. Through this unease I have hoped for qualitative methods, including ethnography and auto-ethnography, to be a part of the process of unearthing the contextualised messiness of people's lives. Once upon a time I lectured in applied sport psychology. I had started doing qualitative research stuff within the framework of my own PhD and quickly sensed that there is more to people than meets the eye. Some time before I had also concluded that there was more to applied practice than mental training, and, through the hard school of applied sport psychology practice, I came to understand that I needed to 'do more' if I was to really help people. Associated with this I also wanted to understand more about other people, to help them it was clear to me that I needed to know more about them. From all of this I began to conclude that I owed it to them to, first and foremost, try to understand myself:

****

160

Odd how quickly things can change. One minute you're 'flying' the next, everything just unravels. At least that's how Lee would explain it. A few short weeks ago his life was top drawer, now, it stinks. Everything used to be so straightforward. Lee liked his coach his coach liked him. The team played two banks of four he understood that. Now his old coach has gone and Lee doesn't trust the new coach, Lee thinks the new coach doesn't like him...sometimes he mulls over his relationship with new coach...always concluding that, "No...he doesn't like me not one bit". Two banks of four have gone...Neanderthal apparently....new coach plays three at the back...Lee grumbles into his training bib "Three at the back...this is league one football man...league one...no-one plays three at the back....not ever...never-ever-man-never".

It's just the phone call a newly accredited sport psychologist wants to get...a nice straightforward intervention...easy peasy, new coach tells Simon (the psychologist) that he's worried about Lee...he thinks that he looks lethargic, he thinks that Lee's has a problem with his motivation, new coach has wide-angle eyes, he sees things, notices little things, he's noticed that Lee has become tense before games and he ends the diagnostic phone call with a list of problems, outbursts during open play, rants in the changing rooms, a withdrawn persona...new coach thinks Lee needs his head "straightening-out" that he needs to "toughen-up and get-at-it". Simon smiles and as he flicks his hair slightly to the left he tells new coach... "well that's the kind of thing I do". Phone call over Simon's blue eyes raced across his neat alphabetically organised books resting side-by-side on pine-wood shelves...all stacked to the brim with applied practice books. Simon's got loads of books, his office is neat, he is neat, he wears nice soft suits and has a bobby floppy hair. On the debit side he wears his hands inside his pockets and this is ill-advised. Male models do this in photo-shoots but they aren't moving. Simon's hands remain 'pocketed-in-movement' and a rather unsettling gait ensues; Charley Chaplin-esque in fact, regardless, he thinks he's cool and that's always risky especially when around footballers.

Lee was sure he'd get a new contract, get another year...now he's not so sure. He's got all the attributes, pace, physical presence, he can pass a neat channel ball, he's good in the air...fair-play he knows he could do with working on his first touch but most players could say the same. Now he's un-hinged...he's unlike the Lee he knows...he hates feeling tense before games, he never used too, most of all he hates losing his cool, Mum says that's "just not our Lee"...Mum might not have a UEAFA A-coaching-licence but she's right enough...these are not normal Lee-type reactions he never used to react to competitive pressure. If only new coach could have seen him in pre-season...flying he was...so good, so in-control, his teammates called him 'the boss'...imagine that... 'boss-man'.

Simon's students have learned that it is wise to dish-out a few compliments, suits, hair, whatever...that said, it is generally agreed that top marks result from comments on his book shelves...they laugh in the student bar "I said...you seem to have your own library there Charley...he's so vain...he just dangles out his leg so ya can piss up it". Credit were credits due, Simon does have nice hair. On the down side his suits do have unfeasibly long pockets. The big winner, the swinger dinger, the fact no-one can dispute, is that, he has a lot of books. All his texts all sell the same message of theory-led mental training interventions...they form Simon's template for 'evidence-based practice', a mantra he trots out to anyone and everyone he meets, the phrase 'evidence' featured in the title of his PhD thesis, a thesis backed by scientific principles.

When Lee and Simon met, Lee knew Simon had been told to see him by new-coach...Lee did not really trust new-coach, so, he decided, initially, not to trust Simon. Lee told Simon that he'd been getting "a-bit" tense before matches and in-matches too...Simon seemed to listen...so, Lee warmed to Simon a little, he thought about telling him that he did not trust new-coach but as he looked across he could see that Simon had stopped listening...in fact Simon had not been listening for quite a few seconds and, if we were to untangle the process of person-to-person interaction we would have to conclude that Simon he had not really listened at all and, while he stopped (pretending to listen) his scholarly mind had gone back to the phone call with the coach it had locked-onto the scientifically derived literature... the literature that linked somatic anxiety elevation with the application of physical relaxation techniques...more specifically he linked in-match anxiety with the cognitive intervention technique of self-talk. Lee was always keen to learn so he listened. Simon, now back in the moment, got 'all-scientific', he was in his element now and with hands safely nestled in silk-lined pockets he talked Lee-through the ideas behind mental training, "You see Lee your brain is like a muscle it can get stronger with training". Lee understood what Simon was getting at straight away he's a bright lad, well he's bright enough. He'll use them new techniques because Simon's going to tell the coach everything he said, and, he wants that contract, and, to be fair, he hates being tense...boss-men don't get tense.

In philosophical terms Simon has never really explored the nuance of what 'scientific principles' might mean but, for Simon, anything science-related just did the trick. It was strange how the word 'science' had somehow meshed itself into every aspect of his self-satisfied-self. In the morning Simon would emerge from his scientific slumber, clean his scientifically whitened teeth and eat his scientifically sound breakfast (lots of fruit!). As he drove to his 'sport science department' he would conduct himself with the certainty common amongst 'sport and exercise scientists' oh yes, he's a scientist no question...he's done ANOVA...post hoc too!...his techniques are scientifically proven...based on scientifically derived evidence...Simon just loved his certainty, loved his paradigm, loved his practice, Simon loved himself.

Lee had a meeting in the local pub with Steve...his best-ever buddy...they go back ages...since school. Steve is not a scientist, he's a more practical type, painting, decorating, he can turn his hand to most things. Lee's Mum loves Stephen (as she calls him) to bits and when he calls around the house she wastes no time in re-telling him how well he did to come top in his fourth year metalwork class, with Lee a close second. Steve's biggest attribute is being sensible...Steve is sensible all the time...his nickname, 'Sensible Steve', tells you all you need to know.

162

Sat in a dingy corner around a round, dusty, sticky, wooden table Lee told Steve about the last few weeks with new coach, about how knackered he was, about the contracts, about the stupid, stupid three at the back system, about how he's started getting tense and pissed-off, he talked more about how knackered he was, he talked about his meeting with Simon, about how he suddenly seemed to stop listening, how his hands never seemed to emerge out of his pockets, and, how he had taught him some new skills, then, he went on and on about how knackered he was over and over again. For nearly an hour Steve said nothing, nothing at all...he just listened, sipped his pint and chewed his way through two packets of salted peanuts. When Lee had finished Steve got up to buy another round...with two fresh pints placed on the table he sat back down...neither man spoke for a few minutes then Steve said:

"...Lee mate...forget the contract stuff...if it happens it happens...and...how do you know the coach doesn't like ya?...and...have ya thought about talkin to the bloke to tell im you don't understand how three at the fuckin-back works? and if I've old ya once I've told ya a dozen-times ya need ta get ya lazy arse out'a that shit-flat and away from that spot-faced rock drummer..."

****

LITTLE THINGS

One of the ways I have sometimes chosen to describe critique, my own and the critique of others is that they are like 'voices in the mist'. In that sense I see critique as being difficult to find, disparate, by and large, isolated, unconnected and disconnected from what might be deemed mainstream. That might be a description that many qualitative researchers, especially those who practiced in the 80's and 90's might associate with. It is, however, a positive experience to listen to someone who has worked-out critical issues *for themselves*...they have not stumbled across an old critical text...they have not heard a grumpy old-git moan away at a conference... they have looked at their work-place and sensed something to be wrong. This is hard enough when your discipline is broadly in-line with the social sciences but imagine the trauma when the doubts are to be found in a practitioner who works in the 'hard sciences'. This creative non-fiction draws from someone's work-based life, from Phil's life (from the second author's life). It reflects also onto aspects of my own past-life in the applied psychology field...like Phil and his alter-ego Steve (our cunningly and auto-ethnographically derived fiction character), I knew the theories well enough, I had read the famous papers written by those famous names but my early applied experiences never felt right, something was missing. Phil did not begin life as a scientist in fact his first degree was humanities based. He came to look back sceptically on that first degree questioning whether it represented 'real' learning. He wanted more he wanted cold hard facts, the certainties, the answers to life's big questions and it was science he felt that might offer him all these things. As his-own athletics career drew to a premature close Phil entered a career in coaching, but it was to science that he turned for the answers on performance. Initially he placed this form of knowing above the day-to-day evidence from his own athletics career – one brought to an abrupt end by injury problems...injuries that no-one had an answer to... Phil takes up the story...*Failing to acknowledge that this is simply how it is, I made up my mind that none of my athletes would ever be left without answers to their questions. In this quest science was to be my guide and I embedded all that I did in evidence based practice. As my knowledge and experience grew I gained confidence in my ability to write what I thought were the perfect training programmes. I poured all that I knew into my programmes, secure in their ability to deliver success to those I coached. Like my failure to acknowledge the 'little things' which played a part in ending my own career, I also remained ignorant of the 'little things' which impacted on the careers of the athletes I coached. The story to follow was written, as noted earlier, for a paper on evidence based practice. It emerged from an auto-ethnographic piece which reflected on my own journey as a coaching practitioner. The version presented here represents the product of a writing collaboration between myself and David. In this tale Steve's journey very much echoes my own growing realisation that perhaps it is the 'little things' that are the most important...*

****

LITTLE THINGS

Those with the power to teach, to select what they teach, to convey knowledge, spoke in the language of science and as Steve listened, as Steve learned, as he wrote the essays, completed the lab reports, sat the examination papers, he came face-to-face with the multi-layered, inter-disciplinary nature of his own failure, the bad advice, ill-informed advice, the advice that ensured injury would compound on injury on injury on injury until the very act of running itself became impossible. In those moments of crystallization he would drift away from his student friends, find a corner and engage his anger.

Now his-own coaching practice leaves nothing to chance. His athletes' training schedules are worked-out with care and precision. In his mind, in one part of his mind, sprinters function according to the law of machines, complex, integrated machines. As they move he watches and questions the biomechanics of gait, he interrogates the sinew and fluidity of physiology. Synthesis of knowledge is key, Steve understands the inter-face between this two disciples, he knows his stuff and he knows (now) how little other practitioner's know, how those he once shook hands with, those he once trusted, he appreciates how little they knew.

There are times in life when reflecting on self is not an option, often the present is so busy that there's no time, no space, for the past, So, as a life based on his own physical capacity for speed came to a close another, based on science, took over and

Steve gave his studies every ounce of energy, every percent out of one hundred that he could muster. Now he festers, grumbles, on imponderable things, on little things.

His life allows him the odd quiet moment here and there and it is then that his mind wanders into the mist, nothing seems out of bounds; he asks himself tough things 'why do I go 'down to the track?' sometimes. When at the track his inner voice asks 'Why are you here?'. In the grain of such questions his mind returns to his own pain, to his frustration, to all those false hopes and promises; a quietly spoken man meeting his own failure head-on...These moments always end the same way, he moves outward from his own head and looks at his athletes, he stops thinking biomechanics, stops thinking physiology and starts thinking people, they're living lives, they have homes, relationships, they have hopes and dreams, they're just like him, he looks once more. Sally has pain killers in her bag again, Beki's mind is miles away...

In the world beyond his reflections friends often comment on his meticulous nature, they admire the way he applies science-based knowledge to his practice, he has built a reputation as an applied sport scientist who deploys evidence grounded in science, in peer review evidence. Steve knows this is his recommendation and he believes in his practice. He does his applied thinking and planning late at night, when the house has gone quiet. Sat in his study he types in progressive sprint drills, works out rep-times, tweaks gym sessions all the time drawing on years of professional study, a process of self-motivated pedagogy that continually builds his professional knowledge of human performance. His home-based thinking and planning space is crowded with the same scientific texts that helped him write essays and sit exams years ago...years ago!...time has moved on...once upon a time he ran (very fast) now he helps others run as fast as they can. Once he was taught about science now he teaches those who want to be scientists. These changes happened over fifteen years, he's no spring chicken, he's been around the block a few times himself, got his hands dirty, taken his fair share of knocks, and, he has his memories.

Like a second library, this personal stuff has been filed away, hidden from view, now it's emerging once more, available for reference. In his student days his own life never featured as part of his essays and rarely part of his lectures, until recently that is. Now his reflections, his inner voice, sends a cold chill of uncertainty through his mind...something is happening...his eyes are opening to other possibilities to different forms of knowledge...certainty is nice, uncertainty is not...so, as he listens to his own thoughts his body shrinks into a strange dark place, with frowning eyes he replays moments from years ago, then he clicks 'fast-forward' reliving moments from the track session last week, reels of film connecting his old life to the present...when he tells others what he's started to think he talks quieter than he normally would...an ontological whisper. Steve gets the big theories; he gets the big disciplines, but what about other things? everyday things? what about the little things?

At his working desk Steve contemplates his challenge, he's not coached this athlete for long, he's a keen lad with a history of injuries and, with this history in mind Steve has done the usual step-by-step analysis with a wide range of performance assessments.

He tested for testing strength, power, and speed, then, he went further, assessed the athlete's movement quality opting to use using the Functional Movement Screen (1) Then, as always, his systematic application of science-to-practice began...back at home Steve made himself a cup of tea and retired to his study, turned his computer on, reached for a few textbooks and lifted them down from the shelves; He looks in his work bag before dragging out a few more peer review papers (all contemporary).

It's late, the family are all asleep, Steve takes a deep breath and carefully spreads out a conviction-of- science onto his desk, the process of constructing a training programme has begun...this is professional knowledge writ large...up-to-date training theory in-action...it might be late but Steve's in the zone, a bad-ass scientist on speed, first the macro stuff (preparation, competition, and transition phases), then meso (general and specific preparation; pre-competition and competition), his cup of tea has gone cold and he never had a sip, the heating has clicked off, but there's no stopping Steve now, next micro cycles (weekly training assignments), and finally daily training units...this is hot stuff...textbook application...The strength work was worked through with forensic precision, the general preparation phase focused on anatomical adaptation and hypertrophy of key muscle groups (Steve had identified this area as one badly in need of additional development). He had identified that the posterior chain muscles, in particular, the gluteals, were in need of development (he knew they had been shown to be key to effective sprint performance).

One o'clock in the morning now, against all odds his pace seems to increase, he shuffles through page after page of supportive texts...always drawing on the latest scientific literature...serious work by a serious scientist...do his athletes appreciate all this effort all this precision? Let's be clear, one last time, it takes knowledge to work at this level...this is not something you can guess at, Steve's good...and deep down he knows it...he knows he gets the science thing, he's secure...so why ponder? Why scrabble? Why worry when everything is sorted? Why beat yourself-up when everything is so comfortable? Why bother with all that doubt? His nights work all done, he turns off the lights...and as he makes his way upstairs he thinks about the athlete, about the way he turned away from him a few times...just a little thing!

He woke early the next morning, the sun was shining so, he got out of bed before the alarm rang, down-stairs now he wandered into his study, picked-up his PhD proposal, went outside and sat on a garden bench. Today's decision time, he needs to hand this application in and get going or just leave it...you might be thinking that Steve's PhD would be into velocity, or power, the list is endless and all would 'help' make him a better coach (maybe)...he wants to be a better coach, a more effective coach, he goes down the track to help people, he has always known the answer to his own questions, but knowing the answer is one thing, recognising the consequences, well, that's different.

Steve's PhD proposal is a consequence and it would surprise many, for it is based around an auto-ethnographic exploration of a coaching-life, of his life. In this moment in his living it is social science that draws him in, that meets his need for a way of exploring a different way of knowing...that's what he needs, that's where he is. Why Steve wonders has he got those pain killers?...Why is she always miles away?... Why did he turn away from me like that?... What are their lives like?...Steve knew all their physical data...but...he understood he needed to know about their 'lives' as well.

Maybe if you have kids and they want to run as fast as they can...maybe if you have kids and they want to go to university to learn how to make others run as quick as they can...maybe you would want them to come across Steve...and, if you think that in those terms it is also (maybe) worth taking a few moments to ask yourself why it is that Steve would be a good man for your kids to know?

FINAL THOUGHTS

All these stories reflect back and tell me a little more about myself, they help me get to know myself better and I think writing has helped Phil also. I would like to thank Phil for his time, his critical thinking, his caring thoughts and for his permission to allow me to co-write alongside him to help bring fictional Steve into being. In fact it was writing and re-working Phil's tale that led me to think about the possibilities offered by the fictional re-working of auto-ethnographic matters. My experiences suggest to me that a part *of me* resides in almost everything I write and that includes in stories that maybe have *began* as fiction.

My recent experimentation with short stories, and with fictions more generally, have led me to draw from w what I know and, of course, I must be a part of that. The finding of 'self-in-fiction' is a maybe best described as an *informal act of reflective analysis* as process that might let you know a little more about yourself and so share a little more of what you are *in-essence* with others who might read what you write. The self-in-fiction theme would appear, inevitably maybe, as a much more covert process of auto-ethnographic writing than the overt auto-ethnographic piece can ever be; but that does not suggest, to me, that it might be less revealing, that is not my experience at all. In all of this reflecting and writing and drafting a sense of a personal truth might emerge, similar, maybe, to an understanding of self building as a consequence of therapy. This does not suggest to me that any kind of all-knowing truth is to be found, it is more that what you truthfully feel in your own sense of being becomes more and more difficult to ignore as the writing process moves forward (months to years and so on). I also sense that truth, on one day or in one phase of time, might not be seen as truth as time goes by. In that regard this personal sense of knowing seems to be forever in flux, in development. The value and or point in sharing these truths, at any one time, requires, it seems to me, an acceptance that there is little here that is permanent. In sharing then, a moment is shared and those who read engage from the back-drop of their own progressing lives. There is, I believe, some point in paths crossing in this way for they might just open-up new possibilities, or confirm direction or critique and there would seem to be some merit in such interactions.

NIGEL P. SHORT

DIDN'T YOU USED TO BE ...?

The role of serendipity and sagaciousness. A reflexive account of a 31-year
career in the English National Health Service.

just like a crack in the pavement
opening fractionally wider every day
with the promise of something concealed
Walking on the Ceiling
Jean Sprackland (1997)

What follows is more a personal nomadic drift than a detached chronological history.
These narratives have been distilled though much reflection into their current forms.
I shed light on the first few months of my retirement from the English National
Health Service (NHS), weaving in some accounts from the NHS and associated
accompanying histories. As the different Nigels look back on this 31-year career,
there was a slow realisation that serendipity and sagaciousness had played a major
role in my multiple lives. Whilst it is not necessarily a goal of this chapter, I wonder
if by revealing and unveiling some of the serendipitous events in my life, you may be
encouraged to be on the lookout for your own serendipitous moments, an area that I
would propose is seldom addressed. As Wolcott (2010) says,

> *'the term suggests more than just luck, it implies good fortune and even, as*
> *my trusty dictionary informs me, a certain aptitude for making desirable*
> *discoveries by accident' (page 45).*

SPRING 2010

This new two-storey building sits in the middle of a recently developed
business park. Here I stand, alone, upstairs in the warm sun filled boardroom.
I am staring out of the wide double glazed windows. A cool draft seeps in
from one of the opened windows; this welcome breeze gently sways several
damaged cream coloured slats of the vertical blind. Opposite, on the other side
of the unadopted road, I can see a couple of middle-aged bricklayers; they are
building a new factory. Their well-worn sleeveless leather jerkins are secured
round their midriffs with strong white twine. They are working on the second
lift. A bright orange steel ladder rests against the scaffolding. A young bloke is
climbing confidently up the ladder; a hod full of pug (mortar mix) rests on his
right shoulder. I remember my days working on the 'line'. My left index finger
still bears the scar where I accidently sliced off the tip with my brick trowel.

N. P. Short et al. (Eds.), Contemporary British Autoethnography, 169–186.

Beyond the brickies are the ancient rolling emerald baize folds of the South Downs. Small fluffy white clouds leave their shadowy impressions on the hills below. Up there, tucked in the creases of the Downs sits Butts Brow. The small moving indistinguishable dots are people walking their dogs; both exercising their limbs and minds. I can just about make out well worn paths; grooved tracks made by human action. How I want to be up there with them, away from these fake shenanigans.

Here I am, lying low, hiding away. The imagination only works when it is free.

Henry Purcell's 'Triumph for the Universe' is playing on the lime green Apple iPod my daughter brought me on my last birthday. In the operas quieter moments, I can just about make out the faint muted muffled sounds of people downstairs; they are celebrating. I remove the earphones. I hear the sounds of glasses being charged and the grandiose congratulatory toasts being offered.

Downstairs, near the entrance, the curtained covered commemorative cartouche waits to be revealed. I am at work; a new mental health service is being officially launched. The building has suddenly become a magnet for many dignitaries.

As I look down, outside the building, on the pavement below are about twenty 'significant' members of the local National Health Service (NHS) Trust. They are being robustly choreographed into position by the Trusts official photographer. I recognise them all, Executive Directors, Senior Managers, a sprinkling of PA staff and tucked away at the back, is our Clinical Lead.

'Where are the clinicians? The people who work at the coal face' I ask myself.

It was at this very moment that I decided to end my full time career in the English NHS; a career which had begun in January 1980 as a Nursing Auxiliary with no recognised qualifications and concluded as a senior accredited Cognitive Behaviour Therapist with an award of a Professional Doctorate.

Meditation of St. Francis — Francisco de Zurbarán

Some questions are raised about the positioning and repositioning of self within the fluidity of moving back and forth between working class family roots, professional and academic colleagues and friends. I try to understand my stories through reflection, reflexivity and use this *writing* as inquiry. I am regularly reminded however, as Ferudi (2007) discusses, that:

> *'Individuals make sense of their experiences through reflecting on their specific circumstances and in line with the expectations transmitted through prevailing cultural norms'. (Ferudi, 2007, p. 237)*

I have tried to make this writing a living ever-developing piece, providing a meandering and schematic perspective with limited conclusions. However, as a potential framework for thinking and feeling, it offers a path towards reconsidering relationships with the concepts of retirement. A further aim is to demystify the process of retirement and to make my continuing journey visible, as Pelias (1999) says our 'texts are modest attempts to resist silence' (Pelias, 1999, p. 9).

I provide the reader with an opportunity to witness some stories from some of my many lives, some from my time in the NHS and some from the first few months of my retirement. A chance to move away from traditional held views where retirement is often seen as a period of, for example, a well-earned rest following a (possible) lifetime of industrious employment. I aim to understand the process *of* and adjustment *to* retirement as part of an important process of my ageing. This autoethnography attempts to contribute to the literature on ageing, retirement, and wellbeing in later life in general by providing one account; my account. I examine how ageing, retirement and associated adjustments to retirement and later life, however, are all closely woven with social contexts (Phillipson 2004) and social constructs.

1ST MARCH 2012

Here I am walking along the old wharf at Salford Quays in Manchester. I am on my way to the new Lowry Arts Centre. I can feel the cold northeasterly breeze biting at my face. I am resisting putting my hands in my pockets; I just want to see if I can go one winter, just one winter, without resorting to the warmth of my pockets. The harsh wind is creating small white crested waves on the water's surface. A gaggle of huge Canada geese pecks away at the miserable grey unrewarding gravel. The walk is inspiring; I remember the ever-changing coastline of my home town of Brighton. I invite my mind to peer through a telescope, to explore the imagery and history of the sea, past and present. This magnificent Manchester canal, which when opened was the largest river navigation in the world. It would have been visited by large cargo ships from around the world.

I sit down. I can feel the icy cold slats of the metal bench through my thick Levi jeans. I contemplate notions of place and time, and consider my changing associations with water and relationships. Memories of swimming on many 25th's of Decembers with my children in the uninviting greyish azure of the

171

wintry English Channel. Swimming off Rock a Nore, Hastings in the summer months with my son after we have both finished work for the day. Imagine. He arrives in his dust covered brickie tee shirt, shorts and cement coated Dr Marten Boots; and there is me; navy blue linen trousers, white linen shirt and Birkenstock Arizona black leather sandals. The disappearing sun is turning the chalky white cliffs into a beautiful patchwork quilt of pinks, oranges and tangerines. We are in the last throws of the day's warmth, splashing, chatting and diving for pebbles in the gentle turquoise briny. Co-creators of a wonderfully beautiful unique enterprise.

I am interested in the subversion of social spaces: old wharfs morphing into posh accommodation, old bank buildings transforming into pubs and restaurants.

*Do **all** people have opportunities to 'transform' who they are?*

This text is cracked and fractured, passages of broken memories. I report from various professional positions; some marginalised, some disenfranchised, some collegiate and some of power. I suggest that personal identities are not fixed and neither are our stories. I call upon bits and pieces of memory; some memories seem unchanging and some wander around depending on where I might be when I have the recall or intrusion. People experience themselves as many selves, 'each of which is felt to have a life of its own' (Lincoln, 1997, p. 40) and 'multiple selves demand multiple texts' (Lincoln, 1997, p. 42). What I present, moves away from conventional reporting and distances itself from the often-associated retirement criteria of time management, low income, loss of status and poor health (Mein, Higgs, Ferrie & Stansfield, 1998).

December 2012

I wrote this when remembering a trip I had made to the Blue Mountains in Australia in 1978. I had bumped into a sculpture by Henry Moore.

Moore's Humility

Leave the busy expense of the coffee bar
And the huge untouched glass vessel of carrot juice
With its rotating blades
The grotesque gift shop, full of objects
That you never knew you never needed

And then, suddenly, there it is!
Unsignposted, untitled and untouched
As he had desired
What Moore can you want?
To remind you of the spontaneity of lifes
Rich unpredictableness

There amongst the blue translucent blue gums
Settled in the sandstone, near Katoomba
Was an early carving
That reminded me of the
Reclining Figure

Take the Great Western highway
Maybe the Bells Line of Roads
Or the train that makes
Its way through to Orange
All this from a man who
Was refused passage to join
The International Brigade
And help the republicans

Would this have changed his modelling?

For most working people, retirement can be a profound change to many aspects of lifestyles, although more recently, retirement is being regarded as an evolving process rather than a single step. In particular, early retirement and accompanying part time work can be seen as a preferable alternative by older people facing an uncertain future in the labour market or redundancy (Phillipson, 2002) and the removal of any fears of redundancy or getting the sack and the removal of responsibility for others.

You may notice many different voices; these voices have emerged from a wide range of different types of experiences. It may not be always clear whose voice you will be hearing. You may of course recognise your own voice echoing through the pages. What I have reported is a reflection of what I think is fair analysis of what I think I remember happened. As Julian Barnes (2011) discusses in his book 'The Sense of an Ending':

> 'That is one of the central problems of history, isn't it, Sir?' The question of subjective versus objective interpretation, the fact that we need to know the history of the historian in order to understand the version that is being put in front of us.' (Barnes, 2011, p. 12)

IT'S DECEMBER 1979. BRIGHTON

I have just returned from a nine-month trip to Morocco. I had been working for a company from Brighton called Camp Africa. Imagine a Butlins holiday camp on the shores of the Atlantic; we were pitched just north of Asilah. Each week 200 hundred people arrive at Tangier Ibn Battouta Airport from Gatwick Airport, England.

Along with four other colleagues, I helped to 'entertain' them for two weeks; Camel treks, beach parties, coach trips to Fez.

I remember one week a bloke asked me on his arrival, how he could get to Marrakesh by bus. I was envious.

Prior to this engagement, I had been travelling for a few years and this sojourn in North Africa is a welcome warm rest. During a coach trip south to Marrakesh I made an uncomfortable, but what seemed like an inevitable decision; I needed to settle down with a 'proper' job.

JANUARY 1980

I started work as a Nursing Auxiliary at Bevendean Hospital in Brighton. One of my younger sisters, having left her position at Bevendean, had gone off to the Brighton School of Nursing to commence her nurse training; I applied for her vacancy and was successful. At the time, I thought it would see me through until I found that 'proper' job.

SEPTEMBER 1980

I had no recognised qualifications and had to sit the General Nurse Council's entrance exam. There are four of us in the room. As I sat down at the brown, laminated surfaced school-type desk, a nurse tutor aggressively plonks a metronome on the table next to my exam paper. The irritating tick, tock, tick bloody tock.

I pass the exam and am offered a place on the next course, which commenced later this month. I start my State Registered Nurse (SRN) training.

SEPTEMBER 1983

I successfully completed my nurse training. I secured a job on an orthopaedic ward. I work on nights for a year.

SEPTEMBER 1984

I start my Registered Mental Health Nurse Training at the Sussex Downs School of Nursing at Hellingly Hospital; a large Victorian hospital about 12 miles north of Eastbourne, East Sussex. I had an idea I might be OK doing this. I do not think I was 'urgent enough' for general nursing.

FEBRUARY 2011

I take 15 white linen shirts I used to wear to work, to a charity shop in Hastings.

For many years, I have visited a second hand shop in Hastings old town. I have a fascination with collecting photos: photos of people. I have a collection of black and white photographs. These photos are pinned up in my house in various rooms. I do not know the people, but I like the idea of keeping them alive in some way. The photos often prompt conversation when people visit my house.

When I first decided to discard my white shirts, I thought of a male friend who might want them. I wonder if this gesture was a way of keeping my working identity alive through someone else. In the end, I decided not to give him the shirts. The shirts prompt further questions for me; where are they now? Like white sails heading out in an uncharted sea.

31ST OCTOBER 2011

I get a phone call early in the morning from my older sister. My dear old Mum had died. Ivy Jane had passed away during the night; comfortably I am reassuringly told. Mum had incrementally downsized from the family homes in Hove and Brighton, (which had four and six rooms respectively), to a sad single room in a nursing home. What had Mum done with all her belongings?

TUESDAY 15TH NOVEMBER 2011

I am with my Mum in the funeral chapel of the undertakers. Mum (I am unable to write the word 'She'. It sounds and feels disrespectful) looks very peaceful. There she lay, the beautiful yet grotesque coffin. I expect her to wake up and say something. I **want** *her to wake up and say something. Mum looks a lot smaller than I remembered. I am telling her about my day. I touch her left cheek with the back of my right hand. I lean over and kiss her forehead. On the table near her coffin are some violet coloured notelets and some small envelopes. I write her a little message and put the notelet in the envelope. I then very gently place the envelope on her well-worn clasped hands.*

DECEMBER 2011

For some unexplained reason, perhaps like Mum, I feel forced to sort things out in my house. It entails a compulsion to separate my selves from some, if not most, of my belongings; what is commonly called 'casser maison', literally breaking the house. (Marcoux 2001)

JULY 2012

I have never aspired to any material life style; never wanted that fast car, that yacht in the marina or the gold plated taps in the bathroom. Now, even if I had chosen these monetary aspirations, I cannot afford it on my NHS pension. How wonderfully liberating. The simple life for me now, growing veggies in the garden. No pressure just contentment.

I have built myself a veggie box in my garden. I brought half a dozen used scaffold boards. The wooden L shape adjoining the L shapes of the garden walls creates an oblong. The retired Nigel has promised a gardening project. As Mark Bhatti (2006) suggests, the garden can have major significance in the development of 'home' in later life.

Gardening involves tasks: weeding, ensuring enough re-cycled water is in the butts, the reshaping of soil and the associated manipulating of the earth. Thus, the garden is less of a landscape more of a 'taskscape' (Ingold, 2000) and of course, the garden requires the physical tasks of digging, raking and planting. These activities are dependent on me keeping reasonable fit, my dexterity and the use of senses. This new project also evokes emotional responses; my 'caring' side. I tend and care for the plants and myself (Casey, 1993; Cooper, 2006; Hitchings, 2003). In addition, as Bhatti, Church, Claremont & Stenner (2009) remind us, the garden prompts fractured memories, especially, they suggest, of childhood gardens (Bachelard, 1971, 1994; Casey, 2000), gardens where we perhaps hid or played games. I wonder if children have these same opportunities now. Furthermore, the garden is a space that is often associated with notions of solitude, many other spaces that people connect with experiences of nature are often shared and more public, even when we are physically isolated (Bhatti & Church, 2004).

OCTOBER 2011

I hear on the radio four's flagship news programme, the Today programme, about the proposed changes to the NHS. I seek comfort knowing that I will never be made redundant; I will never get the sack. I will never be chastised by managers again. I will never be put in a position again where I am expected, although rarely did, to support an idea at work that I do not fully believe in. I received this realisation with a welcome liberation, the removal of work uncertainty. I had spent many hours during the last couple of years (unnecessarily) worrying that I was going to lose my job. Friends and colleagues were called upon; they regularly reassured me that this unwelcome 'rumination' was just that, rumination with absolutely no substance.

Richard Sennett explores the meaning of insecurity felt by many in his book 'The Corrosion of

> *Character' (1998). He argues that this insecurity has implications for moral identity as well as collective social relationships. Work for me was becoming, as suggested by Strangleman (2007) 'short term, fugitive and ephemeral' (page 85). Continuing his thesis Strangleman (2007) reports that to be a 'good' or successful worker now is to avoid commitment, to be mobile and flexible' (page 85). Whilst I was able to be mobile and enjoyed a flexibly stance I was unable to 'avoid commitment'. My integrity and moral positioning were being regularly challenged at work. I felt unable to continue working with (some) people who seemed unable or unwilling to be committed.*

SEPTEMBER 1986-JUNE 1991

I am regularly told at work that I would make a good teacher.

June of 1991 and I apply to enrol on a teacher training course at Thames Polytechnic. I am successful at the Interview and I am offered a place. My place will be sponsored by the English National Board (ENB) for Nursing. Unfortunately, all of their sponsored places are filled. I will have to wait to see if someone 'pulls out.' Eventually I am told that there is a vacancy and I can join the next course in September 1991.

SEPTEMBER 1992

I am now a qualified teacher. I apply for a teaching vacancy in the Seychelles. The successful applicant will be a qualified Nurse Tutor, an RMN and a RGN with a Nursing degree. The Seychelles wish to develop a post registration course for Registered Mental Health nurses.

DECEMBER 1992

I borrow a suit from a friend; the arms of the jacket are too short and the trouser legs fall far short of my brown twelve eye Dr Marten boots. I attend an Interview at the Seychelles Consulate in Baker Street, London. I am offered the job. The employment is for two years.

The National Curriculum is just about to start in the United Kingdom. I make enquiries about my children's education on the Islands. Either they can join an international school, which complements the English National Curriculum or they can attend a Seychelles school. The International School fees would take about 55% of my wages. We decided, as a family, that without financial assistance from the Seychelles government I would reluctantly have to decline their offer. I often wonder what this experience might have been like.

DECEMBER 2011

I had often asked my elderly Mum
  'What have you been up to today?'
  'You know that drawer in the kitchen, the one near the oven? Well I have spent the day tidying that out'. She might reply.
  I now know what that experience is like. I have tidied out lots of drawers during the last few months. An opportunity to tidy the house, tidy the drawer and tidy my life.
  Finding old photos, old letters and those old filofax diaries from the mid 90's. I disposed of many unwanted items; items I had not seen for years and once tidied away I would not see for another few years. The solution was to give them away or throw them away.
  I did not want all my cognitive behaviour therapy (CBT) journals anymore. I also gave away about ten years worth of the Royal College of Nursing publication, Mental Health Practice. A very good friend had just started a new innovative CBT course at University; I gave her all my CBT text books, they were going to a good home and it was a reminder for me of my self exiled, self imposed evaporating CBT identity. More liberation!

*The idea is not to choose the things we will get rid of, but to choose the things we will keep. A contrasting idea, bit like voting, we sometimes vote people **out** not necessarily vote people **in**.*

The emptying process strikes to the heart of what we call a home. This is the place where we can display our belongings and as a result 'show off' our personal choices and for some, our negotiations with our families. In this way, our home acts as a repository of our relational histories. Our possessions are an integral part of the construction and safeguarding of our identity. To choose what belongs in a home is to play around with our identities; choosing what to keep or erase. The construction of house and home are sites for agency and the negotiation of significant change. Thus the opportunity for transformation continues.

Integral to a sense of who we are is a sense of our past. Possessions are for example, a convenient means of storing the memories and feelings that attach our sense of past. For example, a souvenir may make *tangible* some otherwise intangible travel experience (Schifferstein & Zwartkruis-Pelgrim, 2008).

Some possessions may be anchors, they could help to secure and steady the ship; they might help to maintain our identities or conversely we may be inclined to discard possessions when our 'selves' strength buffers becomes less necessary. Such times are likely when key life stages and rites of passage have occurred, for example leaving school, leaving work and retirement. A further consideration; we may shed our possessions when they no longer fit with our identities. This can occur either because the ideal self-image has changed or because the images of the objects formerly incorporated in extended self have changed (Belk 1988).

As La Branche (1973) noted, we are our own historians. Therefore, another factor in the retention or discarding of possessions that no longer fit our view of ourselves is their fit with our perceptions of our entire personal history. Possessions may show where we have come from and thereby remain valuable as a point of contrast to present an extended self.

Furthermore, some authors highlight the importance of domestic space and everyday objects in the ongoing mundane practices of identity development (Forty, 1986; Kwint, Breward & Aynsley, 1999; Rybczynski 1986). Our belongings have a 'cultural biography' (Kopytoff, 1986, pp. 64–91) and are embedded in frameworks of time and memory (Tilley, 2001). Biographies of things are important in the construction of individual and family autobiographies (Csikszentmihalyi & Rochberg-Halton 1981; Woodward, 2001) Thus, the management of domestic display has been conceptualized both as performance for others and a marking practice contributing to negotiations of identity within a network of relations (Hurdley, 2006).

I THINK IT IS THE SUMMER OF 2000

I am sat in The Wheatsheaf pub in Cooden, east Sussex, with a mate. We had just finished a 'team building' day with a local team of acute care Mental Health Nurses. I have never like team building days; the idea is misleading.

As we sup our Harvey's real ale beers, my mate says:

'There is a vacancy at the Institute of Psychiatry. They are looking for a Nurse Tutor to run their 'in patient' course. I reckon you would be an ideal candidate. You have experience of being on both sides of the fence. I think Wendy would welcome a call. Why don't you give her a ring?

LATER THAT MONTH

I travel up to Camberwell, London.

Having greeted each other, Wendy says: 'Well, the Institute runs a unique course for In patient staff and I think you would be good for the course and for the Institute. The course runs over twelve weeks, the staff come into college one day a week. The bloke who runs it now is off to take up a Nurse Consultants post. It will be a great opportunity'.

'I will have to speak to my manager' I tell Wendy.

I meet my manager and they agree to a secondment for a year.

I change the course structure on arrival. I amend the attendance details. The course members then came into college two consecutive days a fortnight.

MAY 1996

I had been working for a Case Management team in Hastings for about three years. The team helped people with long term mental health difficulties; people who experienced damaging pasts. They were people who had experienced difficulties engaging with statuary mental health services. Many people I 'worked with' had been 'found' in doorways or perhaps sleeping rough under the Hastings pier or in squats; unglamorous environments.

One person I engaged with had profound problems with discarding packaging; empty sandwich packets, empty crisps packets, soap boxes. He would hoard all these types of items. The manager of the care home where he lived was becoming increasingly concerned about the fire hazard associated with this type of collecting. The person also wanted help for this problem. He was worried that he might throw something important away in error.

I would visit him a few times a week. After each visit, I would feel more and more impotent and frustrated. How could I help him?

I decided to apply for the English National Board nursing course ENB 650. This was a course for Adult Behavioural Psychotherapy. The course had just been validated at BSc level.

I attended the interview and was successful. I started this life-changing course in the September of 1996.

This was to be my second BSc degree. I had been awarded a BSc 2.1 degree in Nursing in September 1990. I happen to be from a working-class family, a secondary modern school background.

179

Despite my observable academic achievements, unlike me, I am still aware of the seemingly effortless confidence and effortless charm of most of my grammar school contemporaries.

As I got older and settled in to the middle-class worlds of academia, professionalism and publishing, I was hoping that my low academic self-esteem would evaporate and become less important, it did not, unfortunately.

Eventually, the deep-seated wiring weakened and I pay less attention to the unsubstantiated claims of my teachers and careers masters. The wires of inadequacy are buried deep in dark cavernous labyrinths. I had been unsuccessful with my eleven plus (In the United Kingdom, the eleven plus was an exam administered to some students in their last year of their primary school education, governing admission to various types of secondary school. The exam tested a student's ability to solve problems using verbal reasoning and mathematics. The intention was that it should be a general test for intelligence. Introduced in 1944, the examination was used to determine which type of school the student should attend after primary school; a grammar school, a technical college or a secondary modern). I went off to a secondary modern in my home town of Brighton; most of us had the same expectations and the same *lack of* expectations. This position was reinforced by teachers who seemed to be there to control rather than encourage and motivate. I have tried throughout my life to tackle the extent to which working-class children continue to be denied opportunities open to middle-class children on all fronts by modelling and encouraging people. As Brewer (2000, p. 176) points out:

'Each successive generation of working-class children is seen as being both a threat **to** *and hope* **for** *what society might be. Progress for the children has been framed in terms of disjunction and movement from, rather than a continuum or reproduction of, the culture and values of their parents'.*

18TH JANUARY 2011

I travel to Albania. I had been reading a National Geographic journal about the Balkans, an area I had only heard of when internal conflicts were broadcast on television or national newspapers. I booked a flight and hotel.

The flight was smooth and uneventful. I make a change at Budapest, Hungary. The flight attendant on the journey to Tirana, Josef, had a fantastic well-groomed handlebar moustache. I would guess about twelve inches from tip to tip.

The scenery below was mountainous; with what appeared to be treacherous, roads disappearing into long tunnels.

The hotel is clean, basic with courteous friendly helpful staff. We get along with fractured English and my Albanian phrase book.

I was going to become a tourist; an activity that is often conventionally understood to be motivated by a desire to escape 'normal' life (Rojek, 1993). People usually have a choice in their destination. Tourists are often exposed to the unfamiliar, something

I have enjoyed for many years. Social encounters provide tourists particularly, with the opportunity to gain new information about and to confirm congruent understandings of shared social and cultural landscapes (Harrison, 2003). Association is seen as fundamental to the process of giving meaning to our expeditions (White & White, 2008).

22ND JANUARY 2011

I walk down the Rruga (road) Driten Hoxha and look for a mini bus to Shkoder; Shkoder is a town in the north of Albania. The town's football team are playing Base in their premiership league.

I find a private mini bus. The driver wants 4oo Lek (£2.41). I have been advised to offer 300 Lek (£1.80.) He invited me with hand gestures to join him in the front of the mini bus. We are both now sat on the long seat. I try negotiating with him. We clearly do not understand each other and we laugh together.

I feel a tap on my shoulder.

'Can I help you?' a man asks me in English. 'I am an Albanian, and teach English'.

'Thank you, that would be helpful' I reply.

I tell this gentleman what I am trying to discuss with the driver. They then talk to each other and my new companion helps me, through translation, to negotiate.

'Ai dëshiron të shkojë në Shkodër. Çfarë është fare më e lirë ju do të jap atë? Ai ka 300Lek' [He wants to go to Shkoder. What is the cheapest fare you will give him? He has 300Lek]

Unë zakonisht njerëz të ngarkuar 400 lekë. Por në këtë rast një unë do të ngarkuar atij 300 lekë [I usually charge people 400 Lek. But on this one occasion, I will charge him 300 Lek]

The English speaking Albanian then joins me in the front of the mini bus.

We spend the 3-hour journey talking with each other. Towards the end of the journey, we share our email addresses. I find out that Sander Kola [his name] is an editor of a journal, the Linguistic and Communicative Performance Journal. http:// lcpj.

This was one of a handful of encounters with an Albanian. Crouch (2010) says that *encounters* are at the heart of tourism, a defining and distinguishing feature. These encounters are 'immediate, embodied and geographical' (Crouch, 2010, p.521). Interestingly there is the paradox that if tourism is a desire for distraction from the demands and drudgery of everyday routines (Britton, 1991, p.452–453), the flip side of the coin is that we are displaced and immersed in the unfamiliar environments (unless we go back to the same place each year in order to seek the familiar).

JULY 2011

I am invited by my new Albanian friend to write an article for his Journal.

Short N P (2011) Multiple selves, multiple voices and Autoethnography. *Linguistic and Communicative Performance Journal, Vol 3/2, pages 31–54.*

Since this publication, I have been invited to join the Editorial board and an invitation to become more actively involved in the Journals presentation and production.

MARCH 5TH 2012

I cancel my Royal College of Nursing membership More removal from another identity I am not associated with anymore.

JULY 2005

I attend an interview at the Falmer site of the University of Brighton. I have applied for their part time Professional Doctorate course. The interview is a gentle affair; some difficult inquiring questions from the panel of two. After about 50 minutes, I am invited to sit in the 'waiting area'. The bright red chairs are comfortable. I run over in my mind what I have just heard myself say. Was I convincing? Would I secure a place? **Do they think** *I can do this?* **Do I think** *I can do this?*

I am invited back into the interview room.

I was offered a place; I can start in the October 2005 group.

I put £30.00 on my mobile phone tariff and rang many people. I walked along the promenade in Hastings, the warm breeze blowing through my hair and feeling fresh on my face. Tears are gathering in my eyes and gently trickle down my cheeks.

I had to consider, again, the tensions for a working class bloke heading off to study, particularly at Doctoral level. I had worked through some of these tensions before whilst studying at Bachelor and Masters level courses. I am reminded of what Bourdieu suggests:

> '... objective limits become transformed into a practical anticipation of objective limits; a sense of one's place, which leads one to exclude oneself from places from which one is, excluded.' (Bourdieu, 1984, p. 471)

FEBRUARY 2009

Some builders are removing the bath in my house and replacing it with a shower unit. I can hear them downstairs, they are both whistling along to a Tamla Motown record on the radio. I came down to the kitchen to make some tea. I ask them both if they would like some as well. The younger builder asks me about some of the textbooks that are open on the kitchen table. I tell him I am studying at University. The older one looks at me and says

'You are studying at University? The way you have been talking about our work I thought you were in the building trade'.

I tell him that I was a brickie for a few years during my late teens early twenties.

A dialogue opens up between the young builder and me. We discuss his aspirations; he wants to become a marine biologist. Some modelling perhaps?

The new course was scary and exhilarating. Dews and Law (1995) discuss in their edited book 'This fine place so far away from home' the importance of making differences visible and encourage people from marginalised groups to become visible, 'as invisibility is, in the long run, intolerable' (Denis & Law, 1995, p. 5). I have thought of myself as marginalised and invisible for many years. Do I want to move from being invisible? It is safe here. How would I cross the 'border'? Where I come from and where I hope to go to present differing antagonistic styles. I often felt torn between competing loyalties. I think the way to manage this dilemma is to accept and tolerate being 'nowhere at home' (Overall, 1995).

JANUARY 2011-MARCH 2012

In addition to several-planned walks I do each year with a couple of old school mates and regular walking with friends, I walk many miles unaccompanied.

Maybe Llangollen in north Wales; perhaps Werneth Low in between Stockport and Tameside, the glorious hills of the Brecon Beacons or the rugged coastal path west of Swanage, Dorset.

Andrews and Moon (2005) discuss the benefits of what they call 'therapeutic landscapes'; the psychological attachments that people have to places and spaces. They suggest that these landscapes may vary and might be buildings, wild wildernesses or places formed in our imagination.

MARCH 11TH 2012

I will be 58 tomorrow. I catch a bus to Winchelsea and then walk back to Hastings. In Winchelsea church are many stained glass windows, one is a dedication to lifeboat men of the Mary Stanford lifeboat that lost their lives on November 15th 1928, when they were called to rescue a boat. All but two of the crew perished.

Here is the inscription:.

These men of Rye Harbour, crew of the lifeboat Mary Stanford, having confirmed the habit of a noble service, the courage handed down to them by their fathers, were quick to hear the cry of humanity above the roaring sea, in the darkness of their supreme hour, they stayed not to weigh doubt or danger but freely offering this portion of their life for the ransom of men whom they had never known, they went boldly into the last of all their storms.

An inscription that brings me to tears.

In addition, as Lea (2008) discusses, there is a long history of removing oneself from everyday life in order to rest and recuperate. Particular places have 'achieved lasting reputations for healing' (Gesler, 2003, p.2), such as spas, sacred sites and pilgrimage locations. Personally, I prefer getting away from it all; remote places where I will be alone. I agree with Gesler (2003, p.8), who says:

> *'that (people) can attain physical, mental and spiritual healing by simply spending time out-of-doors or seeking out remote or isolated places where they can 'get away from it all', surrounded by undisturbed by nature'.*

11TH OCTOBER 2010

I sit my viva voce. It lasts two and half-hours. An enjoyable, yet testing conversation. One of the viva panel says 'This is an outstanding piece of work Nigel'. I might finally have my 'ticket to ride'.

CODA

This text has provided me with an opportunity to reflect and be reflexive within the text. I have presented my work to colleagues. The occasions have stimulated debate and if, as Frank (2000) and Ellis & Bochner (2000) have suggested, *thinking with* a story is important, and if dislodging the layers of our histories is important, the discussions that followed suggested that these stories did indeed facilitate reflections, a reconsidering and a heightened awareness of retirement and associated contexts.

REFERENCES

Andrews, G., & Moon, G. (2005). Space, place, and the evidence base: Part I - An introduction to health geography. *Worldviews on Evidence-Based Nursing, 2*(2), 55–62.

Bachelard, G. (1971). *The poetics of reverie; childhood, language, and the cosmos.* Boston: Beacon Press. First published in French in 1960.

Bachelard, G. (1994). *The poetics of space.* Boston: Beacon Press. First published in French in 1958.

Belk R. (1988). Possessions and the extended self. *Journal of Consumer Research, 15,* 139–168.

Bhatti, M., & Church, A. (2004). Home, the culture of nature and meanings of gardens in late modernity, *Housing Studies, 19*(1), 37–51.

Bhatti, M., Church, A., Claremont, A., & Stenner, P. (2009). I love being in the garden: enchanting encounters in everyday life. *Social and cultural geography, 10*(1), 61–76.

Bhatti, M. (2006). When I'm in the garden I can create my own paradise: Homes and gardens in later life. *Sociological Review, 54*(2), 318–341.

Bourdieu, P. (1984). *Distinction.* London: Routledge & Kegan Paul.

Brewer, S. (2000). Who do you say I am?' Jesus, gender and the (working-class) family romance. In S. Munt (Ed.), *Cultural studies and the working class: Subject to change* (pp. 167–179). London: Cassell.

Britton, S. (1991). Tourism, capital and place: Towards a critical geography of tourism. *Environment and Planning D: Society and Space, 9,* 451–478.

Bruno, G. (2002). *Atlas of emotion.* London: Verso.

Casey, E. (1993). *Getting back into place: Toward a renewed understanding of the place-world.* Bloomington: Indiana University Press.

Casey, E. (2000*). Remembering: A phenomenological study.* Bloomington: Indiana University Press.

Claremont, A., Church, A., Bhatti, M., & Stenner, P. (2010). Going public: landscaping everyday life. *Cultural Geographies, 17*(2), 277–282

Cooper, D. (2006). *The philosophy of gardens.* Oxford: Oxford University Press.

Crouch, C. (2010). Geographies of tourism: (un)ethical encounters. *Progress in Human Geography*, *34*(4), 521–527

Csikszentmihalyi, M., & Rochberg-Halton, E. (1981). *The meaning of things: Domestic symbols and the self*. Cambridge: Cambridge University Press.

Dews, D., & Law, B. (1995). *This fine place so far away from home: Voices of academics from the working class*. Philadelphia: Temple University Press.

Ellis, C., & Bochner, A. (2000). Autoethnography, personal narrative and reflexivity. In N. K. Denzin & Y. S. Lincoln (Eds.), *The handbook of qualitative research* (2nd ed., pp. 733–768). Thousand Oaks, CA: Sage

Ferudi, F. (2007). From the narrative of the blitz to the rhetoric of vulnerability. *Cultural Sociology*, *1*(2), 235–254.

Forty, A. (1986). *Objects of desire: Design and society since 1750*. London: Thames and Hudson.

Frank, A. (2000). The standpoint of the storyteller. *Qualitative Health Research*, *10*, 354–365.

Gesler, W. (2003). *Healing places*. Oxford: Rowman & Littlefield.

Gibson, J. (1966). *The senses considered as perceptual systems*. Boston: Houghton Mifflin.

Harrison, J. (2003). *Being a tourist: Finding meaning in pleasure travel*. Vancouver: University of British Columbia Press

Hawley, P. (2010). *Being Bright is not enough: The unwritten rules of doctoral study*. Springfield: Charles C Thomas Publisher, Ltd.

Hitchings, R. (2003). People, plants and performance: On actor network theory and the material pleasures of the private garden. *Social & Cultural Geography*, *4*, 99–113.

Hurdley, R. (2006). Dismantling mantelpieces: Narrating identities and materializing culture in the home. *Sociology*, *40*, 717–733

Ingold, T. (2000). *The perception of the environment: Essays in livelihood, dwelling and skill*. London: Routledge.

Jay, F. (2010). *The joy of less, A minimalist living guide: How to declutter, organize and simplify your life*. Belgium: Anja Press.

Kopytoff, I. (1986). The cultural biography of things: Commoditization as a process, In A. Appadurai (ed.), *The social life of things: Commodities in cultural perspective* (pp. 64–91). Melbourne: Cambridge University Pres.

Kwint, M., Breward, C., & Aynsley, J. (Eds.) (1999). *Material memories: Design and evocation*. Oxford: Berg.

La Branche, A. (1973). "Neglected and unused things: Narrative encounter," *Review of Existential Psychology and Psychiatry. 12*(2), 163–168.

Lee, J. (2008). Retreating to nature: Rethinking 'therapeutic landscapes'. *Area, 40*(1), 90–98.

Lincoln, Y. (1997). Self, subject, audience, text: Living at the edge, Writing in the margins. In Tierney W. & Lincoln Y. (eds.), *Representation and the text: Re-framing the narrative voice*. State University of New York Press, Albany.

Mein, G., Higgs, P., Ferrie, J., & Stansfield, S. (1998). Paradigms of retirement: The importance of health and ageing in the whitehall 11 study. *Social Science and Medicine, 47*(4), 535–545.

Marcoux, J. (2001). The 'Casser Maison' ritual : Constructing the self by emptying the home. *Journal of Material Culture, 6*, 213–235.

O'Neill, M. (2001). Corporeal experience: A haptic way of knowing. *Journal of Architectural Education, 55*(1), 3–12.

Overall, C. (1995). Nowhere at home: Towards a phenomenology of working class consciousness. In Dews D & Law B (eds.), *This fine place so far away from home: Voices of academics from the working class* (pp. 209–220). Philadelphia: Temple University Press.

Pelias, R. (1999). *Writing performance: Poeticizing the researcher's body*. Carbondale: Southern Illinois University Press.

Phillipson, C. (2002). *Transitions from work to retirement*. Bristol: The Policy Press/Joseph Rowntree Foundation.

Phillipson, C. (2004). Older workers and retirement: critical perspectives on the research literature and policy implications. *Social Policy and Society, 3*(2), 189–95.

185

Rodaway, P. (1994). *Sensuous geographies: Body, sense and place.* London: Routledge.

Rojek, C. (1993). *Ways of escape: Modern transformations in leisure and travel.* London: Macmillan.

Rybczynski, W. (1986). *Home: A short history of an idea.* New York: Viking.

Schifferstein, H,. & Zwartkruis-Pelgrim, E. (2008). Consumer product attachment: Measurement and design implications. *International Journal of Design, 2*(3), 1–13.

Sennett, R. (1998). *The corrosion of character: The personal consequences of work in the new capitalism.* London: Norton.

Sprackland, J. (1997). *Tattoos for mothers day.* Liverpool: Spike.

Strangleman, T. (2007) The nostalgia for permanence at work? The end of work and its commentators. *The Sociological Review, 55*(1), 81–103

Tilley, C. (2001). Ethnography and material culture. In Atkinson P., Coffey A., Delamont S.., Lofland J., & Lofland L. (Eds.), *Handbook of ethnography* (pp. 258–72). London: Sage.

White, N., & White, P. (2008). Travel as interaction: Encountering place and others. *Journal of Hospitality and Tourism Management Annual*

Whitty, G. (2001). Education, social class and social exclusion, *Journal of Education Policy, 16*(4), 287–295.

Wolcott, H. (2010). *Ethnography lessons: A primer.* Walcott Creek, California. Left Coast Press.

Woodward, I. (2001). Domestic objects and the taste epiphany: A resource for consumption methodology. *Journal of Material Culture, 6*(2), 115–316.

BRETT SMITH

ARTIFICIAL PERSONS AND THE ACADEMY: A STORY[1]

The house is quiet. The bedroom is dark. Despite the air being cool, my skin is cold and damp. The digital blue alarm clock reads 3.34 am, November 27th. Why, again, do I wake up startled? My body is rapidly caught in a thick blanket of fright. Who *am* I? Who *am I* becoming?

* * *

"Come in," I say in a sharp voice. The undergraduate 3rd year student opens my office door, and pokes her head around it.

"Do you have a few minutes Brett? I've a few questions about my research project."

"Not really. Sign up for a tutorial." Turning my head back to the computer screen and the grant application that was sucking the life out of me, I add, "The tutorial sheet to book a meeting is on my door. See you later."

"Sorry Brett," the student says in an apologetic tone. "I tried signing up for a tutorial yesterday but all your slots are taken for the next 4 weeks. All of November is booked out. I wouldn't normally bother you. I know you're very busy. But it's quite urgent. I could really do with your help."

Turning my head from the computer screen, I say in a flat voice, "Sorry, it's school and university policy to have 2 hours dedicated to tutorials per week. If the slots are filled, then there is nothing I can do. I'm just following school policy. See you."

I turn my head back the screen, and begin typing. The student slowly shuts my door. As she does, I suddenly feel false. "This isn't you Brett. And what about her? How does she feel being treated like that? Does she think I'm uncaring? Does she feel angry, disappointed, and/or frustrated? What will she do now?"

Despite both feeling sick, and knowing the next 30 minutes are lost, I resist the call to act. I recall in my head the voice of the Head of School[2]. "Research and grants are simply what counts. You will not keep your job or get promoted by being good at teaching or caring about students. Forgot about teaching well or going that extra mile with them. We need to toe the line the university has set."

I quickly turn my attention back to writing the grant and resist running down the corridor, catching up with the student, and inviting her back to talk.

* * *

N. P. Short et al. (Eds.), Contemporary British Autoethnography, 187–202.

The warmth from the late September sun kisses my face. I smile again. In my head, as I walk into the university and to my office, I converse with phantom others. "I love the first week of the semester. I feel energised by the students. Their vibrancy is contagious. I *love* this job," I tell them. Still smiling, I inhale the warmth and the rich scent of freshly cut grass. On the grass, students sit in small groups chatting, throw a Frisbee between them, kick a football around, or just sit. I carry on smiling and wander on towards my office.

The automatic doors to the building open and I walk in. Nausea erupts in my body. I run down the corridor to the toilets and dash into the first cubical. Kneeling, my lunch involuntary gushes out of my mouth into the pan. I taste more vomit in the back of my throat, and throw up again. Ten minutes later, after trying to swill the acrid taste away and washing the tears from my eyes, I slowly walk up the stairs to my office. "Welcome back," I say to myself.

* * *

The sound of someone knocking on my door interrupts my writing. "Come in," I say with a hint of anger in my voice.

"Afternoon Brett. Are you coming to the school meeting?" asks Matthew. Matthew was a member of staff who had joined us a few months ago. I warmed to him quickly. He was friendly, eager, and very bright. He spoke with joy about his young family. He appreciated the flexible hours but recognized the need to work hard. He very rarely moaned about the new forms of public management, the rise of neoliberalism, and the steep increase of outcome-based assessment systems for research productivity that pervaded university. He knew it was all a game.

"Thanks for reminding me about the meeting Matthew," I say with a mischievous smile. Saving the paper I'm writing, and then turning the computer off, I ask, "How's things anyway Matthew?"

"Great. I've got my first PhD student. I'm so excited about working with him and the research. Yourself? How are things? I've not seen you much lately?"

"Fine. I've been working at home trying to write a paper and put two grants. I need to pull in a big grant if I'm going to secure my job and get promoted. I've also been told by our Head of School and the Deputy Vice Chancellor that I need to publish my work in higher impact factor journals." As these words come out of mouth, I pull a grimace that makes Matthew laugh.

"You don't go much on impact factors do you Brett," he says to tease me and knowing I'll react.

I can feel my own rush to respond on queue: "Other than they are statistically flawed, are manipulated by editors, and are no indicator of the real quality of a paper, I have no problem with them. Other than knowing they are a social construction and that anyone who believes in them as some indicator of research quality is talking crap, or are deluded, then its fine."

Matthew stands smiling, knowing I have taken the bait. I smile back, but then add seriously, "I know I need to play the impact factor game if I'm too survive in this university. I need to pay the mortgage and eat."

He stops smiling. This is a reminder to a newcomer of a harsh reality he faces in the academy. From his look I know this is not the talk he wants to hear. My moaning isn't pleasurable to listen to. For a while now, I've realised I'm not much fun to be around. Each time this realisation hits me I immediately think of sociability[3] and how that to interact sociably is to interact for the pleasure of interacting in itself.

"Sorry Matthew. Bad day. The last thing I need is to sit in a meeting and be talked at for an hour." Screwing up my face, I quickly add, "Sorry, there I go again."

As I lock my office door, I shift my talk. "So, Matthew how was your weekend? Did you manage to get in a bit of climbing?"

A few minutes later, after listening to his climbing stories, we walk into the meeting room. It is full. Most of the staff within the School either sit chatting to the person next to them or are working, that is, editing their own research paper. As Matthew sits down in the first chair available, I scan the room to look for my colleagues who make up the Socio-Cultural Studies Group. They are sitting together at the back laughing. The tension in my body eases slightly. I navigate the chairs in the room and sit down amongst them.

"What's so funny?" I say to the group.

"You never guess what?" two of them say in unison.

"What!"

"Have you not read the e-mail that was circulated yesterday?" adds Jane

"No. I couldn't bring myself to read it. Bad news?"

Leonard, a senior member in the School and our group looks up to respond.

"Nothing more bizarre than a 'traffic light system' has been introduced to judge us as academics in terms of grant capture and publication quality for the RAE. Basically, green light is good – you are safe. Amber is OK – but you are not safe.

"And red," I say?

"Red – basically means 'DEAD' in this place! You are not up to scratch and will not be submitted in the RAE so can look forward to a hasty exit or a change of contract to a 'Teaching Fellow'.

"Shit." I suddenly feel my body tighten, and the fear swells through me. I feel the power of this traffic light system to define me and my colleagues in the School. Looking at the reactions of my colleagues in the Socio-Cultural Studies Group to the comment made by Leonard, I sense their angst at what this means for them as qualitative researchers in an otherwise quantitative and psychometric environment. They know the low opinion their lab-based colleagues have of their ethnographic and phenomenological work. Some remain mildly tolerant but others openly hold their 'unscientific story telling' in contempt. The power relations of these three simple colours – Red, Amber, and Green, will be played out in this arena. Each colour will do serious things on and people. Those who are defined by the colour ascribed to them know this and, just as importantly, those who do the ascribing know this. That's what they intend.

I slump into a chair.

"Why the hell did I come to the meeting," I silently say.

A moment later Jack, the Head of School, opens the meeting.

"Thanks everyone for coming. This is a big year for us. I know you will all have read the e-mail I forwarded on from the Vice Chancellor. As you might have gathered, a new traffic light system has been implemented by the Vice Chancellor and his senior management team to help us get a sense of where we all stand in the run up to the RAE..."

"And which you are following and exercising without questioning it," I add in my head.

"This new traffic light system means that not only will your individual grant income be given a category, green, amber or red, but also your 4 best research papers will be judged and classified in the same way."

"Jack," asks Leonard in his usual polite and soft tone used in meetings. "It would be helpful if you could offer some guidance to staff on what criteria you and the others will judge the papers by? "

Squirming, Jack replies, "Thanks for that Leonard. The director of research, myself, and two independent external assessors will judge the 4 papers you have already chosen to submit as your best work using the one to four star system as in relation to the criteria. Rest assured, we will all be unbiased and objective."

Raising his hand slightly, and in an inquisitive tone, Matthew asks Jack. "I wondered where teaching fit into this system? Maybe it's gone over me."

Rubbing his face with one of his thick hands, Jack says, "It doesn't play any part. The Vice Chancellor made it very clear to me in my last meeting with him that we have to prioritise research and grants. If we don't produce world-leading research and bring in more research council money, we all know the consequences."

Feeling more irritated, and close to erupting with anger, I want to raise my hand and point out why this is wrong. Instead, I stay silent. I know there would be repercussions if I 'spoke out'. Bullying was common.

"We know the consequences, but that is how it is," adds Jack. Looking drained, and turning the Research Director for support, he continues. "We have to accept that as being part of an elite university. Research and grants are simply what counts. You will not keep your job or get promoted by being good at teaching or caring about students. Forgot about teaching well or going that extra mile with students. We need to toe the line the university has set. I'm only saying all this too you because it is in your best interests."

I sink further in my chair. Leaning slowly forward, I pick up my pen and scribble a few thoughts in my diary. "Artificial persons in action? What are the consequences for education, students, me, and my colleagues?"

* * *

According to Wolgast (1992), artificial persons are those who "speak and act in the name of others, (who) can commit and obligate them" (p. 1). Thus, artificial persons are followers of orders. They toe the line. They speak on behalf of institutional procedures and organisational rules. They are not then 'responsible' for their effects on human lives. Yet, artificial persons, and the people that promote and produce them, do effect people, affecting the significance of actions and influencing "the more fundamental idea of what a person is" (p. 4). Further, as Frank (2004, p. 127) highlights, artificial persons "have administrative utility because they act not on their own authority but to implement an authority that resides elsewhere. This usefulness creates the ethical problem that artificial persons no longer feel personal responsibility for their actions toward others". But as Frank notes, artificial persons do act, and in ways that can commit symbolic violence. This violence can be particularly insidious as the artificial person speaks with an authority deriving from both (their) expertise and (their) claim to be acting in the person's best interests.

Not only can artificial persons inflict damage on and in other people, they can also damage themselves. They can feel that they are becoming, or have become, someone they are not. They can feel morally bankrupt (or maybe corrupt). As a result, they might leave the job that they once loved in order to be who they feel morally best being. Or, they sink deeper into being an artificial person.

Of course, becoming and being an artificial necessarily involves structure. Our choices are unchosen choices[4]. We are constrained by structural matters. But, people do interact in purposive ways, bringing their preferences, desires, back stories, career aspirations, and so on to bear (i.e., agency). In other words, just like 'senior management/ bureaucrats' who purposefully produce artificial persons, the artificial person cannot themselves be let off the hook. Just because someone acts in the name of others, this does not give them an alibi. They do perform harm and are complicit in the production of becoming an artificial person. They do have agency and cannot pretend otherwise.

* * *

I quickly put down my lukewarm coffee on the sticky student union table, slouch into the chair, and hold up the research paper in front of me. Maybe Martin won't notice me, I think. But I'm out of luck as I catch him approaching.

"How did your meeting go with Jack'? asks Martin.

Putting down the research paper, I reply "Fine. The usual. More research published in better impact factor journals, and get council grant money. All predictable." What Martin really wanted to hear was what 'colour' on the traffic light classification had I been given.

"So not too bad then?"

I shrug my shoulders. I am already annoyed by his presence.

"We all really must start hitting bigger journals and bring in more money," Martin adds. "I've just submitted a paper to a top ten mainstream psychology journal that has a big impact factor. I have two grants that will be submitted by the end of the month too."

"OK. Best of luck."

"I've also got two of my Master's students theses published. Not in great journals. It's MSc work after all. But it's all good for my CV. I'm thinking too of asking some more students to volunteer to collect some qualitative data. That reminds me, I must pass on the qualitative paper that I just got accepted. One of my PhD students submitted her first study and it was accepted yesterday. It was a qualitative one. She interviewed 10 elite athletes about their experiences of burnout. Her second, third, and fourth study will be quantitative of course, but you might be interested in this one."

"Thanks. That would be good," I lie. I had read three of his previous co-authored qualitative papers. Each was published in psychology journals that had strong impact factors. But the work wasn't the kind of qualitative research I valued - work built on spending much time with people; work that was heartfelt and compelling to read; work that produced thick descriptions and nuanced insights into the social world from a researcher that was generous, caring, and wants to make a difference; and work that was theoretically eclectic, erudite, and generative.

Like a growing number of papers I was receiving to review for journals, the papers Martin produced were *technically* competent. But, at least in my view, each paper lacked critical thought and was theoretically unimaginative. Data collection and analysis was quick and clean. There was no attempt to deal with the complexities surrounding validity or reliability. The usual 'triangulation' and 'inter-rater reliability checks' were inserted into the methods as if they were uncontested and can do the work each technique promised it's technician it can do. The end result was work that felt cold and pedestrian. It was the kind of work produced by someone who viewed qualitative research as a technical exercise one could learn overnight and reproduce with ease, rather than as a craft and way of being. A fast food burger company would be proud of serving up this kind of work I often thought.

It was however also the kind of research that I was beginning to think about producing. I would not be responsible for this I told myself. I was just following orders from the head of school and Deputy Vice Chancellor. It was the kind of safe work that big impact journal editors seemed to like.

Suddenly I felt sympathy for Martin. Or was it sympathy for me? Maybe this was why I was annoyed by his presence and didn't want to spend time with. He reminded me of who I was becoming, or am.

* * *

Later that night over a beer in my local pub I force myself to compare 'me' with Martin. I go through a mental tick list silently in my head.

1. Martin doesn't offer critical insights during meetings with senior staff. He stays silent in each meeting.
   Tick, that's me now.

2. Martin has a list of slots on his door when he is available to see students. They can sign up only during those limited hours he provides. The discussions are very instrumental in that each is designed to lead to a product that will benefit him. Outside these 'office hours' he is unavailable because he is very busy or says his schedule doesn't permit it. He reminds people often how busy, and therefore important, he is.

   Tick. I start to feel sick with worry.

3. Martin knows his original research passion will struggle to be funded through research councils. He changed his research agenda to fit funding calls or what is currently fashionable within the school.

   Nearly a tick. I've been told by the School's director of research to change my research focus in order to make it more appealing to funders. I'm considering following orders.

4. Martin has taken on administration duties that will benefit him and his research rather than doing them to be collegiate.

   Tick, that's me. Who am I becoming? I'm not sure I'm liking this person, whoever he is. My stomach tightens, and my deep feeling of distress grows inside.

5. Martin aims to supervise as many postgraduate students as he can. This is not because he is interested in them or their ideas. They are extra hands to collect data for him and swell his output of publications.

   No, that is not me. But I've thought about doing this, and I may even do it. It wouldn't be my fault if I did. It's a model 'the School' is promoting and one suggested that I follow if I'm to be successful within the university.

6. Martin believes in impact factors as the main indicator of quality research.

   I know impact factors are flawed. I've stood up at a major conference and offered a critique of them in front of my peers. And, let's not forget, I've read some truly awful research in journals with high impact factors. I know that some of the best research I've read has been published in journals with no impact factor. But, the last two papers I submitted were to journals with high impact factors. I did that simply because of the impact factor the journals had. How different am I then from Martin? Am I really so close to being an artificial person? Am I already there? My stomach tighten further.

7. Martin believes in the 'game' of academia and that there is only one way to play it. But he doesn't seem to know it is a game that is constructed by certain people for various neoliberal purposes, and personal gain. What is also worrying is that he passes the game, and how it should be played (at least as laid out by the university), onto his postgraduate students. He doesn't offer a critique of the game as a social construction infused with power relations, suggest ways to sometimes subvert and deflect it, or offer possibilities to play the game differently when the occasion allows. Martin reproduces the game in his silences, actions, and behaviours to his students. Worryingly too, I now see his postgraduate students reproducing the game, thereby, on the one hand, increasing its circulation further and, on the other, narrowing down even more what research can be and do.

I know academia is a game. I know all the problems that go with believing in it as a natural reality and that there is only one game that can be played. I also feel that reproducing it through the bodies of postgraduates is wrong. Despite this, if I'm honest with myself, I'm not far from being sucked into reproducing the game through my own silences, actions, and behaviours. Another spurt of worry is felt deep inside me.

8. Martin follows uncritically a model of how a student should be supervised. He believes a PhD should always follow the natural science model of 'Do study 1, write it up as a paper; then do study 2, and write it up as a paper; then do study 3, and write it up as a paper; and finally do study 4, and write it up as a paper.' This might work very well for the natural sciences. But Martin doesn't realise (or doesn't care) that this model of 4 studies often does not work for certain projects in the social sciences (e.g., sociology and psychology). It may even be counter-productive to producing high quality research. There is also little or no appreciation of the major difference between a PhD chapter and paper. He never questions the need for 4 studies (why not 1, 3, 7, or 10?). He never worries that if research from the outset is set out in the linear path that the 4 study model promotes, there is the danger that the research produced is predictable, insipid, and simple.

I know there is no universal formula to doing a PhD and fully realise the dangers that go with thinking there is one. But, it's a tempting model to follow. In eliminating a great deal of the uncertainty that goes with doing good qualitative research, and by following a linear route that is easier to supervise than a messy, complex, and emergent journey, I'd boost my publications, get students through in the time the university dictates, and have more and more completions on my CV. Tempting. Young staff like me in our School had consistently been told too that we need more PhD students and quicker completions. It feels wrong, and is. But, as a system of reward for those who follow it, and punishment for those who question its applicability for all scholarship, the model is seductive.

9. Martin has no interest in his colleagues within the School. They are either obstacles to his progress or simply stepping stones along the way to higher things. He will work with someone though if he can get something from him or her that will boost his CV.

Cross. I'm not this person. Yet....Still though, I feel deeply worried. Distress grows and presses against my sides, making me feel sick.

I take a small sip of beer and go through each point again. As I slowly do, I try to rationalise my behaviour or search autobiographical memories for moments that would justify the removal of my mental ticks next to most points. I can't hide though from my body's knowledge. The more I scrutinise the points the more the gouging ache of distress washes through me, coming in stronger waves as I feel my way into the realisation I was becoming someone I did not want to be. The artificial person had worked its way into me. I was putting myself in its neoliberal narrative, and letting it live inside and through me. In the corner of my stomach, I still felt that I had some of 'me' left. Yet 'me' was eroding fast. I put my half empty pint down and leave.

* * *

We tend to look everywhere but in the mirror.

* * *

I look out into the audience as I take a sip of tepid water from the plastic bottle I had purchased from the hospital vending machine that morning. The physiotherapists, surgeons, hospital mangers, clinical psychologists, occupational therapists, nurses, and spinal cord injured people seemed to have been relatively interested in my talk on spinal cord injury and the possibilities of narrative care within a spinal injury inpatient hospital. Drawing on research conducted with my colleague Andrew Sparkes,[5] I spoke about why narratives matter in terms of shaping and conducting the lives of people who had suffered a spinal cord injury through playing sport. As part of this, and drawing on the work of Arthur Frank,[6] I talked about the capacity of stories to take care of people by containing fear and affirming what is valuable. It was highlighted that by witnessing and multiplying stories, both hospital staff and spinal cord injured people might help others who have fallen out of the story of which they were part, and to find a new story of which they can be part. They might also animate a collective story[7] in which a sense of solidarity can be generated that connects people together in ways that challenge feelings of isolation and fear that can prevail following a spinal cord injury.

However, I suggested that doing all this is neither easy nor straightforward. In addition to the problem of limited time people can have to both listen to stories and share these with others in hospital settings, I emphasised that practicing narrative care can be constrained when people operate as artificial persons.

I look once more out into the audience, put the bottled water onto the lectern, and ask if anyone has any questions. Silence. People shift uncomfortably in their chairs. Suddenly one hand springs up.

"Brett, thank you. Joyce, senior nurse here. I was interested in this idea of the artificial person you presented. The artificial person captures who we are being increasingly turned into. I hate it. I can see myself in it. I've lost countless colleagues over the years because of being turned into someone they are not, because they feel that they are more responsible for paperwork than for patient care, because they have ended up losing what propelled them into becoming a nurse. And that was not about money. We entered the profession because we want to care for people."

Most of the audience rapidly nod their heads in agreement.

"I'd agree Joyce," says a surgeon on the back row. "It's hit us too. I'm seeing more and more junior staff not even turning into this artificial person, but entering as already one. Who are training these people? What are we doing to them?"

"Hold on there Harvey," interjects Mark, one of the hospital managers. Turning slight in his chair, and leaning over his shoulder, he adds, "I think we need to get some perspective on this."

In his pause the words, "What the fuck have I opened up", rush through my head.

"I'm sure," Harvey continues, "that there are many nurses, surgeons, physiotherapists and so on who are very content and happy in their jobs."

"And they *are* probably the artificial person," jumps in Joyce.

"Joyce, I can see this has hit a spot with staff," says Harvey.

People nod their heads and few also air their agreements with a raised "Yesssss."

"Brett, you're around this afternoon I believe," Harvey notes.

"I am."

"Can I suggest that you, me, and Joyce find some time to discuss this matter. Contra to what some of you might think, I'm not here to make your lives a misery."

Several people gently laugh.

"I'm happy for other staff to join us, if you're free of course, to discuss this and see if we can find some solutions. I don't want to brush this under the carpet. It's clearly too important and I really didn't realise there was such strong feeling. Let's take some responsibility and do something about it."

* * *

The student union is busy. Mobile phones bleep, students tap at their laptops, others share photographs and post messages over the Internet, and some band I'd not heard of sing in the background. From the corner of my eye I notice a colleague buying coffee at the student union cafe. I recognise him as one of the seven people that interviewed me for the lecturing post I recently started. I'd said hello to him a few times within the building our offices were located in. He was in his mid-forties, and a few years older than me. He was also a highly distinguished natural scientist not just in our School, but as I learned from colleagues within the first few weeks of joining my new university, across the globe.

A few moments later, my new colleague walks over to me, a large coffee in his right hand, and glasses perched on top of his nose.

"Hi Brett," says Trent.

"Hi."

"Would you mind if I joined you?

"Please do," I say with a hint of nervousness in my voice. More of the garbled responses I gave to his interview questions come rushing through my body.

Sitting down opposite me, and putting the coffee down on the table, Trent gently asks, "How are things Brett? Settled in yet?"

"Slowly, yes. But things are great. I've really enjoyed teaching, and am looking forward to collecting data and getting my teeth into a new project."

"Wonderful to hear." Peering down his glasses, and looking down at the page of notes that sit on the table next to my coffee, he says with a small nod, "Sorry if I've disturbed you. It looks serious."

"It is, kind of. Actually, I've a dilemma of sorts."

"Tricky things those. What is it? Anything I can help you with?" says Trent frowning, before adding, "If you don't mind me saying."

"No, no. I'm an editor of a journal."

Trent nods, and says, "I know. I was one of the people on your interview panel. It was only a few months ago!"

"Sorry Trent," I say in a slightly embarrassed tone.

"Seriously, I'm glad you took the job Brett. I'm no expert on what you do, but we need the kind of work you do in the school. It's good that we're appointing more people who do the kind of science like you do."

"Thanks. I think the university might be an exception. I don't see many job adverts for qualitative researchers in sport, exercise and health schools across the UK."

"Terrible shame. Terrible. You do such interesting and important work. Things can and do change though."

"True."

Pointing at the paper scribbled with notes in front of me, Trent probes further, "So, what's this dilemma then Brett."

"I just had a meeting with the managing editor who works for publisher of the journal I edit. She tells me all the signs of quality, for the publisher, are there. It's selling well, has a very submission rate, a high rejection rate, and all that kind of stuff. And the journal is moving into its fifth year. So, I've got to start thinking about getting an impact factor for it, she insists."

Laughing, Trent says "Ahhh yes, our friend an impact factor for it, she insists. A strange little beast. I published a paper in a journal last month that had an impact factor of 19.4. I got the cold shoulder that week from a few colleagues in the lab." Shaking his head and frowning in disbelief, he adds, "Strange. Stranger because it's not even my best work! I published another paper that month in a journal that had an impact factor of 4.2. That work was infinitely better."

I smile broadly, and then add, "Trent, our journals in the social sciences generally have an impact factor of about 1 or in some rare cases, maybe 3 or 4, at best. Publishing a paper in a journal with an impact factor of 4.2 would, in some people's eyes in our world, be like walking on water. But maybe in other people's eyes, that might not be good enough. For sure, we can't compete against natural scientists."

Raising his voice, Trent says, "But why compete anyway. You shouldn't need to. Between you and me, that's what I said in the interview panel when we were making decisions about who to appoint. It was raised that most of your work doesn't come with huge impact factors when compared to work we do. But that was missing the point a few of us stressed. Most of the panel got it. Your work is different and we need to respect that."

"Trent, thanks."

"Stop saying thanks, and tell me about your meeting."

After taking a sip of my coffee, I say, "As I said, the journal I edit is now in a position to apply for an impact factor. I'm caught in a very tricky place, or a game to play. On the one hand, I know that impact factors are flawed and, when used as markers of judgment of research quality, can do harm. I know, for example, the equation a journal's impact factor is calculated from. I know there are arithmetic or algorithmic defects in this calculation. I'm aware too that from the equation the impact factor depends crucially on is based on which article types Thomson Scientific deems as citable. This company is then the sole or key arbiter of the impact factor game." Lowering my voice as if some from Thomson Scientific was sat opposite, I add, "What's interesting is that not only is Thomson Scientific part of a private, for-profit organisation that has no obligation to be accountable to the authors and readers of journals. But as far as I know the company still refuses to make public its process for choosing citable article types." Emphasising the word citable with a change in my voice tone, I stress, "What they deem 'citable'"

"Interesting Brett. I wasn't aware of that. If that is the case, that means research is rated by a process that isn't transparent or accountable to researchers."

"It's subjective too!" I add with wry smile. Taking another sip of my coffee, I continue. "I know too that since a journal's impact factor is derived from citations to all articles in a journal, this number can't tell us anything about the quality of any specific research article in that journal. The article could be poor but because it's in a high impact it might be considered top quality."

"And Brett," Trent adds with a small sigh, "An impact factor doesn't tell us anything of the quality of the work of any author. You know what too, in all my time, I've never had one person outside of academia that deals with sporting policy ask about the impact factor of a journal I've published in."

Feeling a little more confident around Trent, I say, "I've had though over the years lots of researchers who want to submit to the journal ask me what the impact factor is. I've even had to encourage a few people who were just finishing their PhD to *not* submit their work to the journal. Their research was damn good. But I know that the impact factor of a journal is being used by some universities to decide whether or not a young researcher gets offered a position in a department."

"Or if an established one gets promoted or are given tenure," interjects Trent with a knowing side nod.

"True," I reply, before adding, "A lot is riding on an impact factor then. People's career's are on the line over a number that makes no sense, mathematically, ethically, or in terms of accountability."

Smiling, and throwing up his hands, Trent says in voice filled with sarcasm, "If that's the case, get an impact factor and as an editor put in strategies to boost your impact factor. Increase the numerator in the equation by encouraging authors to cite articles published in your journal or decrease the denominator by making such articles superficially less substantial. Force authors to cut down their methods, don't talk about your, what's the word. You mentioned it in your interview and baffled us natural scientists. Epp, epi..."

"Epistemology."

"Yes, avoid talking about that. Tell authors also to reduce the number of references they use, or you as the editor manipulate the impact factor by decreasing the number of research articles published. It's done I hear."

"Or," I add with a small laugh, "I could seek mostly review articles and publish these as they usually get more citations than research articles. I could get a few dodgy papers and later retract them."

"You could," Trent nearly shouts with excitement. "Retraction happens a lot in my field. Ironically a retracted paper often gets more citations than other reliable papers. And even more ironic is the fact its citation contribution to journal never gets subtracted. Retraction Brett is the name of the game!"

Leaning forward slightly, and with a big grin, I say, "Thanks Trent. You've made my day."

"No problem. We should chat more. It would be good to get all the different fields and diverse epistemologies in this School together to chat. But, come on Brett, no sitting on the fence. What are you going to do? Are you going to go for an impact factor?"

"I don't really want to play the impact factor game, but feel I should as without one I wonder if the journal will survive. I might harm careers too. The journal's possible first impact factor should be of interest to me, and is. When will it get one, and how high will it be, is a question that crops up with discussions with editorial board members and authors. I can't ignore them! I really value their thoughts and they deserve to be taken seriously. But impact factors are a rigged game and I'd feel complicit in its reproduction if I went for one."

"You've not answered my question," says Trent, raising his eyes, and turning up the corner of his mouth. "Are you, as editor, going to go for an impact factor?"

With a heavy sigh, I respond with the answer I've known in my bones for some time, "I will go for one."

"Ok. There we go. Why don't you write about it? Maybe open your first issue that has an impact factor tied to it with what we've talked about. Open up a larger dialogue."

"I could, but editorial's rarely get cited, so I'd harm the impact factor," I say with mischievous smile.

* * *

There are two modest purposes behind writing this autoethnography. First, drawing on numerous stories I've witnessed from other people in various universities, in these pages I sought to offer a story that showed a glimpse of the dark side of academia with Britain. As part of this dark side, I aimed to show artificial persons in action and how people can become this person who speaks on behalf of institutional procedures and organisational rules but does not feel responsible for their effects on human lives. Within academia, these effects include damage to family relationships, people's health and wellbeing, and university staff-student relations. Artificial persons also harm the process and products of research. Under their gaze, and within webs of power, one kind of knowing is privileged and rewarded. Diversity is rarely celebrated. What counts as research by the artificial person, and the managerial culture of academia they speak on behalf of, is defined narrowly as 1) work published in journals with a high quantified impact factor, 2) work with high citation counts, 3) work funded through full economic costed grant income. Thus, when read simply through such quantifiable outcome-based assessment systems and a private business model, qualitative research in general and autoethnographic work in particular, from the very outset, is deemed 'poor research' and the author a failure.

Does this then mean that we abandon this work? No! Does it mean we place ourselves in a victim narrative and complain amongst ourselves that we are misunderstood and that 'others' just don't get creative analytical practices (Richardson, 2000) like autoethnography? No! What then might be done?

My second modest hope is that this story animates opportunities for all kinds of scientists - regardless of subject area, discipline, tradition, or paradigm - to engage in critical dialogue about academia and develop a collective resistance against the various forces (e.g., artificial persons, bullying, and academic value being based simply on a range of metrics) that are shaping professional and personal landscapes in unacceptable ways. Of course, such dialogues across differences and efforts to come together are not easy or will be straightforward. But, there is a growing number of scholars (e.g., Burrows, 2012; Holligan, 2011; Shore, 2008; Sparkes, 2007) who *are* engaging in a critical dialogue, and when joined together, evoke collaborative efforts to develop different ways of thinking about scholarship, academia, and who we might be. This autoethnography, I hope, adds another voice to such a growing community made up of different scholars.

In offering another voice, and modestly expanding the critical dialogue on academia and how it is being shaped in unacceptable ways partly through the rise of artificial persons and an obsession with metrics, it is hoped that this story shows that becoming and being an artificial person is *not* a person's destiny. We might be predisposed or bred by supervisors, Professors, Directors of research, Heads of School and so on to act in particular ways, and we are certainly constrained by structure and power relations, but predisposition, breeding, structure, and power is never determination. To think in deterministic ways is to be seduced into believing you cannot resist or subvert being an artificial person. Choices are unchosen yet we are actors in the drama of academia too.

Thus, becoming and being an artificial person necessarily involves both structure *and* agency in some balance. University academics themselves can resist being an artificial person. They may need to sometimes play 'the game' in order to survive and flourish within academia, but joining with others and collectively resisting living as an artificial person on most occasions is possible. Equally, when academics are artificial persons and desire this way of being, or see no reason to be otherwise as they benefit from being this person within academia right now, there is the danger that they reduce their own student's belief in their own capacity to make a difference and think that there is no other way of being. But there are other ways. Students can and do act differently. They don't have to mimic their supervisor and turn into another artificial person who, upon entering academia, then breeds more when they later themselves supervise. Here, then, we return to responsibility: What can we— each of us, in our daily work—do to make any difference? How can academics avoid feeling caught in some vast machinery in which there can be no personal responsibility?

As part of a critical dialogue, one possibility is to be (even just sometimes) what Foucault (2001) termed the *parrhesiast*. The parrhesiast is a particular kind of truth teller. He or she literally speaks truth to power; for example, highlighting in a meeting that there are many different ways of doing research, and that none of these are inherently better or worse than another; discussing with staff about who they want to be, and might be, in academia in ways that celebrate diversity, compassion, and equity; highlighting that metrics are a (flawed) construction and game; and voicing concerns over academics simply being valued in monetary terms or other kinds of (masculine) metric they can be easily measured on and suggesting that we play an important role in promoting civic justice and social care. Of course speaking such truths is not easy. People ought to be afraid. But truth can overcome fear and animate personal responsibility, which is are ethical imperatives of parrhesia.

As this autoethnography has shown, we live in troubling times. But, as the story also has testified, people can and do act, choosing who they want to be in the process. Becoming an artificial person isn't destiny; it can be resisted. People within academia can live differently. They can celebrate compassion, diversity, social justice, and equity whilst also promoting and doing high quality research.

ACKNOWLEDGMENTS

Thank you to Andrew Sparkes for his invaluable comments on the chapter.

NOTES

[1]   In what follows is a story about the academy in general and artificial persons in particular. It is based on experiences, interactions, emotions, and events I have heard *other* people talk about from *different* universities. As such, the story is a construction that weaves together multiple voices I've witnessed as a narrative researcher about lives lived within the culture of academia. It is *not* based on any person I currently work with.

[2]

[3]   Simmel (1971)

[4]   Bourdieu (2000)

[5]   See Smith, 2008; 2013, Smith & Sparkes, 2002, 2004, 2005, 2008, 2011; Sparkes & Smith, 2002, 2003, 2009, 2011a, b).

[6]   See Frank (1995, 2004)

[7]   See Richardson (1990) and Phoenix & Smith (2011)

B. SMITH

REFERENCES

Bourdieu, P. (2000). *Pascalian meditations*. Stanford, CA: Stanford University Press.
Burrows, R. (2012). Living with the h-index? Metric assemblages in the contemporary academy. *The Sociological Review, 60*(2), 355–372.
Foucault, M. (2001). *Fearless speech*. In Pearson J. (ed.). Los Angeles: Semiotext(e).
Frank, A. W. (1995). *The wounded storyteller: Body, illness and ethics*. Chicago: The University of Chicago Press.
Frank, A. W. (2004). *The renewal of generosity*. Chicago, IL: University of Chicago Press.
Holligan, C. (2011). Feudalism and academia: UK academics' accounts of research culture. *International Journal of Qualitative Studies in Education, 24*(1), 55–75.
Phoenix, C., & Smith, B. (2011). Telling a (good?) counterstory of aging: Natural bodybuilding meets the narrative of decline. *The Journals of Gerontology Series B: Psychological Sciences and Social Sciences, 66*(5), 628–639.
Richardson, L. (1990). *Writing strategies*. London: Sage.
Richardson, L. (2000). Writing: A method of inquiry. In N. Denzin & Y. Lincoln (Eds.), *Handbook of qualitative research* (2nd ed., pp. 923–948). London: Sage.
Shore, C. (2008). Audit culture and illiberal governance: Universities and the politics of accountability. *Anthropological Theory, 8*(3), 278–298.
Simmel, G. (1971). *On individuality and social forms: Selected writings*. In D. N. Levine (ed.). Chicago, IL: University of Chicago Press.
Smith, B. (2008). Imagining being disabled through playing sport: The body and alterity as limits to imagining others lives. *Sport, Ethics and Philosophy, 2*(2), 142–157.
Smith, B. (2013). Disability, sport, and men's narratives of health: A qualitative study. *Health Psychology, 32*(1), 110–119.
Smith, B. (2013). Sporting spinal cord injuries, social relations, and rehabilitation narratives: An ethnographic creative non-fiction of becoming disabled through sport. *Sociology of Sport Journal, 30*(2), 132–152.
Smith, B., & Sparkes, A. C. (2002). Men, sport, spinal cord injury, and the construction of coherence: Narrative practice in action. *Qualitative Research, 2*(2), 143–171.
Smith, B., & Sparkes, A. C. (2004). Men, sport, and spinal cord injury: An analysis of metaphors and narrative types. *Disability & Society, 19*(6), 509–612.
Smith, B., & Sparkes, A. C. (2005). Men, sport, spinal cord injury and narratives of hope. *Social Science & Medicine, 61*(5), 1095–1105.
Smith, B., & Sparkes, A. C. (2008). Changing bodies, changing narratives and the consequences of tellability: A case study of becoming disabled through sport. *Sociology of health and illness, 30*(2), 217–236.
Smith, B., & Sparkes, A. C. (2011). Multiple responses to a chaos narrative. *Health: An interdisciplinary Journal for the Social Study of Health, Illness & Medicine, 15*(1), 38–53.
Sparkes, A. C. (2007). Embodiment, academics, and the audit culture: A story seeking consideration. *Qualitative Research, 7*(4), 521–550.
Sparkes, A. C., & Smith, B. (2002). Sport, spinal cord injuries, embodied masculinities, and narrative identity dilemmas. *Men and Masculinities, 4*(3), 258–285.
Sparkes, A., & Smith, B. (2003). Men, sport, spinal cord injury and narrative time. *Qualitative Research, 3*(3), 295–320.
Sparkes, A. C., & Smith, B. (2009). Men, spinal cord injury, memories, and the narrative performance of pain. *Disability & Society, 23*(7), 679–690.
Sparkes, A. C., & Smith, B. (2011a). Inhabiting different bodies over time: Narrative and pedagogical challenges. *Sport, Education & Society, 16*(3), 357–370.
Sparkes, A. C., & Smith, B. (2011b). Narrative analysis as an embodied engagement with the lives of others. In J. Holstein & J. Gubrium (Eds.), *Varieties of narrative analysis* (pp. 53–73). London: Sage.
Wolgast, E. (1992). *Ethics of an artificial person: Lost responsibility in professions and organisations*. Stanford, CA: Standford University Press.

ANDREW C. SPARKES

AUTOETHNOGRAPHY AT THE WILL
OF THE BODY: REFLECTIONS ON
A FAILURE TO PRODUCE ON TIME

INTRODUCTION

The invitation came. This was my promise to the editors. My abstract of abstraction called: "The embodiment of father and sons: In bits and pieces of flesh, memory, time, and place".

In this chapter I seek to generate what Ellis (2009) calls a meta-autoethnography. This is an occasion when the author revisits an original representation, considers various responses to it, and writes an autoethnographic account about the autoethnography. I do so by reflecting upon an autoethnographic piece I wrote in 2011 that was eventually published in the journal *Qualitative Inquiry* (Sparkes, 2012). This piece explored the dynamics of father son relationships by calling upon bits and pieces of memory and representing them through poetic forms and vignettes. Issues of embodiment, health, ageing, social class, masculinity, sport, and vulnerability as multilayered and interrelated phenomena pervaded the text. The constraining and enabling influence each of these had on emerging senses of body-self and how they are transmitted across generations was hinted at throughout. At the time, I invited the readers to add their own bits and pieces in the full acknowledgement that memories are tricksters and shape-shifters. But of course, as its author I am also a reader of my own autoethnography and life moves on beyond my text. For example, shortly after I had corrected the proofs for the paper, in October 2011, my 17 year old son ruptured his anterior cruciate ligaments in a rugby match and had to have major surgery, followed by rehabilitation for 9 month before he could play sport again. Likewise, shortly after the paper was published in February 2012, in the January, my 87 year old father collapsed, was rushed to hospital with a heartbeat of 25 and given a pacemaker. This may explain his confused state in the months prior to his collapse, or it may have accelerated a gradual shift into the world of vascular cognitive impairment or 'dementia'. Right now we don't know. Both of these events were foreshadowed in my published paper which I now reflect on in the light of what has happened, not sure if it is a case of life imitating art or vice versa. Regardless, these corporeal ruptures in the lives of my father and son have saturated my own flesh, shifted my vantage point for reading my previous

N. P. Short et al. (Eds.), Contemporary British Autoethnography, 203–211.

autoethnography, and raised questions about the dynamics of our relationships over time against the memory traces of what has gone before. It also raises questions about the value of autoethnography as a means of exploring and analysing these dynamics in ways that illustrate the complex connections between different kinds of bodies, selves and subcultures. Hence my desire to generate an autoethnography of an autoethnography, even though I know that, once again, the memories I draw on are tricksters and shape-shifters.

I recognise the 'me' speaking through this abstract of a future text. He is rational, detached, coherent, academic, consumer- publication- and product -orientated. This is an assumed cognitive 'normality' before the writing begins. But it's not and it doesn't. Despite numerous attempts the story has yet to arrive on the page in publishable form (whatever that might mean). It is still there, with me, in me. I am waiting.

The editors of this book twice extended my deadline for submission. They can wait no longer given their contractual arrangements. I worry, not wanting to let them down. Significantly, I get increasingly annoyed at the story that I know is there waiting to be told but which will not reveal itself to me on time and on schedule. But, then I think: Why should it? I think back to the title of Frank's (1991) book *At the Will of the Body* (in which he explores his experiences of developing heart disease in early middle-age and then, as he is getting over this, of discovering he has testicular cancer). Then I ask myself what can be learned from this refusal of a story (or stories) to be told by me, in me, and through me, in relation to the autoethnographic enterprise as an embodied process rather than just a textual product with a predictable publication date. What does this tell me about the ways that my stories are at the will of my body and those of other bodies that shape my life? To explore this question, I offer what Ellis (2009) might call a meta-autoethnogaphy of the 'not yet' or of the 'waiting to be told'.

FEELING ETHICAL DILEMMAS IN THE BODY

As the abstract of my promised paper indicates, anxieties of various kinds have inhabited my body both during the writing of and the 2012 publication called: *Fathers and sons - in bits and pieces.* Anxieties instigated by seeing the fear, confusion and bewilderment in my father's eyes when he is in hospital waiting for a pacemaker to be fitted with, as yet to be diagnosed with vascular cognitive impairment or 'dementia'. Him not knowing why he was there, thinking it was a prison, refusing to take his medication from nurses because it was poison being administered to kill him. Learning that during the night he tries to flee the ward and has to be forcibly held down by security guards in his bed prior to the administration of chemical sedation. Gazing at the deep purples bruises on his forearms while my Dad tells me how they were inflicted during the night by 'terrorists' in black uniforms. Me holding his shaking hands trying to make his demons go away.

Watching my younger brother by eight years watching my father agitatedly trying to re-arrange the furniture in a hospital room post-op, thinking he was back in his own home but with everything in the wrong place. Then, both of us helping him to do it, concurring with his 'misplaced' reality. Watching as my brother talks to the nurse about this episode with concern, copiously crying as he tries to ensure Dad's safety and the most appropriate treatment. Watching my brother's eyes scan the room as we sit with Dad during his time in a hospital psychiatric unit waiting for an 'assessment' to be made. Laughing with him as humour breaks through when one of us refers to various scenes from the film 'One flew over the cuckoo's nest' starring Jack Nicholson. Watching the different pains of a father and two sons unfold and intertwine in a volatile space occupied by other fathers, mothers, sons and daughters, all equally lost and seeking salvation in their own ways.

Sharing our relief at getting Dad into a decent care home where we feel he is looked after, safe, warm and fed. The shards of guilt seeing my brother stressed and fatigued as, due to geographical proximity he carries the load of regularly visiting Dad and sorting out the economics of care by selling his home to pay the bills. More guilt as a new job takes me even further from Dad in mileage terms, making my visits to him sporadic, as is the care I can offer. The desolation of hearing him ask: "What have I done to be *here*. I've committed no crime". To realise, that despite naming all the members of football teams he played for in his youth that he can't remember what he had for breakfast or how to find his way from the dining hall to his room. The haunting moments of knowing he gets lonely, bored, and confused, that he often feels imprisoned. My ongoing worries about the 'quality' of his life are constant.

But, there are 'second chances' to be celebrated. My brother reworking what has been a difficult relationship with my Dad over the years and being openly appreciated by him now in a way that was not possible before. I am also given the privilege of being able to recognise and acknowledge the love, compassion, courage, honesty and dedication displayed by my brother in these tough times. My Mum, putting aside her resentments and anger accumulated in the years during and after their acrimonious divorce, to welcome my Dad as a guest into her home, cooking a meal for him, listening to him, gratefully accepting his thanks and compliments. Recognising his confusion and feeling compassion for the father of her sons. And for me, the chance to take my Dad out for drives, to buy him lunch or bread and milk for his fridge, to ring up the care home to ask them to put his TV on the right channel when there is a football game being shown, to sit with him and listen to his stories of when he was a young man, to hear him on his good days crack jokes about the world around him, to tell him I love him and to know he understands this. There are good days. We hug a lot now.

There are also moments of learning and insight that offer themselves as gifts to anyone who will accept them. My brother tells me of a visit to Dad, sitting with him in the dining room while he eats his lunch. On a nearby table sit three elderly women waiting for their food to be brought to them. They often sit quietly together not saying much just enjoying each other's company. Betty puts down her teacup and says in a clear tone to her companions, "Does anybody know why we are here?" Neither comment. Following a significant pause Violet responds with "Not a clue.

I don't know". There is some more silence before Doris emphatically adds "No one's ever told me." My brother and I laugh at the story but then consider the profundity of Betty's question and the responses by Violet and Doris. We reflect on how often we ask the same question about our own hectic, confusing lives and how so often we echo the same dismayed responses.

The doctoral thesis is a fascinating autoethnography that explores the experiences of being bullied in the work place. It is an evocative, insightful, analytical and harrowing read. Acting as the external examiner I explore with the candidate a range of theoretical and methodological issues as part of our intense scholarly engagement in the two hour viva voce. The candidate is successful. She is happy and so am I. The university is a three hour drive from my own but only an hour drive from Dad's care home so I journey over to see him. He's not in his room. I go in search of him to the lounge where I find a local church group conducting a carol service with some of the residents. My Dad is shy and does not normally get involved in such gatherings so I am delighted to see him sitting by the window. I wave to catch his attention. He recognises me so I move quietly to give him a kiss on the cheek and sit on the windowsill behind him.

Olive who is seated next to my Dad holds her hymn sheet upside down and is singing the wrong tune. She asks me to help her. I do so, and turn the hymn sheet the right way up. Olive smiles and thanks me before turning it upside down again and continuing to sing the wrong tune. She is happy and so am I. The hymn being sung ends and the choir leader announces that the next one will be 'Silent Night'. She asks if the residents know it. Some mumble a response other remain silent. My Dad is one of the latter. The choir leader then looks directly at my Dad and asks him if he knows the tune to this hymn. Without hesitation he responds, "Know it? I wrote it!" The choir and her laugh as do my Dad and me. This dry humour is so much a part of him and I love it when it springs forth. He is happy and so am I. In such moments my Dad teaches me the importance of living in the immediacy of the present with him. It is a gift to be treasured, and I gratefully accept it.

Beyond, between, and enmeshed in all of this there is my son - Alexander. The angst described in my 2012 paper relates to my worries over spinal cord injury in rugby and of my concerns about this happening to him. Thankfully this never happened but an anterior cruciate ligament injury did. Out of the blue, without any contact or impact with another body, just a simple sidestep, and that was it. This was followed by MRI scans, surgery, and 9 months of intense rehabilitation. Then there was the watching of his frustrations early on as he re-learns to use his leg and body. Watching his school let him down by an absence of care and concern. Watching his determination when working with the physiotherapist to get back to full fitness. Watching him in the gymnasium doing his exercises in strict form. Watching his progress. Watching him move now, his body lean and powerful. Watching him enjoy movement and his body once again but also his doubts about playing contact sports in the future. And, being part of all this, being a father to a son in the new and different spaces his injured body propelled us into. Simply, being thankful for the opportunity of being there to care and for what we have both learned about each other along the way.

Given what I have revealed so far, it would seem that it might not take much more to deliver on my promise and produce a meta-autoethnography for consumption. There are several related factors that act against this. The first is ethical in nature. When I wrote the abstract I was, having previously produced autoethnographic work (e.g., Sparkes, 1996, 2003a, 2003b, 2007, 2012; Sparkes & Smith, 2012), acutely aware of the associated ethical issues dilemmas. After all, our stories are not our own. In the process of writing about ourselves, we also write about others. In this act we run the risk of making those we write about not only recognisable to others but recognisable to themselves in ways they might not feel comfortable with or agree to even if they have given their informed consent (whatever this might mean) for the story to be told. Ellis (2007) makes the following observation.

Central to relational ethics is the question "What should I do now?" rather than the statement "This is what you should do now." Relational ethics requires researchers to act from our hearts and our minds, to acknowledge our interpersonal bonds to others, and initiate and maintain conversations. As part of relational ethics we seek to deal with the reality and practice of changing relationships with our participants over time. If our participants become friends, what are our ethical responsibilities towards them? What are our ethical responsibilities toward intimate others who are implicated in the stories we write about ourselves? How can we act in a humane, non-exploitative way, while being mindful of our role as researchers? (Ellis, 2007, p. 5)

Ellis (2007) goes on to provide a number of thinking points for ethical consideration in autoethnography. These include the following.

1. You have to live the experience of doing research with intimate others, think it though, improvise, write and rewrite, anticipate and feel its consequences.
2. No matter how strictly you follow procedural guidelines, situations will come up in the field that will make your head spin and your hearts ache.
3. Think about the greater good of your research – does it justify the potential risk to others? And, be careful that your definition of the *greater good* isn't one created *for your own good.*
4. You do not own your story. Your story is also other people's stories. You have no inalienable right to tell the stories of others. Intimate, identifiable others deserve as least as much consideration as strangers and probably more. You have to live in the world of those you write about and those you write for and to.
5. Be careful how you present yourself in the writing.
6. Be careful that your research does not negatively affect your life and relationships, hurt you, or others in your world.

- Hold relational concerns as high as research. When possible research from an ethic of care. That's the best you can do.

More recently, Tolich (2010) constructs ten foundational ethical guidelines for autoethnographers that go beyond procedural ethics and into the domain of ethics in practice. One of the categories he focuses on, in order to anticipate and attempt to minimize harm from the outset, relates to the vulnerability of both researcher and participants arising from internal confidentiality and from researcher self-harm. With regard to vulnerability, the following guidelines are offered.

- Beware of internal confidentiality: the relationships at risk are not with the researcher exposing confidences to outsiders, but confidences exposed among the participants of family members themselves.
- Treat any autoethnography as an inked tattoo by anticipating the author's future vulnerability.
- No story should harm others, and if harm is unavoidable, take steps to minimize harm.
- Those unable to minimize risk to self or others should use a nom de plume as the default.
- Assume all people mentioned in the text will read it one day.

As I reflect on these think-points and guidelines I react at a visceral level. I can feel the needle pain as the inked tattoo is marked on my skin and I am left wondering what kind of tattoo and what textures of pain my Dad, Mum, Brother and Son and others might experience in the story waiting to be told if I force it into being right now and ask them to read it. I feel anxious about the confidences that might be exposed about them and about me in the telling, affecting our lives and relationships, hurting them, or me in the process. I'm confused as to what 'informed consent' might mean for my dad now living with vascular cognitive impairment or 'dementia'. Right now, I'm also suspicious of any rationalisation I might provide about the 'greater good' of me producing an autoethnography that seeks, in 'academic' terms, to illuminate the impact of interrupted body projects in relational and generational terms within a society that valorises youthful non-impaired bodies and stigmatises aged bodies and mental illness. All this, within a public health system that is underfunded and unable to provide suitable care for those living with such conditions.

I'm wary that in crafting this story from an academic perspective and getting it published in a scholarly volume such as this one that my definition of the greater good might well be one created *for my own good*, for example, in curriculum vitae terms. Finally, like Allen-Collinson (2012), I know that engaging in the autoethnographic *process* itself can constitute an emotionally painful and potentially self-injurious act. Like her, I realise that just as I must consider carefully how to protect and care for those I write about in my stories, so I must also devote the same attention to protecting myself in the research process should this prove necessary. Right now, I think it is necessary because my body instinctively tells me so. It doesn't *feel* right. To force a story into being would cause me undue harm.

REFLECTIONS

The ethical dilemmas I have outlined above connect me to the bodies of intimate others in my life and to my own corporeal being. I feel these dilemmas deep within my flesh as the story ebbs and flows in my sinews reminding me that knowledge is inevitably of the body and that knowing requires the existence of a body. As Uotinen (2011) points out, this bodily knowledge does not necessarily presume consciousness. She distinguishes general bodily knowledge from knowledge acquired while unconscious, by introducing the concept of *unbeknown knowledge*. For her, this refers to the "specific type of bodily knowledge that is formed while one is unconscious or which, at least, is not mediated and signified by conscious, intellectual activity' (p. 1308). Uotinen suggests it is possible to know without knowing and that unbeknown knowledge is first and foremost of the body.

> *Unbeknown knowing is unfiltered, raw knowledge that is produced by our body and senses. At the same time, it is inevitably fuzzy, vague, and difficult to reach or analyze. Bodily knowledge is constantly produced, but when we are in our normal condition it remains hidden, avoids analyses and significations, and it is difficult for us to become aware of, even if we wanted to. (Uotinen, 2011, p. 1312)*

The unbeknown yet-to-be-told story is currently circulating within me at the pre-objective, multi-sensual and carnal level. It is not yet ready for language to take its hold. Before this can occur, in Vannini, Waskul and Gottschalk's (2011) terms, there is *somatic work* to be done. For them, this refers to the range of "linguistic and alinguistic reflexive experiences and activities by which individuals interpret, create, extinguish, maintain, interrupt, and/or communicate somatic sensations that are congruent with personal, interpersonal, and/or cultural notions of moral, aesthetic, and/or logical desirability" (p. 19).

This is precisely what I underestimated in producing my original abstract. I knew that I could, and would, perform such somatic work according to a negotiated set of somatic rules that are personal, interpersonal, contextual, cultural and historical. The mistake I made, however, was to assume that I controlled the pace and form of this somatic work as it operated on, in, and through my story at the carnal level. I believed I could tell the story when it should be ready so that I could then craft it in written form as a chapter for this volume. In so doing, I forgot the 'will of the body' in the process which would not be rushed to reveal itself in symbolic form and on demand at a pre-specified point in time. As Vannini and his colleagues rightly point out, "Humans can know, sense, and thus craft meaning carnally, without the necessary aid of abstract symbols. We then filter these sensory qualities by deploying the qualifying practices of somatic work" (p. 20).

For Winterson (2012) "there are two kinds of writing; the one you write and the one that writes you. The one that writes you is dangerous. You go where you don't want to go. You look where you don't want to look" (p. 54). This was something else I overlooked, even though this was how I had experienced much of my previous autoethnographic writing. Before, in a real sense, the story had already written me and the somatic work had been done. Then I put the story in the public domain by submitting it to a journal or offering it in response to an invitation by an editor for a book chapter. In contrast, for this book, it was the first time I had ever promised to produce an autoethnographic story that had yet to be written, and where I was writing 'it' and the somatic work had yet to be done. Naively, I thought that once the abstract was framed that the story would by definition emerge as planned, in some kind of orderly sequence, and most importantly, on time. Clearly, for the reasons I have outlined, it did not.

Some might argue that if we wait for the will of the body to release its story that many autoethnographies would never get produced. In one sense, they are right. Indeed, this may be no bad thing in certain circumstances. Saying this, I recognise the dilemmas this raises for scholars in the current audit culture that frames university life which involves the quantification of output over time (Sparkes, in press). It also raises dilemmas for undergraduate and postgraduate students who opt to produce autoethnographies for their dissertations or theses as these have definite deadlines for submission. Trying to make the case to a supervisor that the submission is late because the body has not yet released the story in full would be a difficult task indeed!

My questions in the face of all this, however, would include the following. If we override the will of the body and force the story into textual form then what do we actually end up with? What kind of autoethnography do we get? Indeed, what kind of autoethnography do we (whoever this 'we' may be) want? While some audiences might be satisfied with a forced and premature story, where does this leave the author in terms of their relationship to their corporeal being and how they feel about themselves? What does this forcing say about how our scholarship privileges the cognitive over the carnal as a way of knowing? What are the consequences for the autoethnographic author of denying or by-passing these carnal ways of knowing? How does all of this act to deny the dynamics of the senses in action and the accomplishment of somatic work in the unfolding over time of an embodied autoethnography? There are many other questions I could ask and I am sure that readers will add their own to those I have offered so far.

When students come to me to discuss their dissertation or thesis proposal and they mention the work 'autoethnography' I feel obliged to inform them that this is not the easy option they so often think it is. I warn them that it's not just about 'them' and of the need to consider the ethical dilemmas that go with this approach as outlined by Allen-Collinson (2012), Ellis (2007), and Tollich (2010). Likewise, I discuss their motivations for choosing autoethnography and ask them to consider their emotional readiness to engage in this demanding and potentially disturbing scholastic endeavour. To date, however, I have not asked them to consider that the story they wish to tell might be at the will of their body and that this will cannot be forced without radically altering the autoethnographic process and end-product in ways that they may not find comfortable, satisfying or desirable. In this regard, I hope that my 'failure' to produce my promised autoethnography on time will not only act as a case study for consideration but also provide a stimulus for further explorations of the carnal dynamics involved in the autoethnographic enterprise.

ACKNOWLEDGEMENTS

My thanks to Kitrina Douglas and David Carless for their comments on an earlier draft of this article.

REFERENCES

Allen-Collinson, J. (2012). Autoethnography: Situating personal sporting narratives in socio-cultural contexts. In Young, K., & Atkinson, M. (Eds.). *Qualitative research on sport and physical culture* (pp. 191–212). Bingley, UK: Emerald Group Publishing Ltd.

Ellis, C. (2007). Telling secrets, revealing lies: Relational ethics in intimate research with others. *Qualitative Inquiry, 13*, 3–29.

Ellis, C. (2009). *Revision: Autoethnographic reflections on life and work.* Walnut Creek, CA: Left Coast.

Frank, A. (1991). *At the will of the body.* Chicago: Chicago University Press.

Sparkes, A. (1996). The fatal flaw: A narrative of the fragile body-self. *Qualitative Inquiry, 2*, 463–495.

Sparkes, A. (2003a). Bodies, identities, selves: Autoethnographic fragments and reflections. In Denison, J., & Markula, P. (Eds.), *"Moving writing": Crafting movement and sport research* (pp. 51–76). New York: Peter Lang.

Sparkes, A. (2003b). From performance to impairment: A patchwork of embodied memories. In Evans, J., Davies, B., & Wright, J. (Eds.), *Body knowledge and control* (pp. 157–172). London: Routledge.

Sparkes, A. (2007). Embodiment, academics, and the audit culture: A story seeking consideration. *Qualitative Research, 7*, 519–548.

Sparkes, A. (2012). Fathers and sons: In bits and pieces. *Qualitative Inquiry, 18*, 167–178.

Sparkes, A. (in press). Qualitative research in sport, exercise and health in the era of neoliberalism, audit, and new public management: Understanding the conditions for the (im)possibilities of a new paradigm dialogue. *Qualitative Research in Sport, Exercise & Health.*

Sparkes, A., & Smith, B. (2012). Narrative analysis as an embodied engagement with the lives of others. In Gubrium, J., & Holstein, J. (Eds.). *Varieties of narrative analysis* (pp. 53–73). London: Sage.

Tolich, M. (2010). A critique of current practice: Ten foundational guidelines for autoethnographers. *Qualitative Health Research, 20*, 1599–1610.

Uotinen, J. (2011). Senses, bodily knowledge, and autoethnography: Unbeknown knowledge from an IVU experience. *Qualitative Health Research, 21*, 1307–1315.

Vannini, P., Waskul, D., & Gottschalk, S. (2012). *The senses in self, society, and culture.* London: Routledge.

Winterson, J. (2011). *Why be happy when you could be normal?* London: Vintage Books.

LYDIA TURNER

THE EVOCATIVE AUTOETHNOGRAPHIC I: THE RELATIONAL ETHICS OF WRITING ABOUT ONESELF

Shall I write my story
And yours
Our lives which bump and collide
Divide and meet in intimacy
Shall I tell the world
Our my secret life, our secret life
In which you play a starring role
At this moment, you're my story
And I contemplate telling all
The hurt and longing
The intimacy and joy
In my story of my self
The self I share with you

Autoethnographic writing has often encompassed the kinds of experience we might not ordinarily talk about publicly. Autoethnography has been a vehicle for sharing thoughts, feelings and experience, which might only be witnessed by those close to us, or perhaps kept to ourselves. The death of a father through his son's eyes (Wyatt, 2005, 2006, 2008; Wyatt & Adams, 2012), growing up with a disabled mother (Ronai, 1996), experiencing mental ill health (Grant, 2006; Short, Grant & Clarke, 2007), exposure to physical ill health (Sparkes, 1996), difficulties in the relationship with weight and food (Tillmann-Healy, 1996), and undergoing an abortion (Ellis & Bochner, 1992), are just some of the examples of evocatively written accounts that take the reader into the private cultural world of the author. While these are all personal experiences, they involve others, family members, partners, ex-partners, friends, bystanders, people who know the writer, and people who might have 'gone through' these experiences with the writer. In order to behave in an ethical way as an autoethnographer, should I be seeking permission from all those people involved in my stories, or perhaps just some of them. Should I be anonymising all other persons described within my cultural experiences, or even changing descriptions of the stories themselves? My accounts also involve the audience, the readers or recipients of these evocative stories. As an author of evocative autoethnography, I won't know

N. P. Short et al. (Eds.), Contemporary British Autoethnography, 213–229.

if my writing upsets, hurts, offends, angers, pleases, delights, causes anxiety or leaves the reader indifferent to my story (unless they tell me), and what if the same piece of writing upsets one person, angers another and comforts a third? Where does this leave us as writers and researchers within the field of autoethnography, trying to research and write in an ethical way?

> *I finished the paper with tears rolling silently down my face, something I only noticed when watery splodge appeared on the page in front of me.* (Turner 2012, p. 91)

So what are ethics? The Concise Routledge encyclopaedia of Philosophy (2000) describes the concern of ethics as the system of morality "which involves notions such as rightness and wrongness, guilt and shame" (p256). We might think broadly that ethics are a way of being, ethical practice a way in which one 'ought' to act, either through moral character, thought for the consequences of ones actions, or by abiding by ethical rules associated with an undertaking. That is, in a virtuous way or with religious morals of friendliness, compassion, truthfulness and modesty, trying not to do harm to others, and treating others as we would like to be treated ourselves. However, my notion of a personal morality, which dictates that I shouldn't do anything that is upsetting to others falls apart in light of my beliefs in a constructed reality, in which we each might construct shared experiences differently.

Autoethnographic writers describe autoethnographic work in various ways, for example as "highly personalised accounts that draw upon the experience of the author/researcher for the purposes of extending sociological understanding" (Sparkes 2000, p.21), or a process which involves "a back-and-forth movement between experiencing and examining a vulnerable self and revealing the broader context of the experience" Ellis (2007, p. 14). Although we might have different ways of describing what we think autoethnographic writing or research is, perhaps, ethically, we might need to think about *why* we are using this particular methodology or way of writing, *why* we wish to tell the world about us. An autoethnographic piece of writing might be an academic study in the form of a thesis, it might be an academic article, or perhaps it may be a rant or a catharsis (Pillow, 2003), or the author writing to heal (Ettorre, 2010; Frank, 1995; Georgio, 2009). It might be any or all of these things when it 'starts', and might transform or become something(s) else, either through iterative processes on the part of the author(s) or experience on the part of the reader(s).

In keeping with Kant's 'categorical imperative', Rawls' (1971) 'rational intuitionism' appears to posit that there can be a societal truth to a moral position that is known and upon which a course of action can be based. In other words, we can know what is right and what is wrong. Deontological ethics appears to support this view by suggesting that the morality of an act is not *just* defined by its outcome, but by the idea that some things *are* morally wrong. We might consider deontological ethics to represent the rules of ethical behaviour and the way in which we have a *duty* to others, a sociological experience where if we follow the rules the consequences will take care of themselves. Within utilitarian ethics (Bentham, 1781/2000; Mill, 1879/2004), where we look for the greatest good for the greatest number, a generic blurring of individual boundaries can occur where we are herded towards what's 'good for us', and are more concerned with the overall outcome or consequence than the motivation behind the action.

So why do I need/want to tell you about me, about my experiences? To help me emotionally? To move my thinking on? By telling the world their story, the author might receive some unheard validation of their experience, an experience that might hitherto have been left invalidated. Or, in the name of research, to move your thinking on? To help you? Perhaps we write autoethnographically for all of these reasons or perhaps for none of them. Perhaps our reasons for doing what we do changes as we do it, as does the reader's ideas about what (and why) they might reading what they are, in a continually emerging, becoming assemblage between reader and writer.

It wasn't until we were walking home from being dropped off by the school bus that we remembered. I had turned 14 a week or so beforehand and my sister, 12 about three weeks before that. We looked at each other briefly, each acknowledging that we had managed to forget. How had we managed to forget? We turned right and wandered down the lane, out school shoes crunching on the gravel, ash and clinker from the fires and central heating boilers located in the houses down the lane. I sensed a reluctance from my sister to go home. Our pace was slowing. We are going to have to just go in I said to her, Dad will know we're supposed to be home from school around this time.

As we came to the bottom of the lane, the drive was full up with cars. All packed together, there was going to have to be a bit of reversing to get everyone out. We walked past the lounge window and saw people standing around inside. "Ready?" I asked my sister, she nodded and I pulled the key from the depths of my school shirt and undid the Yale. I took it out of the door and left it hanging outside my school jumper as I pushed open the lounge door. Everyone stopped and looked at us, as we stood in the doorway. There were a lot of people I didn't recognise. A woman in in a WRAF uniform was the first to move, walking over to my sister and I and offering her had to shake. We took it in turns, and she told us she was sorry. After that I moved through the crowded lounge and into the kitchen where my Dad was talking to someone and there were ladies from the village making tea and washing up.

We didn't know quite what to do. We had been asked if we wanted to go to the funeral (my Dad said we were old enough to be treated like adults now), and it just seemed easier to say no. There had never been any discussion about my Mum's illness, her likelihood of dying and then her actually dying. I had guessed (of course) and when my Dad told us she was dying, while we sat in the car park at Addenbrookes hospital, and I told him that I knew, he told me how brave I was for keeping it to myself. After that we never mentioned it again. My Mum gradually got more and more ill, spent more and more time asleep upstairs in bed. My sister and I started looking after ourselves, and doing the household chores and my Dad went to the pub a lot.

Then, when she had been in the hospice for a few months, my Mum died. In the last couple of weeks, my Dad had been picking us up from school at lunchtime and driving us to the hospice where we would try to feed my Mum, or help her to sit up, and then we would be taken back to school. No discussion, no expression of feelings. I can remember realising that I had forgotten how to feel. I felt nothing. I hadn't felt for months and on the day of the funeral, I still didn't feel. I didn't feel for a couple of years after that, then spent my later teenage years and early twenties, feeling far too much of everything all the time.

We might think therefore, about the *right* thing to do, or the *right* way to be, dependent on the moral rules that guide us or the or the imagined consequences, but this suggests a binary in which there is a wrong way to act or indeed a wrong way to be. Surely, we can't be as clear cut as to define action of being as *right* or *wrong*. What I might consider my ethical rights might conflict with someone else's ethical rights; where does that leave us? As Roth (2009) suggests, "even the most narcissistic piece of writing that we might imagine already implies the Other". Autoethnography is a relational pursuit. We study our selves within our culture(s). Our self-narratives stray into and cross over the paths of others, and our autoethnographic stories become part of other's lives. Can we always be ethical in our autoethnographical practices and writing behaviour? If we can't, should we continue to try knowing that we may well inevitably 'trip up'? And is being ethical a socially constructed concept any way?

In her address to the British Educational Research Association Annual Conference Delamont (2007) suggests that autoethnography *cannot* be published ethically. The main premise of her argument appears to be that autoethnography in telling stories about the author, inevitably leaks in other 'participants', those people who were a part of the author's written or performed experience, and that those people might not have given explicit permission for *their* story to be included in *our* work. People 'pop up' in our stories. We don't live in relation-less worlds. We have parents (dead or alive) children, friends, partners, people we interact with in the day to day comings and goings of our lives. People who make an impact on us, in all sorts of different ways.

"No I'm not giving you the key", I said

He pushed me into the huge bathroom and slammed the door behind him. The bathroom was dark and he turned quickly to lock the door and turn the light on, I saw his outline silhouetted against the door, before I had to turn away from the glare of the overhead strip light.

"Give me the fucking key", he said, his voice echoing around the large bathroom

I was sprawled on the floor back hard against the curve of the wall where the floor covering rolled up the wall acting as a kind of waterproof skirting board. To my left was the huge bath, one of two on this floor of the nurses home and I grasped the top of it to stop myself slipping on the shiny floor, not moving my eyes from his face.

"You've got one more chance to give me the key", he said

I wondered what I was doing here, why didn't I just give him the key. I was making a stand I guess, if I gave him the key he would go back into my room, lay on the bed, probably turn on the TV and act as if nothing had happened. Although he probably wouldn't speak with me, until he wanted something, that is. And I couldn't say no, fuck off, don't treat me this way, I'm worth more than this. The last time he punched me, his mate John told me that I must have done something to piss him off or he wouldn't have had to hit me. Hmmm, I probably did. It had become quite habitual, all this. He disappeared when we were supposed to be meeting, sometimes for days, he flirted, kissed (I had seen him) and (I suspected at the time and found out later) screwed other girls, and if I said anything, he denied it. It's a good way to turn someone mad, I saw him snogging a girl in the pub once while I stood there, he didn't even try and hide it, his mates were there. I remember standing there stunned and disbelieving. He finished kissing her and then sauntered back over to me as if nothing had happened. She confidently walked past me with a big grin on her face, barging into my shoulder as she passed, nearly knocking me flying. I turned and tried to ask him why he had just kissed her. He told me that he didn't know what I was talking about and that I was being paranoid. I turned and pleaded with John to back up my story and he just shrugged and told me he didn't see anything. He told me years later that of course it had happened, but that he wasn't going to be disloyal to his mate.

This was what I was trying to take a stand against, me being me, me being weak, not being able to stand up for myself, not being able to say I'M NOT GOING TO LET YOU TREAT ME LIKE THAT.

"No", I said

So he hit me. A punch to the left side of my face. I was lucid and quick enough to whip my glasses off my face, I didn't really want them broken, or banged into my face, I couldn't afford a new pair. I grasped the side of the bath to steady myself, as my head hit the wall he towered over me, left hand out to receive the key, and right hand curled into a fist, ready to hit me a second time. I remember seeing flashing lights before my eyes and musing that this must be what people meant when they said they saw stars. I handed him the key, and heard him go out of the bathroom, then unlocking and opening my door across the corridor. I didn't hear him come out again and pictured him lying on my bed watching my little black and white portable. I knew that sooner or later I would get up off the floor and go into my room, and that nothing would be said.

So, who should we consider when we are writing autoethnographically, who is worthy of our ethical concern? The people who we may recruit into the research? The 'audience' of our experiences; our readers? Ourselves? The people in our lives who end up appearing in our stories? Or perhaps none of the above? I might write about another person, but protect their identity, change their name, gender and the circumstances around the event I am describing, so I will tell you a kind of 'factional' story (Richardson & St Pierre, 2005, p. 961). Alternatively, I might write about my childhood, citing my parents as participants in my parenting. These descriptions of my experiences of my early life might not be as my parents remember them. My descriptions might critique the way I was brought up, or expose elements of childhood that would otherwise remain unsaid and dormant in my family narrative. If asked, my parents might never have agreed to have *their* role in *my* story told to the world. It might be that someone in my story is dead and cannot be asked, or alternatively that I am estranged from them in some way and my relationship with them is such that I wouldn't be prepared to discuss my writing with them. Where, then, does this leave the ethical considerations for my (implicit, explicit, dead, estranged) 'participants'.

Hello Dad

I hope you are well. I thought I'd get in touch. I know it's a couple of decades since we met, and that time moves on, but I'm only now becoming skilled, skilled enough to see how emotionally unskilled I am. You brought us up to be tough and stoic, stiff upper lip and all that, and Mum, while she was alive, wasn't the most demonstrative of people, now I look back on it, but she did her duty by us. She appeared enthusiastic when we showed her pictures we had drawn, disciplined us when she thought we were being naughty. I remember I hit Sarah with a 'swing ball' bat once because she was annoying me. Mum must have seen me do it and stormed out of the house and caught me a cracker around the face, then turned and stormed back into the house. Sarah and I carried on playing 'swing ball'.

It was amazing how little emotions were discussed in our house. In fact they weren't discussed at all. Shown sometimes but not discussed, unless our emotions culminated in us 'misbehaving', then we were punished. Sarah was forever getting told off for being too excitable, not sitting still and touching things when she shouldn't have. I remember she also had that facial twitch and grunt that you were very intolerant of. No amount of telling off made her stop, if anything it seemed to make her worse. Then there was that time you shouted at me because I couldn't spell something or recite my times tables, something of that nature, I can't remember now. That was particularly effective: you shouted so loud I went blind in one eye! It stopped you shouting at me, for a while at least, and I had days off school to go to the hospital for years afterwards, even though they said that there was nothing physically wrong.

You changed tack after Mum died. I think you lost your fight and shouting; even talking to us in a steely tone didn't seem to satisfy you anymore. Instead you adopted the silent approach. That was far more effective, I must say, especially when we had to work out what we had done to incur your displeasure. Sometimes it took days of discussion between Sarah and I. I remember waking up on those mornings and feeling fine until I remembered that you weren't talking with us, and this knot of anxiety would grip my stomach. It was much easier when we realised what we had done, then we could do something to make it OK again. I think my favourite was when we lost the garage key in the snow. You were steely in your disappointment, but you did talk to us, at least to let us know of just how disappointed you were in us. The good thing was that we knew what we had done that time, but it took several days of searching in the snow before we found the key and another week or two after that before we were forgiven.

I think, with a compassionate head, trying to imagine what it was like for you, you had no idea how to bring up two daughters, and didn't particularly want to. You tried to kick us out on a number of occasions, I remember, before we actually left home for good, and then you were quite happy to bury yourself in the countryside and leave us to our own devices.

Now I'm well into my forties and far too emotionally unskilled for a woman of my age. I have spent my life continually striving to be good enough and never quite making it. I've been able to get myself into (and fortunately out of) several abusive relationships, and I still get it wrong, frequently. I'm too attracted by the fairy tale promise of 'real' love and commitment and often end up lonely and insecure. Still, at least I now know what I'm unskilled at, and the trouble it gets me into, and I generally keep on the straight and narrow. I've even got a doctorate now; you'd be impressed after all those years of me never quite living up to your expectations.

I know you did the best you could do with us Dad, but unfortunately it fell short, and despite my acquired knowledge, parenting skill and experience, and the support of some good people, I'm still not there (sane and skilled I mean), and to be honest I'm not even sure whether I ever will be. I will carry on trying though, if only so that I stand a small chance of someday feeling worth it, and being able to sustain relationships where I'm not constantly in danger of being irritating or hard work. You never know, I might get there one day!

Anyway, take care

Lydia

And time passes......

Dear Lydia

Reading what you wrote then, today, leaves me feeling sad. Do you really have to be so bitter about your childhood? Weren't your parents doing the best they could for you and can't you forgive them for their mistakes? Does your hurt need to bias your memory and thinking all these years later; hurt begets hurt.

219

Your experiences have left you feeling vulnerable and ashamed. I know that, you know that, but why are you telling the world this? To resonate with others? To move their thinking on? To move your thinking on? Maybe this letter is proof of that. Perhaps it is restorative, I wonder if it's important for reader to share that idea?

Or...

Maybe it changes. Did you write it feeling bitter, or rather, knowing you, just very sad, and perhaps in my reading of it now I am experiencing it as bitter.

Its difficult stuff to read, even for me, and I'm not sure if its OK that you've written it here, and now.

Lydia

If I am to write about some of my experience, which just happened to have 'participants', other 'actors' in my scenarios, I can still only describe my experience of their words, actions or presence in my story, an experience in which me and another, or me and several others, might have be involved, filtered through my own selves. Perhaps a little more controversially, if I am to reveal a person's identity alongside their words, it is still *my* experience of their words, filtered through my own selves. Furthermore, if I were to write about *my* reflections on others' words to or about me, asking permission from the originators of these words might be a moot point. I would argue that my experience is my construction of events. Within a constructed ontology, there ceases to be 'factual' accounts which can be identified as the 'true' version of events, there are just different constructions of an event, or moment in history.

What's with all this fucking auto stuff? Being authentic while being ethical. Authenticity to Rob might mean pissing people off. To Sarah it's supposed to be more compassionate. She tells me that we 'should' be thinking about the effect, we have on others around us, but then appears to be blissfully unaware of how her behaviour affects others, how it affects me. Rob's argument is that when he is being authentic, he can say what the hell he likes and if others don't like it than it's their look out. Sarah is the same. She has no regard for how her actions impact on others, and apparently on me in particular? She is just being herself and if I have a problem with that then it is my problem, not hers. She is so fucking exclusive. I'm tucked neatly into a box of sex and chats. She doesn't want me in the rest of her life; I don't crop up in her work, anywhere! I find out what she is up to by reading her latest draft. All this 'considering participants' taking care of those people you talk about in your auto is just bollocks; what about the people who are left out. The 'participants' who share your life and aren't mentioned. What about their ethical rights???

Within autoethnography the researcher/researched, or author/authored, tells us about him or herself, they tell us the evocative bits, the emotive bits, the painful bits, and the happy bits, but they choose what to tell us. They may be experiences that they wanted to share with the reader, or ones that acted as a vehicle for other unutterable words. Writers of Autoethnography might see themselves as marginalised within society (Grant, 2010; Holt, 2003; O'Neill, Giddens, Breatnach, Bagley, Bourne & Judge 2002; Short & Grant, 2009; Tierney, 1998; Toyosaki, Pensoneau-Conway, Wendt & Leathers 2009), or they might just be speaking out loud, those thoughts and feelings experienced by many in a similar way, but rarely discussed outside a close circle (Adams, 2006; Ellingson, 1998; Sparkes, 1996; Turner, 2012; Wyatt, 2005, 2006, 2008).

Arguably, once words are spoken or actions performed; once they 'leave' the mouths or bodies of those who are part of the shared scenario in which I'm included, they become part of *my* experience. 'Ownership' of these words and actions are passed out into the wider world to be interpreted and reinterpreted until they fade into dust. However, do I need to seek permission to convey *my* experiences of those people beyond our joint experience? Perhaps not, if the originator or originators of the words or actions are not made explicit, nor their authenticity or context justified. However if I were to discuss experiences from my childhood, which might include commentary on my experience of my parenting, or direct examples of my experience of past relationships, should I seek permission from my parents/partner/friends or ex-partners/ex-boyfriends/former friends? It may well be no party would have agreed. Barthes (1977) as quoted in Burke (1998) proposes that "linguistically, the author is never more than the instance writing, just as I is nothing other than the instance saying I" (p.16). In other words, he is suggesting that once words have been uttered, the recipient, whose interpreted meaning may or may not be the same as the author of those words, may and almost certainly will construct their meaning for themselves. Whether my words speak of others, they are still my words.

Having said all this however, It might seem reasonable that taking some responsibility and accountability for the impact of your writing/performance on another, would form part of the ethical framework surrounding autoethnography, but is it practical, or viable even? Perhaps it means that we can carry on writing the way we write or perform what we want to perform but that we give some thought to others. If we don't consequentially temper our performance or reword our narrative, what's the point in thinking about the impact on the recipients.

"I felt very hurt by your actions"

"I'm sorry you are disappointed that I do not behave the way you want me to"
(Turner 2012, p96)

221

Dear Reader

I'm going to tell you about me(s), about me(s) in my culture(s), the present, the past, the pain, my political narrative of marginalisation within my culture(s), my accounts of my value laden performance, the flawed workings of my basic life skills, laid bare for you to use to facilitate your own thinking, should you care to do so. I'm going to hope that it might move your thinking on, and mine.

Dear Writer

Such self-indulgence! Why should I read what you have to say, your story, your life, what does it have to do with me. Why should I be interested in your outpourings, your grief, your secrets, YOUR way of looking at YOUR world!?

I'm going to tell you how my past and my present moulds and shapes me, and me it. How I don't fit, how I fuck up (again and again), and how (I have let) others have fuck(ed) me up (again and again), the repeating huge thunderous wheels of my life patterns, which I lean and strain against, trying to divert them in a more healthy, less repetitive, direction.

And.....? Your point is? So what if your life has been difficult, so what if its been OK, happy even. Why are you telling me, why are you publishing YOU, giving the world access. What has it got to do with them and, while we are on the subject, is this rigorous scientific study?

Perhaps, though I ought to tell you some nice things, so things that might make you smile or even laugh, perhaps it's not nice of me to inflict my pain on you. What if I upset you, or irritate you, what if you believe that what I have to say is best kept to myself. What if my writings become tiresome to you, losing their evocative remit? What if I make myself vulnerable, and....... what if you discard my writing and me(s)?

You won't know will you? How can you ever know what the reader thinks, unless they tell you, and they might I suppose. They might publish a review. A review in which they dismiss your outpourings as trite, as meaningless, as inconsequential to the scientific community. What then eh? How will you feel then? Is it really worth all this laying yourself-bare stuff? Exposing your friends, family and others who happened to get caught up in 'your story's' to the world, exposing the world to your friends, family and these other random people? What if you make me upset, irritated, bored? And what about the characters in your stories, these stories might be theirs as well. Is that fair on them, on us?

And what if, through my evocative writing, I just manoeuvre those thunderous wheels back into line again, ensuring that I repeat those patterns I am seeking to move away from? What if I make things worse for me through writing like this? I find writing autoethnographically hard, it can drain me. I think and think and think, I think about things that upset me, I visualise scenes in which I had felt hurt or angry,

I daydream about happy times and this constant reflecting and reflexive nature of the writing leaves me like a child never quite able to catch its own shadow.

Or on you?

But today I feel happy. Its funny how my mood affects my writing. Today I don't feel anxious, or wretched, today I'm not downtrodden and worthless. Today I'm strong and independent and capable.

Ok, so what are you going to tell us about then. What will I learn from hearing your 'happy stories'? I might become bored, that was something you were worried about before wasn't it?

So what do I say when I'm OK, what do I write about. Perhaps I'll show the way things change. Can writing be evocative if it doesn't involve distress of some kind or another, somewhere along the line.

Hmmm good question. The ethics of writing about happy things. You are less likely to upset people, more likely to make them smile. The people in your stories might not mind being included so much (if they were to find out it was them you were talking about). Perhaps you could tell us about falling in love, without getting your heart broken, or the joy of bringing up your kids without the tough bits.

Yeah I could, but it's unlikely.....

So, remind me, what is the point of autoethnography again?

Neumann (1996) argues that autoethnographic research "democratize[s] the representational sphere of culture by locating the particular experiences of individuals in tension with dominant expressions of discursive power" (189). (So the power game begins). Dominant discourses challenged by the lone narrative which seeks to 'speak up for the little man', the marginalised, the lone narrative providing volume for the quiet or silenced voice. The equilibrium once more restored, Goliath brought to his knees by David, thus 'reinforcing social power' (Ellingson, 2006), leaving a narrative or indeed performative landscape safe to roam in without fear of stricture or repression. I wonder, however, if this *is* where the 'battle' leaves us. Foucault (1977) argued that truth, meaning, and thus the perception and enactment of power, are created through discourse. I wonder therefore, does autoethnography seek to establish an alternatively powerful and dominant discourse though its opposition to mainstream research. If we argue against a regime, a practice, a dominant discourse, in favour of an alternative 'way of doing things' then perhaps we just seek to overthrow those we see as having the power, in favour of creating an opposing dominant discourse, an alternative power base. Is it ethical to think that my story is more valid than yours?

"I can't dictate how you will feel or what you will think when you read my work. Your feelings are not my responsibility"

"But you upset me, with your poetic words describing loneliness, and your beautifully painted pictures of pain and suffering, your stories of frustration and hopelessness...you left me feeling like this"

"I didn't leave you feeling any such way, you did that all by yourself, and anyway, you didn't have to carry on reading"

"No I didn't have to, but I did...I was captured."

It may be that what autoethnography endeavours to do, is to scrutinise rather than dismantle those dominant narratives, suggest alternatives and proffer viewpoints previously discarded as unhelpfully subjective, an innocent narrative laying out its brightly coloured wares in the market place, tempting and attracting with its familiar yet idiosyncratic nature. The signs which read "try this, see what you think" in stark contrast to the neighbouring stalls which advertise their "guaranteed ways forward" and "credibility with certainty". The dominant discourse, a sure clean cut respectable way to proceed if there is difficulty tolerating the almost inevitable uncertainty of 'being'
or
autoethnography the 'alternative' slightly hippy, probably ought to get its hair cut, middle aged (now) rebel.

"I think we should consider the people who are involved in what we are writing about, those who were participants in our experiences, those readers who know us...and those people who don't know us but read our stories....."

*"Hmmmm, we might consider them, but these are **our** experiences; we are entitled to write about **our** experiences, surely, and if someone gets upset, or angry or happy or sad, what can we do about it?"*

"Nothing, I guess, but I still feel we should think about the feelings of the people we might be writing about, and, furthermore, the feelings of the people who will read our work while we are writing. I don't want to upset anyone"

"Yes but you might, is it realistic to think that if you are writing about something that has been deeply upsetting for you, that it might not be upsetting

225

*for someone reading your story 'thinking with you'. We won't know what our readers think, unless they let us know. But whether they do or not, it's **their** construction of what we write. They are responsible for their construction, not us. If we have been marginalised, mistreated, hurt or upset by someone or something, if those experiences have been evocative for us, then that is what we write. Our writing is about the experiences we have found evocative and our writing should be evocative. I don't want to produce a sanitised, bland version of my experiences for fear of upsetting someone."*

The self might be the focus of research, but the self is porous, leaking to the other without due ethical consideration. (Tolich 2010, p 1608)

Autoethnographic writing or performance will always have limitations in terms of those events, evocative or otherwise we choose to speak about or not. Those events most evocative for me might be relational, and it is those events, which are the hardest to include ethically. I might not want to discuss incidences with my children or rows with my partner. I wouldn't want to expose them (or me), break their confidence or trust, tell the world about 'them', this is my story to but "what is conscious and in awareness can be articulated, but this will always be both complete and incomplete and as such presents a partial view" (Freshwater 2005, p.311–312). Is it ethical to the audience to leave parts out, withhold descriptions that might help the reader make sense of my narrative, they won't know what I don't tell them. Perhaps we can leave gaps, spaces where things weren't said . Or maybe we can use other forms of 'storytelling': analogies, stories, poetry, scripted drama's, movement, photographs, thus disguising identities and context, conversations and events, while still retaining the integrity of the experience. Arguably, autoethnography will always be an "incomplete, interpersonal, embodied lived experience" (Gannon 2006, p.477). Returning for a moment to being relationally ethical practice, how do we "honour our relational responsibilities yet present our lives in a complex and truthful way for readers" (Ellis 2007, p. 17), perhaps all we can do is try.

It was the gaps in her words

That shouted the loudest

She didn't tell me,

(or us)

Where the real pain lay

Instead we found it

Clinging to the underside of her other words

Like cobwebs tucked into winter hedges

Only noticed in the early morning fog

When the water droplets,

Add so much weight to the fragile structure

You fear it might rip apart

> *Your prose described the fullness of the moon*
> *Reflecting off the snow*
> *Lighting the scene as if I were daylight*
> *A monochrome setting for your story*

> *But not that she was there*
> *And that you sat together in the snow*
> *Stubbornly refusing to answer her questions*
> *As the delicate flakes melted with her tears*

> *You told us of the sorrow*
> *The pain and the anger*
> *Following the dismissal*
> *Of your heartfelt argument*

> *But not the way you set about amending your discourse*
> *To better meet*
> *The changing environment*
> *Of your new world establishment*

> *And finally, You laid bare your contemporary selves*
> *The inner workings of the man*
> *On the page for all to see*
> *Or so we thought*

> *But you didn't share the past*
> *The present or the hopeful futures*
> *Felted in and around the man*
> *There was just too much, you see*

Why do you tell me one story and not another?

So where does this leave us? I don't want to upset anyone. Nevertheless, this is all socially constructed isn't it? What I read might have upset me, but not others, what I write might upset some people, might irritate others, and might bore some readers depending on their interest in the subject and what else might be happening in their lives at the time of reading. I can't make people think or feel a certain way, and I don't wish to try. I would argue that autoethnography has ethical value of over other forms of research which might take an 'arrogant' position of 'telling the truth' or informing people of 'facts', to me it feels a bit like art. I'll put it out there and you can make of it what you will.

REFERENCES

Adams, T. (2006). Seeking father: Relationally reframing a troubled love story. *Qualitative Inquiry*, *12*(4), 704–723.

Berger, L. (2001). Inside out: Narrative autoethnography as a path toward rapport. *Qualitative Inquiry*, *7*(4), 504–518.

Bochner, A., & Ellis, C. (Eds.). (2002). *Ethnographically speaking*. Walnut Creek: AltaMira Press.

Burke, S. (1998). *The death and return of the author: Criticism and subjectivity in Barthes, Foucault and Derrida*. Edinburgh: University Press.

Concise Routledge Encyclopaedia of Philosophy (2000). London: Routledge.

Delamont, S. (2007). Arguments against auto-ethnography. *Qualitative Researcher 4*. Retrieved 3 March 2009 from http://www.cardiff.ac.uk/socsi/qualiti/QualitativeResearcher/QR_Issue4_Feb07.pdf

Ellingson, K. (2006). Embodied knowledge: Writing researchers' bodies into qualitative health research. *Qualitative Health Research*, *16*, 298–310.

Ellis, C., & Bochner, A. (1992). Telling and performing personal stories: The constraints of choice in abortion. In C. Ellis & M. Flaherty (Eds.), *Investigating subjectivity: Research on lived experience* (pp. 79–101). Newbury Park, CA: Sage.

Ellis, C. (2007). Telling secrets, Revealing Lives: Relational ethics in research with intimate others. *Qualitative Inquiry*, *13*(3), 3–29.

Ettororre, E. (2010). Nuns, dykes, drugs and gendered bodies: An autoethnography of a lesbian feminist's journey through 'good time' sociology. *Sexualities*, *13*, 295–315.

Foucault, M. (1977). What is an author? In D. F. Bouchard & S. Sherry (Eds.), *Language, counter-memory, practice* (pp. 124–127). New York: Cornell.

Frank, A. (1995). *The wounded storyteller: Body, illness and ethics*. Chicago: The University if Chicago Press.

Gannon, S. (2006). The (im)possibilities of writing the self-writing: French poststructural theory and autoethnography. *Cultural Studies Critical Methodologies*, *6*, 474.

Giorgio, G. (2009). Traumatic truths and the gift of telling. *Qualitative Inquiry*, *15*(1). 149–67.

Grant, A. (2006). Testimony: God and aeroplanes: My experience of breakdown and recovery. *Journal of Psychiatric and Mental Health Nursing*, *13*(4), 456–457.

Grant, A. (2010). The evidence base and philosophical Debates in CBT in A. Grant, M. Towend, R. Mulhern, & N. Short, N. (Eds.), *Cognitive behavioural therapy in mental health care* (2nd ed.). London: Sage.

Holt, N. (2003). Representation, legitimation, and autoethnography: An autoethnographic writing story. *International Journal of Qualitative Methods*, *2*(3), 1–22.

Muncey, T. (2010). *Creating autoethnographies*. London: Sage.

Neumann, M. (1996). Collecting ourselves at the end of the century. In C. Ellis & A. P. Bochner (Eds.), *Composing ethnography: Alternative forms of qualitative writing* (pp. 172–198). Walnut Creek, CA: AltaMira.

O'Neill, M., Giddens, S., Breatnach, P., Bagley, C,. Bourne, D., & Judge, T. (2002). Renewed methodologies for social research: Ethno-mimesis as performative praxis. *The Sociological Review*, *32*(1), 69–88.

Pillow, W. (2003). Confession, catharsis, or cure? Rethinking the uses of reflexivity as methodological power in qualitative research. *Qualitative Studies in Education*, *16*(2) 175–196

Rawls, J. (1971). *A theory of justice*. Cambridge, MA: Harvard University Press.

Richardson L & St Pierre. (2005). Writing: A method of inquiry. In Denzin N., & Lincoln Y. (Eds.), *The Sage handbook of qualitative research: Third edition*. London: Sage.

Ronai, C. R. (1996). My mother is mentally retarded. In C. Ellis & A. Bochner (Eds.), *Composing Ethnography: Alternative forms of writing*, 109–131. Walnut Creek, CA: AltaMira Press.

Roth, Wolff-Michael (2009). Auto/Ethnography and the question of ethics. *Forum Qualitative Sozialforschung / Forum: Qualitative Social Research*, *10*(1), Art. 38, Retrieved 7 September 2012 from http://nbnresolving.de/urn:nbn:de:0114-fqs0901381.

Short N., Grant A., & Clarke L. (2007). Living in the borderlands; writing in the margins: An autoethnographic tale. *Journal of Psychiatric and Mental Health Nursing*, *14*, 771–782.

Short, N. P., & Grant, A. (2009). Burnard (2007): Autoethnography or a realist account? *Journal of Psychiatric and Mental Health Nursing, 16,* 196–198.

Slattery, P., & Rapp, D. (2002). *Ethics and the foundations of education: Teaching convictions in a postmodern world.* Boston: Allyn & Bacon.

Sparkes, A. (1996). "The fatal flaw": A narrative of the fragile body-self. *Qualitative Inquiry, 2,* 463–494.

Sparkes, A. (2000). Autoethnography and narratives of self: Reflections on criteria in action. *Sociology of Sports Journal, 17,* 21–43.

Sparkes, A. (2007). Embodiment, academics, and the audit culture: A story seeking consideration. *Qualitative Research, 7,* 521–550.

Tierny, W. G. (1998). Life history's history: Subjects foretold. *Qualitative Inquiry, 4,* 49–70.

Tillmann-Healy L. M. (1996). A secret life in a culture of thinness. Reflections on body, food, and bulimia. In Bochner, A. P., & Ellis, C. (Eds.), *Composing Ethnography. Alternative Forms of Qualitative Writing* (pp. 76–108). Walnut Creek, CA: Alta Mira Press.

Tolich, M. (2010). A critique of current practice: Ten foundational guidelines for autoethnographers. *Qualitative Health Research, 20*(12), 1599–1610.

Toyosaki, S., Pensoneau-Conway, S., Wendt, N., & Leathers, K. (2009). Community autoethnography: Compiling the personal and resituating Whiteness. Cultural Studies. *Critical Methodologies, 9*(1), 56–83.

Turner, L. (2012). *Nursing and worth: An autoethnographic journey.* Unpublished doctoral thesis, University of Brighton, United Kingdom.

Wallace, S. (2005). Addressing health disparities through relational ethics: An approach to increasing African American participation in biomedical and health research. In Trimble, J., & Fisher, C. (Eds.), *The handbook of ethical research with ethnocultural populations and communities.* California: Sage.

Wyatt, J. (2005). A gentle Going? An autoethnographic Short Story. *Qualitative Inquiry, 11,* 724–732.

Wyatt, J. (2006). Psychic distance, consent, and other ethical issues: Reflections on the Writing of "a gentle going?" *Qualitative inquiry, 12,* 813–818.

Wyatt, J. (2008). No longer loss: Autoethnographic stammering. *Qualitative Inquiry, 14,* 955–967.

Wyatt, J., & Adams, T. (2012). Introduction: On (Writing) Fathers. *Qualitative Inquiry, 18*(2), 119–120.

THE THREE EDITORS (TURNER, SHORT & GRANT)

CODA

Lydia: So what have we come across in the book that's interesting for us?

Alec: I was struck by how in my own and Brett Smith's chapters there are the organisational problems around... sometimes people call it new public management in the public sector, sometimes it's referred to in broader, politico-economic terms as neo-liberalism, and just the effect that has ...... whether that makes it difficult to do critical enquiry in higher education, as opposed to concentrating on just training, training facts.

Nigel: Yeah, I think David Gilbourne touches on it.

A: Yeah, the valorising of evidence based knowledge.

N: It's interesting that some of the contributing authors are quite significant players in the university system isn't it?

L: So some authors have the difficulty of not only writing about organisations but working in the organisations they are critiquing...

A: Yeah.

N: How can we tie it...I'm being deliberately provocative here I think...how can we tie that in with the view that these are just stories aren't they?

A: What are?

N: Well the stories that people are giving us about the difficulties in their organisations.

A: I think that often people who are dismissive of narratives, autoethnographic or otherwise, say 'oh, they are just anecdotes', 'they are just stories'. I think they are narratives, yes, but they have material bases. People get upset don't they? There's a materiality to it.

N: Yes but I'm teasing out whether that needs some discussion I think, to get around that idea about people dismissing it because they are just stories.

A: Ah right, yeah.

L: But then we don't want to get stuck in a binary of either these are facts or they're not.

N: I think we can get round that I think, but you're right. It avoids the emotion of it. Just because people are feeling it doesn't mean that its not...

A: That its not valid, legitimate. It's not 'just their story. Just one story among loads of others'.

N: And the fact that we didn't request these stories and they've come in, haven't they.

N. P. Short et al. (Eds.), Contemporary British Autoethnography, 231–240.

A: Yeah.

N: Whether that says something not necessarily about the individual but about the dismissal of emotional intelligence and integrity.

A: Yeah that's right. That's a good point, yeah.

L: So I guess we're back to some of Ellis's stuff on how do we measure the validity of research in autoethnography?

N: Yeah, which fits in a way with REF stuff, which Brett discusses, where that's often avoided. We just want to know about the facts and the figures... and how limiting that is.

A: Yeah.

N: They are probably well rehearsed and dull and they've been out there for a while, these arguments. But if we are talking about what we are finding, what we've discovered...

A: People often talk about the truth value, don't they, of something. Let's prove in qualitative research terms the equivalent of validity and reliability and credibility and all that kind of stuff, just to make sure this is good qualitative research. But I think - as opposed to conventional qualitative inquiry - autoethnography, especially in its poststructural and experimental forms ... I think Andrew Sparkes wrote about this a few years ago... needs a different kind of...that it needs a connoisseurship approach rather than a scientific kind of checklist.

N: Yeah, I suppose the difficulty... and you experience this Lydia, or we all have to a degree, how if you are using a homogeneous measure of applying it to different disciplines it just collapses doesn't it.

A: Yeah. Are you saying that people could be writing autoethnographies of universities that are just kind of irrelevant?

L: What I'm saying is that it may be that our measures, kind of like Carolyn Ellis's ideas on how you measure the robustness of autoethnography versus standard qualitative research?

N: Do you mean measure or do you mean evaluation?

L: Yeah, evaluation is probably a better way of putting it, a more helpful construct.

N: Okay, I think the evaluation of something is determined by what it is you are evaluating so there are different tools for different things aren't there?

A: There's a whole literature on evaluating qualitative research, for example Lincoln and Guba, Ellis and Bochner, Richardson, and Sparkes with his connoisseurship notion. The point that Andrew makes I think is that the list forms of evaluation can constitute normative policing of the boundaries, keeping everything the same. They don't allow for out of the box stuff, so that's why you need to have a flexible shifting non-standard, non-listy, way of, you know, moment by moment, piece by piece, a bit like trying to aesthetically evaluate art... there's not a kind of list of its got to be this, it's got to be that.

232

N: I'm just wondering how to include this, because it might be obvious to us, but I think David Gilbourne and Phil Marshall... their chapter is a good example of non-listing, isn't it. It hasn't got what the others have got, that is references, but that's Okay.

A: I think it's more than Okay.

L: So how does that work then? We've got a chapter that hasn't got a single reference in it, so how does that work in terms of thinking about academic writing and theoretical underpinning.

N: I think it's approaching some of the answers to those questions in a different way

A: Yeah, Derrida for example wrote fantastic scholarly work in the form of love letters and postcards. Big name scholars, some classical, were talked about, and to paraphrase him he abused more than used references. References pre-suppose that you are submitting to some kind of foundational academic authority to back up your argument, right?

N: So it implies in a way that what you are referring to is valid in some way and it has a truth and a validation criteria.

A: Or there might be references that are kind of implicit. It's just a convention isn't it? You don't have to include lots of references.

L: I'm just thinking about some of the people that might be reading this book, some of the students who are sat in some of these higher education organisations, going back to what we were saying earlier, that work in accordance with these traditional academic rules. How are they going to argue that they don't need references?

N: I suppose in a sense it becomes what we were arguing before, that it doesn't have to be this traditional representational qualitative stuff. I was thinking that if I read the David Gilbourne and Phil Marshall chapter and it resonates with me, I think that's a reference enough.

L: But isn't that just a story, isn't that just somebody's story?

A: You might read someone's autoethnography that is referenced, but it might be shallow and not resonate. To me that's 'just a story'.

L: Okay. So for example, we had a conversation about Julian Barnes' Book, Levels of Life, Nigel, of which a part of him is talking about his experiences of bereavement. I finished reading it and said to you this is autoethnography, and you said how come? And you were arguing that it wasn't.

N: I suppose I was first mooting that it was autobiography, so then we had the conversation about the contrast between autobiography and autoethnography.

A: Culture, cultural interrogation, is autoethnography.

L: Okay, so I was suggesting that his culture was that of a widower husband

N: Yeah, and I think we ended that conversation agreeing that it was autoethnography. I just hadn't thought about it in that way when I was reading it before, because I was so engrossed and embedded in the story.

L: I'm not trying to say, see I told you so, I am trying to play devil's advocate. How come David and Phil's chapter isn't just a pile of stories?

N: Well I suppose at one level it is, literally, it is.

A: But there is culture implicit in the background.

N: In Barnes' book, there are references. He makes references to poets or other novels but they aren't dated.

L: So what you are telling me is if you get 'pulled into' a story then that is another way of evaluating the 'worth' of writing?

A N: Yeah..

L: Even without explicit academic references?

N: I guess the essays that you might get in your work as a lecturer aren't necessarily stories. So it goes back to the idea that the methodology and the theoretical underpinning would be influenced by a student's research question in relation to onto-epistemological issues.

A: Not just that but there is a whole technology of representational practices that are associated directly with scholarship which appear to be foundational but are actually arbitrary and contingent.

N: Different methods of evaluation are used for different purposes. So for example if you read statements that are unsubstantiated in a case study, for example '... everyone with anxiety experiences....', it might be 'true' but it is unsubstantiated. So I'd want them to go and check what they are using for evidence.

A: If we go back to Bruner, he talks about two modes of thought. One mode is the logico-empirical mode and the other is a narrative mode about stories, drama... believable, but not necessarily validatable historical accounts. It feels like you have got respectable science versus stories, but...fundamentally they are both stories, even the results of empirical science are stories.

N: But then that opens up questions about...

A: But there isn't a neat dividing line between the humanities and literature and autoethnography. Richardson, Bochner and Ellis, etc.... all these people are saying you must at least be as influenced by the arts as you are by the social sciences.

N: I think what you are saying is a good point. So this seems to tie in with our conversation about Julian Barnes book and how that was an example for me of how we might emotionally engage with writings differently. I found it evocative. I wept, so it was evocative in that sense but I suppose I hadn't translated it in my mind to be an autoethnography. I think that's relevant to this conversation in that it's how people read texts differently.

L: So are we saying it's not the way it's written but the way it's read?

N: What's important for me is the way in which I *engage* with what is written, which relates to an ethics of readership. For example, taking the text seriously, giving it time and consideration......

L: So what's that got to do with whether we use references or not?

A: Okay, I think that if the use of references is tied up with representational practices which are assumed to be foundational but which are not, then it may be legitimate for autoethnographic writers to transgress those practices as a form of academic cultural critique.

N: So what we are saying is that scholarly writing needs to be taken seriously whether it has references or not and that writing can be scholarly without references?

A: So the idea that its either scholarly or its not scholarly relates to the attempt in our book to go beyond or transcend conventional boundaries and binaries. If you are stuck in binaries, and you ask is this biography or is this autoethnography, is this scholarship or not, is it literature or is it social science... this is either-or arguing that doesn't make sense to me anymore. I think Julian Barnes is a brilliant autoethnographer. But you don't even have to use the term autoethnography – more a text that you engage with seriously and thus learn important things about life.

L: It is difficult though....there are binaries going on in both your chapter Alec, and mine, maybe not so much Nigel's. So we are saying one thing and then doing another.

A: (laughs) But, equally, binaries can be useful can't they, in different places, and when appropriate used strategically and rhetorically.

N: So that ties in with your work at university Lydia. Sometimes we need to use different approaches. It depends on what you are trying to evaluate. Sometimes it's necessary to be a positivist, for example drug trials, exhaust emission levels, etc.

N: So what comes next?

A: For me as well as thinking post binary it's about continuing to move on and build on the work of others.

L: So there are some things or authors that we might have moved on or away from and then there are others such as Bruner, for example, who still holds 'true' and is timeless.

A: I wonder if that's because, in addition to his depth and timelessness, he's not paradigm- entrapped, or narrative-entrapped?

A: In keeping with the discussion about binaries, I remember I used to have terrible battles with another lecturer at a different university years ago who was the external examiner for the degree I was leading. This was because I was moving away from a lot of orthodoxies, and I was trying to encourage students to be creative and think outside the box, and he was kind of policing a narrow line which didn't move on and in my view had become tired and jaded.

N: There's something about being respectful to those that have come before us but it doesn't mean that we have to keep repeating it in that way.

N: You know, if you had said to me 10 years ago 'guess what, you are going to write or edit a book', I would have said you were having a laugh. But incrementally I've got to this place. Its something I wouldn't have thought

I'd been able to do years ago. So when we meet students that don't believe what they can achieve then this demonstrates that there are opportunities.

A: There's an idea about being stoic isn't there. If you want to run a marathon, you have to run, and if you want to write autoethnography, you have to write. That's what Laurel Richardson writes about. You have to practice creative analytical writing to be able to do it. What you seem to have demonstrated Nigel is a commitment to regular practice, thus challenging yourself to achieve greater expertise as an autoethnographer.

TEA BREAK

L: I've been thinking over the tea break... I guess the struggle I have, it comes and goes, is why should anyone want to hear about me, about my crap, about whatever? It's self-indulgent and embarrassing and elbow chewing for someone else to read it. So there's that versus all those ideas about writing this someone might read it and their thinking might move on, and isn't that what research is all about?

N: This is important isn't it? There might be other people reading this who think 'what's the point?'.

A: If you're investigating subjectivity all these ideas are going to come up aren't they?

L: Yes, and it needs to be a transparent process. You need to be showing your working out, so while you are writing you are showing that you are reflecting on what you are writing, thinking about the implications and then reflection has an impact on what you write. You need to show yourself working out... be transparent about it.

A: A sort of meta reflexivity thing.

N: Even if the answer is 'wrong' you need to show your workings.

OUR REFLECTIONS ON THE WORKINGS........

L: When reading Kitrina's chapter, I read it very quickly without breathing. It felt like she wrote it at a million miles an hour and I read it at that same pace, realising I had to remember to breathe every so often. It went here and there, and over there, and back there......so perhaps we have something about the balance between content and process.

L: So maybe one of our emerging themes are the various styles.

N: Yeah, and celebrating the different styles.

N: So there's something about style, presentation and reflexivity. So I guess we've tried to embrace the approach in a way.

A: And going back to David and Phil, you could call it their implicit style. Their chapter seems to us to be about ambivalence around what constitutes being an academic.

A: There's a kind of rapid fire in Kitrina's work, staccato sort of delivery. I find your writing....Nigel....

N: Soporific (smiles).

L: To me if feels like it very much contrasts with Kitrina's.

A: It's more stolid and slow paced for me.

N: It's a very interesting idea that words on a page can be read so differently. I think we all experienced Kitrina's chapter as being quick, but it's the way we read it rather than the way its written. We don't know how it's written. It's interesting that I didn't write mine to be read slowly, but it's clearly presenting one of my slower self(s). It was unintentional.

L: Hmmmmm. So as much as I had to remember to breathe with Kitrina's, with yours there was a bit of me wanting you to hurry up. That probably says more about me than you!

N: It is interesting because they are ONLY words on a page aren't they? But somehow style conveys speed.

Another tea break

A: In chapter one we talked about the risks of writing autoethnography, especially when one's own organisation is being critically interrogated. I think that Mike Hayler, Jess Moriarty and Brett Smith's chapters are exemplars in this regard.

L: You do this too Alec, in your chapter.

A: I think we are all attempting to humanise higher education, and challenge the perceived idea that you have to write in concordance with postpositivist values.

L: I was thinking, some chapters are fractured and rhizomatic, for example Nigel's and mine, and some are more chronological and methodical, such as Jess's and Brett's.

N: The different presentations raise issues about style again. Barthes argued that people are conditioned to expect comfortable reads which don't require any kind of exercising of concentration and fit into an orderly pattern of emplotment, and another readerly possibility is one that requires more concentration and demands more of the reader in co-authoring what they read. I heard a programme he other day, where three people were reviewing a book. One of the commentators suggested that she didn't enjoy it because it didn't have a tail that she could grab onto and the other two said that was exactly *why* they enjoyed reading it, because there *wasn't* a tail.

A: I think you've both hit the nail on the head. there are quite a few of our chapters, mine included, which don't have a neat start: here's what I'm going to do, get to the end, its resolved type of thing. Its more zig-zaggy. Do autoethnographic tales have to conform? What if they don't?

L: No, absolutely, they don't

N: Someone could read yours Lydia and think it's a bit disjointed. Its the responsibility of the reader how they want to experience how they engage with what they read. This is another example of the significance of readerly ethics.

L: Yeah sure.

N: Maybe our discussion adds to the idea of there being many possible styles, including stories that are chronological, post-linear, or a combination of the two, so there might be value in knowing the route as well as being secure in uncertainty, that life is a bit like...you are walking down the road and suddenly....

A: Life can be messy, rhizomatic, more like a maze than a motorway...

N: I do take your point Lydia that its difficult to know how far to go in explaining. It raises the questions as to how much you explain to the reader, thereby depriving them of using their imagination when reading.

L: When I think about how I experienced what you wrote in both your chapters Nigel, because I felt you were going at a much slower pace when I was reading, to save me standing around and thinking where are we going next, you provided pointers - for example, dates and situational descriptors. I needed that, because of its slower pace, I needed more gentle direction. A sort of gentle invitation to follow you. This is in contrast David Carless's chapter, which also provided pointers but felt as if it moved at a quicker pace. His pointers had a qualitatively different function for me.

A: It seems to me that you are both attempting to articulate the demands on readers to engage emotionally with autoethnographical writing.

L: I suppose I'm thinking in experiential terms. For me, Alec, when I read your chapter it was like you had grabbed me by the arm and shown me what was going with a sort of 'look at this, look at what's going on here!'.

A: What I was actually intending in my writing Lydia was demanding that you, as reader, witness what I feel are social justice violations.

L: With yours Nigel, there was a bit of 'c'mon, let's just wander down here, and then go down there'. with Kitrina's, I was running to keep up with her and I suppose with Mike's and Jess's I felt I walked with them from the other side of the road. But that's Okay: different chapters, different experiences. With David Carless's and Brett's, I was there with them, and from my cultural position I found their chapters a little uncomfortable.

A: It raises issues about readers' cultural positioning, readerly ethics, engaged and non engaged voyeurism, social justice, 'come and look at this because its awful', or 'I don't care whether you look at this or not, I'm just telling you'.

L: David Carless's chapter was challenging for me. It was culturally very different from my own life experiences. There was also perhaps a gendered thing there for me. It was evocative for me to be invited into a world that I don't usually inhabit.

A: A kind of cultural estrangement?

A: There is a sense that you are inviting the readers into a sort of cultural critique, out of their cultural comfort zones to 'come and have a look at this. You might be shocked, it might be new to you, you might need to develop new templates, have you got the schemata to deal with this?'

L: If I think about Jonathan's it made me feel quite sad. I felt I was there with him just gently walking with him, so no big emotion but gently evocative.

N: I suppose I related to his chapter in that he was talking about disengagement, letting go of work.

A: He was. I thought about you Nigel when I read that

N: Yeah, two different ways of letting go and moving on, transforming. This might sound ethereal, but I had an image about walking down the path, about being in the waiting room.

A: Is this because of you both being psychotherapists with a similar cultural background, with similar observations and reflections?

N: And about nature. I spoke in one chapter about my garden, and he walked us down his garden path. I suppose we walked similar cultural paths; that would be a good metaphor.

N: In contrast, in the Ken Gale and Jonathan Wyatt chapter we are introduced to a different style again in the context of assemblage writing. I was thinking about the difference between single and co-authored chapters. I was interested in how their assemblage co-authored chapter was created and it raised questions for me about how it represented on paper how assemblage is normally conducted, that is there is often more than one author but we usually only read one.

A: Yeah, Jonathan writing alone is given an opportunity to present a different side of his representational subjectivity.

N: We often only have the opportunity to hear the voice of one person's account and here we have an opportunity to witness a co-authored, co-constructed piece of narrative, which shows how conversations might develop.

A: Their co-constructed chapter was very meticulous, precise and moment by moment.

L: I think for me it felt fascinating. I was intrigued by the way in which the text rhizomatically developed and felted before my eyes.

L: With Kitrina's, it made me a bit uncomfortable but it was almost like I didn't have time to stop and think about it at the time. I needed to wait until I got to the end and then reflect on what she had written.

N: What we are describing and discussing now is something about deliberately NOT directing the reader.

A: It's interesting... I am learning new stuff having this trialogue and hearing about the ways in which you have both experienced the chapters. One of the things we haven't talked about yet specifically, or perhaps explicitly is a better word, is the ethics of writing autoethnography.

A: Your chapter, Lydia... got me thinking quite a lot about the ethics of writing autoethnography, over which you seemed to take very great care.

N: And the importance of paying attention.

L: What do you mean Nigel?

N: I suppose that because both my chapters focussed primarily on me, with minimal obvious involvement of others, it was helpful to be reminded of the importance of paying attention to the consequences of what we write about and the impact of our writings on other people.

L: Hmm, but there might be implicit involvement of others, if only from a readerly perspective, and I know we've touched on this before. Both you and Alec included distressing reference to your stays in hospital.

A: When I read what Andrew Sparkes had written in his chapter about his father in relation to formal warnings to autoethnographers about relational ethics in their writing, I thought again about what you had written Lydia. I kind of feel that I might be a bit reckless or cavalier in some of my writing.

N: There's something that might remain unresolved about this isn't there. There needs to be some kind of self-selecting at the end as to what is going to be included or not. Its something that is ever present.

A: I personally think it's an irresolvable concern. When I read Andrew's chapter, especially Tolich's prescription list for ethically attuned autoethnographers, I thought to myself that its never as clear cut as a neat list would remedy. There's a good case to be made often for what Ellis once described as 'writing mean', where the social justice consequences outweigh concerns over possible damage to specific individuals. It seems to me that if you followed the prescription lists to the letter, what you might end up with often are bland, anodyne and boring autoethnographies.

N: This conversation that we've had seems really important, not only for us as editors to perhaps draw some ideas from the text but for me... it also feels a worthwhile exercise in that some of the things we have discussed are often hidden from autoethnographic texts.

A: Or silenced.

L: Hmmm.

EDITORIAL TEAM/CONTRIBUTING AUTHORS

Nigel P. Short: I retired in January 2011 from a 31-year career in the NHS. During this time, I was awarded my RGN, RMN, BSc (Nursing), ENB 650, BSc (CBT), MSc (CBT), PGCE (HE) and Nurse Tutor qualifications. In 2010, I was awarded a Professional Doctorate with a thesis entitled: *A Mental Health Professionals Development; An Evocative Autoethnography.* I spent the last 12 years of my career practising and teaching Cognitive Behaviour Psychotherapy. I have contributed numerous articles to Mental Health Nursing literature and co-authored Cognitive Behavioural Therapy in Mental Health Care [2004, Sage] (with Alec Grant, Jem Mills and Ronan Mulhern) and Cognitive Behavioural Therapy in Mental Health Care. 2nd edition [2010, Sage] (with Alec Grant, Michael Townend and Ronan Mulhern). Since retiring, I have occupied my time with autoethnographic writing, gardening, learning (very slowly) to play the bass guitar and getting good use out of my National Trust card.

Lydia Turner, RMN, ENB 650, MSc (CBT), D. Nursing, is a Consultant Psychological Therapist at Sussex Partnership NHS Foundation Trust and Programme Director for the MSc/PG Dip in Psychological Therapies at the University of Sussex. Lydia recently co-authored *Managing Anxiety with CBT for Dummies* [2012] (with Graham Davey, Kate Cavanagh, Fergal Jones and Adrian Whittington) and completed a Professional Doctorate researching Nursing and Worth using evocative autoethnography as a methodology. Lydia has a particular interest in working with people with low self esteem, and those who have been given a diagnosis of Personality Disorder, and currently spends her time teaching CBT and supervising CBT therapists in training. Lydia is Mum to four teenage boys and enjoys new places and experiences.

Alec Grant, BA(Hons), MA, PhD, Cert Res Meth, PGCTLHE, RMN, ENB 650, FHEA is a principal lecturer in the Faculty of Health and Social Science, at the University of Brighton. Among other duties, he leads, teaches and supervises postgraduate qualitative research education, and with Mike Hayler co-founded the *Altogether for Autoethnography* group. His interest and involvement in investigating subjectivity and related methodologies began around 1995, forming a significant strand to his critical ethnographic PhD. Over the last decade, these interests have developed and coalesced around his simultaneous experiences as mental health user-survivor/academic/researcher. Most of his published work in this period relates to this and includes several autoethnographic articles - two co-written with Nigel Short - and two edited narrative collections, of the lived experiences of madness and institutional psychiatric treatment and of suicide respectively. In his other lives, it's fun for him to be a grandfather, a father, a husband, a friend, a folk fiddle player and, although he doesn't always get it right, overall a decent gentleman of a certain age.

***

CONTRIBUTING AUTHORS

David Carless, PhD, is a Reader in narrative psychology in the Institute of Sport, Physical Activity and Leisure at Leeds Metropolitan University in the UK. His research – which draws on psychology, sociology, and the performing arts – uses storied forms of communication to understand and represent human experience. Through a variety of narrative, performative and arts-based methods, David's work explores how identity and mental health are developed, threatened or recovered in sport and physical activity contexts. His work has been disseminated internationally through keynote lectures, live performances, books and invited book chapters, and has been published in a number of interdisciplinary journals.

Kitrina Douglas: My background in professional sport has resulted in me charting a somewhat different path to many of my academic colleagues. Before beginning my academic studies, I had played golf on the Women's European, Japanese, Australian, & LPGA tours, was awarded "Master Professional," by the PGA, worked in broadcasting and the media, and was a published author. I am currently an Ambassador with the National Coordinating Centre for Public Engagement, have a fractional appointment at Leeds Metropolitan University and am a Visiting Fellow at the University of Bristol where I completed my PhD in 2004. My research interests are in the areas of physical activity & mental health, narrative inquiry and creative performative methodologies. I have carried out research for a variety of agencies including, the Dept' of Heath, NHS Trusts, UK sport, the Addiction Recovery Agency, and the Women's sport and fitness foundation.

Ken Gale: works in the School of Education at Plymouth University and has published widely and presented at a number of international conferences on the philosophy of education and narrative approaches to education practices. His co-authored books include, *Between the two: A nomadic inquiry into collaborative writing and subjectivity, Deleuze and collaborative writing: an immanent plane of composition* and *How writing touches: an intimate scholarly collaboration.* With Jonathan Wyatt, he has recently edited a Special Edition on collaborative writing for the *International Review of Qualitative Research.* He is an associate member of the Higher Education Academy, a member of the International Association of Qualitative Inquiry and the Narrative Inquiry Centre at the University of Bristol, where he is also a Visiting Fellow. Ken has three children, Katy, Reuben and Phoebe and a grandson, Rohan James: he lives, nurtures and sustains his soul in Cornwall in the UK.

Professor David Gilbourne is presently Professor of Qualitative Research in the Department of Sport, Health and Exercise at the University of Hull. He initiated and co-directed the 1ˢᵗ and 2ⁿᵈ International Conferences in Qualitative Research in Sport (2004-2006) and co-founded and now acts as Advisory Editor to *Qualitative Research in Sport, Exercise and Health*. David's research interests include critical reflective practice and the practice of critical social science; specialising in the representation of qualitative research through creative mediums such as storytelling, auto-ethnography, poetry and theatre.

Mike Hayler is a senior lecturer in the School of Education at the University of Brighton working mainly with students who are preparing to be teachers. He is an associate member of the international *Self-Study in Teacher Education* special interest group and a member of the *Altogether for Autoethnography* group at Brighton. His book *Autoethnography, Self-Narrative and Teacher Education* was published by Sense Publishers in November 2011.

Phil Marshall is a lecturer in strength conditioning and undergraduate director of studies for the BSc Sports Coaching and Performance programme at the University of Hull, UK. He has over 17 years of experience as a track and field and strength conditioning coach and has worked with athletes from grassroots through to elite level. Phil's research interests centre on autoethnography and the sociological aspects of sports coaching. He is currently undertaking PhD study exploring autoethnographical accounts of his own, in the field, coaching experiences.

Dr Jess Moriarty is a senior lecturer at the University of Brighton where she specialises in Creative Writing. Jess won a Teaching Excellence award for her workshops with undergraduates that focus on building inspiration and motivation with the writing processes. Jess has been interviewed by the Times Higher Educational Supplement about her workshops and won an Innovation Award for her retreats where participants are encouraged to develop confidence with writing and speaking. For her thesis she produced an analytical autoethnodrama about the pressures of life in a fictional university and the impact of the perceived publish or perish culture on some academics motivation and desire to write for academic publication.

For more information please go to http://arts.brighton.ac.uk/business-and-community/work-write-live

Brett Smith, PhD, is Reader in Qualitative Health Research and leads the psycho-social health and well-being strand within the Peter Harrison Centre for Disability Sport at Loughborough University. His theoretical and empirical research interests concern disability, health, and physical activity; the development of qualitative research methods; and narrative theory. He has published extensively on each of these topics in various journals, books, and handbooks. Brett's research is regularly utilised by health professional's, disability user-groups, and sporting governing bodies to inform policy and health practices. By invitation, on several occasions he has presented his research on disability in the UK Government Houses of Parliament. Brett is Editor-in-Chief of the international journal *Qualitative Research in Sport, Exercise, and Health* and serves on eight editorial boards. He is co-author (with Andrew C. Sparkes) of the book *Qualitative Research in Sport, Exercise, and Health: From Process to Product*.

Professor Andrew C. Sparkes, PhD, Andrew currently is with the Research Institute for Sport, Physical Activity and Leisure and a member of the Carnegie Faculty at Leeds Metropolitan University. His research interests revolve around the ways that people experience different forms of embodiment over time in a variety of contexts. Recent work has focused on performing bodies and identity formation; interrupted body projects and the narrative reconstruction of self; ageing bodies in sport and physical activity contexts; and sporting auto/biographies and body-self-culture relationships. These interests are framed by a desire to develop critical forms of understanding via the use of life history, ethnography, autoethnography, and narrative approaches. Andrew's work is nomadic in nature, operating across disciplinary boundaries and flourishing in the fertile spaces between them. Whilst respecting traditions he seeks to trouble standard notions of method and aspires to represent lived experience using a variety of genres.

Jonathan Wyatt is Senior Lecturer in Counselling and Psychotherapy at the University of Edinburgh. His research examines the entanglement of self and other within and beyond the therapeutic assemblage; and it troubles what we mean by 'self' and 'other'. He undertakes this research through autoethnography, collaborative writing as inquiry and, latterly, through bringing these together with dance/movement, performance and film. His most recent co-authored book is *How Writing Touches: An Intimate Scholarly Collaboration*, published by Cambridge Scholars.

Lightning Source UK Ltd.
Milton Keynes UK
UKOW04f1320300814

237792UK00003B/151/P